*Barnstorming
to Bush Flying*

Barnstorming to Bush Flying

BRITISH COLUMBIA'S AVIATION PIONEERS
1910-1930

Peter Corley-Smith

Sono Nis Press • Victoria, B.C. • 1989

Canadian Cataloguing in Publication Data

Corley-Smith, Peter, 1923-
   Barnstorming to bush flying

   Includes bibliographical references.
   ISBN 1-55039-020-1

   1. Aeronautics - British Columbia - History.
I. Title.
TL523.C67 1989   629.13'09711   C89-091491-5

First printing December 1989
Second printing June 1994

Publication of this book has been financially
assisted by the Canada Council Block Grant Program
and the Ministry of Municipal Affairs, Recreation
and Culture through the British Columbia Heritage
Trust and British Columbia Lotteries.

Published by
SONO NIS PRESS
1745 Blanshard Street
Victoria, British Columbia V8W 2J8

Designed and printed in Canada by
MORRISS PRINTING COMPANY LTD.
Victoria, British Columbia

To those pilots who flew in aircraft with sluggish and sometimes unpredictable controls, and engines that quickly lost by overheating what little power they had. And to those later pilots and air engineers who, though their aircraft were more responsive, powerful and reliable, set off without any navigational aids over country that was frequently unmapped and sometimes unexplored. All of them were richly endowed with what later military bureaucrats were to call "moral fibre."

Foreword

In these days of time management, one needs to have aims and objectives. I am told that objectives are the goal posts, and aims are how you intend to go about trying to put the ball between them. My objective was to write a readable and reasonably comprehensive narrative history of the development of aviation in British Columbia from 1910 to 1930. My aims were to find primary sources whenever I had the resources, or the luck, and so avoid not only making my own mistakes of interpretation, but adding to past ones.

The search for these primary sources can be sometimes rewarding, more often frustrating. As an example, the Richmond Museum is located almost within shouting distance of the old Minoru Park race track, where all the very early aviation action took place. I went there full of optimism, only to find virtually no written material about aviation and only two photographs: one the much published photograph of Charles Hamilton's Curtiss pusher biplane; the other a blurry image, just recognizable as a Curtiss JN-4 with two unidentifiable people standing beside it.

In my bush flying days, when someone was expressing dissatisfaction with his lot (water from a leaking tent dripping on his sleeping bag, or the dead mosquitoes in his coffee), one could always provoke a spark of rage by reminding him that it was all part of the challenge of the North. My colleagues are pleased to remind me that much the same thing is true about research. Writing a book is always a challenge, and these disappointments fade quickly when the occasional rewards materialize — the finding of a World War I pilot's log books; or the personal diary of a participant in an attempted round-the-world flight in 1924 — and in any case, the big finds invariably come just after one's book has gone to press.

Meanwhile, I look forward to writing about the next phase of aviation pioneering in British Columbia: the great era of bush flying of the 1930s and the development of the airlines into the 1940s. Then it will be a question of selection as much as searching.

Peter Corley-Smith
Victoria, B.C., 1989

Terminology

As with any technology, aviation has a jargon of its own. I have tried to avoid using much of it; or, at least, to make the meaning as clear as possible by the context. However, some of the early terms could be very confusing. As one example, the Wright brothers used the word "drift" for what we now call "drag." Aircraft had many names: first it was aerodrome, later adopted to describe an airfield; then it was aeroplane; and finally, airplane.

I was curious to discover when this last change came about, and I stumbled on a more or less definite date by accident while researching Ernest Hoy's 1919 flight across the Rockies. In the Vernon *News* (August 7, 1919) I found this paragraph tucked away on page 6 under the heading "'Airship' or 'Airplane'":

Washington, Aug. 2—To settle the linguistic difficulties which have arisen with the development of aeronautics, the air service has officially decided to use the word "airship" only to designate dirigible balloons and other lighter-than-air types of craft. All heavier-than-air types of craft will be designated as "airplanes."

The Canadian press, which has always slavishly obeyed any dicta on style or spelling from south of the border, promptly abandoned the current Canadian term, which was aeroplane, and substituted airplane. However, some time was to pass before aviators themselves did so, and I have attempted to suit the terminology to the times.

Acknowledgements

One of the rewards of writing a book like this one is to meet people while researching the topic — interesting and helpful people — many of whom were there to see the history of aviation unfolding, while seldom realizing that they were part of that history, and most having documents, photographs and mementoes they had not looked at for years. I have had a great deal of help from them. I can only hope I have done them justice. My sincere thanks go to: Ted Cressy, Maurice McGregor, Page and Ethel MacPhee, Keith and Margaret Rutledge, Bill and Joan McLeod, Clark Seaborn, Geoffrey Rowe, Pam MacAlister, John Mac-Leod, Norman Hoffar, Irene Reid-Hoffar, Ted and Doris Coombes, Bill Mckee, David Maude, Pat Phillips, Howard White, Diana Kennedy, Margaret Mae Johnston, Gordon Brown, Peter White, Richard Cooper, Margaret Sawyer, Paul Ferguson, Peter Locke, Jack Fleetwood, Martin and Jane Lynch; and especial thanks to Henry Stevenson, who has saved me much travel time and expense with his research into the aviation history of the Kootenays, which he has generously allowed me to use.

Among the many institutions that have helped by giving me access to their collections and allowing me to use those collections, I owe the biggest debt to the one in which I have the privilege to be a Research Associate — the Royal British Columbia Museum (RBCM). My thanks to Director Bill Barkley and Assistant Director Ted Miller for their support. In addition, I have received nothing but assistance and courtesy from the following institutions: Provincial Archives of British Columbia (PABC), Victoria; British Columbia Legislative Library, Victoria; British Columbia Ministry of Forests Library, Victoria; City of Vancouver Archives; Maritime Museum, Vancouver; City of Victoria Archives; Maritime Museum of British Columbia, Victoria; Vancouver Public Library; University of Victoria Library; National Museums of Canada, Ottawa; Public Archives of Canada, Ottawa; Yukon Archives, Whitehorse; Science Museum, London, U.K.; Richmond Museum-

Archives; David Thompson Library, Nelson; Nelson Museum; Nicola Valley Museum-Archives, Merritt; Kootenay Lake Historical Society Archives, Kaslo; Nakusp Museum; Creston Valley Museum; R. N. (Reg) Atkinson Museum, Penticton; Kelowna Centennial Museum; Greater Vernon Museum-Archives; Atlin Historical Museum; Boundary Museum, Grand Forks; Revelstoke Museum; Cowichan Lake Museum, Duncan; Railway Museum, Cranbrook; Rossland Mining Museum; Consolidated Mining and Smelting (COMINCO), Trail; Fraser-Fort George Regional Museum, Prince George; Kitimat Centennial Museum; Dawson Creek Station Museum; Hudson's Hope Museum; Bulkley Valley Museum, Smithers; North Peace Museum, Fort St. John; Whistler Museum; British Columbia Aviation Museum, Sidney; and Pemberton Museum — all have been generous with their help.

As always, I am deeply indebted to my friends and colleagues, Dave Parker and Bob Turner; Bob for making me work much harder than I intended to find primary sources, and whose proof-reading comments carry enough sting to force me to re-write what I have said so that it makes some sense. Dave for making free not only his extensive aviation files, but also his enviable knowledge of the subject. He could not hope to preserve me from all error; but he has frequently helped me to avoid really egregious mistakes.

My friends at Sono Nis Press and the Morriss Printing Company, especially Dick Morriss, Patricia Sloan and Jim Bennett have made what can be a traumatic involvement into an enjoyable experience in friendly co-operation.

And finally, to my wife, Nina, I must give thanks for the tolerance that made it possible for me to chase down that last, all-important validating reference — and then spend the hours working at my word processor I should have spent helping her in the garden.

Contents

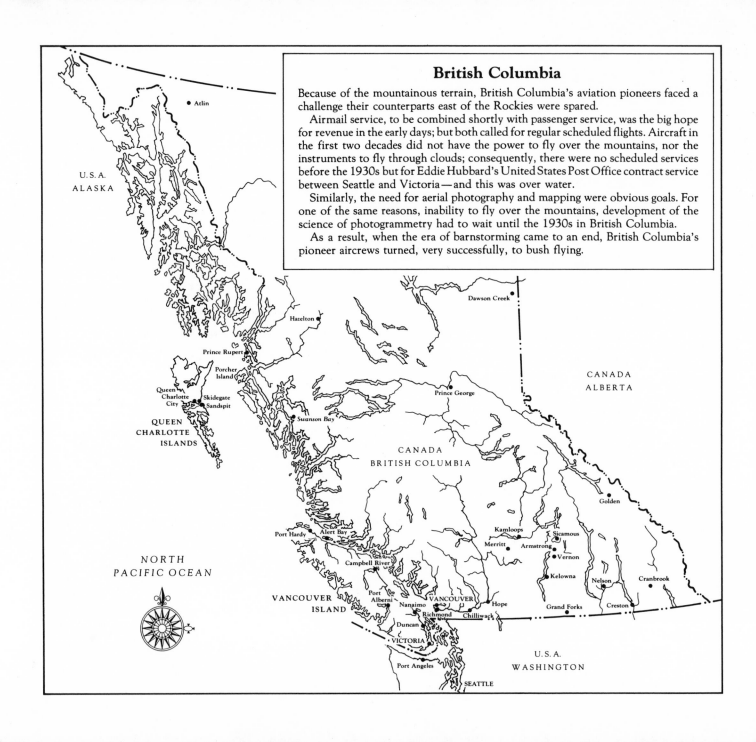

British Columbia

Because of the mountainous terrain, British Columbia's aviation pioneers faced a challenge their counterparts east of the Rockies were spared.

Airmail service, to be combined shortly with passenger service, was the big hope for revenue in the early days; but both called for regular scheduled flights. Aircraft in the first two decades did not have the power to fly over the mountains, nor the instruments to fly through clouds; consequently, there were no scheduled services before the 1930s but for Eddie Hubbard's United States Post Office contract service between Seattle and Victoria—and this was over water.

Similarly, the need for aerial photography and mapping were obvious goals. For one of the same reasons, inability to fly over the mountains, development of the science of photogrammetry had to wait until the 1930s in British Columbia.

As a result, when the era of barnstorming came to an end, British Columbia's pioneer aircrews turned, very successfully, to bush flying.

Chapter One

Beginnings

"...as gradual and graceful as the rise of an unstartled pheasant."

THE VANCOUVER *Daily World*

GERRY WELLBURN

The first manned "flight" recorded in British Columbia was an ascent in an unpowered hot-air balloon by Professor LeClaire, on June 9, 1880. LeClaire rose from the Skinner Street show grounds in Nanaimo and landed in the harbour. Nearly 30 years passed before the first controlled flight on October 14, 1909 when Harry Ginter flew a Strobel dirigible at the Provincial Exhibition grounds in Queen's Park, New Westminster.[1]

These events provoked a good deal of local interest, but it was the advent of the aeroplane that brought a genuine hope of fulfilling one of mankind's most enduring dreams: to fly like a bird. On December 17, 1903, the Wright brothers made what is generally conceded to be the first controlled, powered flight of a heavier-than-air machine. It was a brief accomplishment—the first flight, a few feet above the ground, covered some 120 feet (36.5 m)—and it took time for the news to spread, more time before people realized that this was the real thing. But when they did, they were genuinely excited and seized by the desire to see this phenomenon for themselves. In British Columbia, they had to wait until an early spring day in 1910.

On March 25, 1910, an American pilot, Charles K. Hamilton, demonstrated in a small Curtiss biplane that the dream really had come true. Hamilton had only recently graduated to aeroplanes; he had begun his flying career in 1906 as a dirigible pilot. He and Lincoln Beachey had performed in a series of exhibition flights from as far as Montreal and Winnipeg in the north, to Montgomery, Alabama, in the south.

It is worth pausing for a moment to recall this era. Flying a dirigible, a powered and controllable balloon, at the turn of the century may not have called for a great deal of judgement and co-ordination, but it clearly required agility and courage. The gas bag (filled with some 8,500 cubic feet [240 m³] of highly combustible hydrogen), was shaped like a large, pointed sausage, approximately 60 feet (18 m) long by about 18 feet (5.5 m) in diameter. In the earlier models, the gas bag was covered by a net. Cords from this net supported a triangular framework made of spruce. This frame, typically 36 feet (11 m) long and 30 inches (76 cm) high, was hung apex up about five feet (1.5 m) below the bottom of the bag. Frank Goodale, who accompanied Hamilton as a helper in 1907, and became a pilot the following year, describes what it was like to fly one:

I DROPPED OFF AT OTTAWA.

GERRY WELLBURN

The operator, or "aeronaut" as he was called, rode astride the frame in which the five-horsepower motorcycle engine was mounted. To preserve the balance, the engine was about a third of the way from the front of the frame and connected to the propeller by a long hollow steel tube used as a shaft.

The rudder, mounted at the rear, was built of bamboo fish poles such as we used up the creek in our boyhood days. This was covered with unbleached muslin and operated by a long endless line of cotton sash cord run through a pulley placed just ahead of the engine.

So, when ready to ascend, we find our hardy pioneer of the air sitting astride an inch and a quarter spruce pole, his feet perched on two similar poles, and a piece of quarter-inch sash cord grasped firmly in each hand as his only hand-hold, and at the same time his only means of controlling the horizontal direction of the craft.

The "ship" being weighed off so that the bag was just sustaining the weight (not lifting), the operator gave the word and the motor, after a lot of coaxing and priming, started to sputter with the spontaneous abandon of a bunch of firecrackers. This produced a violent reaction along the entire length of the frame-work, causing the aeronaut to vibrate with the rest of the machine. This was neither pleasant nor reassuring, but one became used to it as part of the game after a few experiences in the air.

After the motor was warmed up long enough to indicate an intention to continue to run, the aeronaut slid back along the frame about two-thirds of the way aft, and the word was given to the men who had been holding the frame shoulder high off the ground to, "Let go, everybody." As this was done, the weight of the aeronaut caused the nose to incline upward at an angle of fifteen degrees and the pull of the propeller drew the ship upward.

When the desired height was reached, the aeronaut slid forward in a series of hops and jerks until the ship was on an even keel. He then had nothing to do but steer with the tiller rope, balance himself and the ship like a tightrope walker, pump oil with a hand gun every three minutes, test the internal pressure of the gas bag by snapping his index finger against the round belly that was only a foot above his head, and keep a careful ear tilted towards the motor for any signs of asthma or the croup with which all these motors were chronic sufferers.[2]

Charles Hamilton, in his Curtiss pusher biplane, presided over a far more sophisticated control system. Now, too, he had to judge his speed (without an airspeed indicator), for the aeroplane relied on forward speed to maintain lift and stay in the air. As a result, an engine failure became a much more urgent problem than it had been with the airship, when the pilot could float with the wind until he found a suitable place to land before venting gas to descend.

Charlie Hamilton was an interesting character. Realizing that dirigibles were becoming passé at aviation exhibitions, he looked around for a chance to switch to aeroplanes. At that time there were really only two practical options (unless he started from scratch to design and build his own aircraft, and teach himself to fly): he could either go to the Wright brothers, or to Glenn Curtiss. The story sounds far-fetched, but here is how aviation historian Harold Morehouse describes Hamilton's initiation into heavier-than-air flying:

He heard of the great Channel Crossing by Blériot, and of Glenn Curtiss's feat, winning the Gordon Bennett Cup Race at Rheims, France. These events apparently influenced Hamilton, for he went to Hammondsport in mid-October [1909] to learn to fly. However, Glenn Curtiss stated there were no airplanes available; he could not be taken on as a student. With that settled, Curtiss left on a trip. Hamilton remained. Without asking anyone, and as soon as the next new airplane was out of the factory, he took it up and down the field making several small hops. He was at this practice the next day when Curtiss returned, to be furious, but also amazed, for it was obvious that Hamilton had an instinct for flying. Curtiss allowed him to stay on, gave him some instruction and in November, having made a flight of some 25 minutes Curtiss took him on as an exhibition flyer.[3]

In fact, Hamilton started with a big advantage. He was frail and skinny, weighing only a little over 100 pounds (45 kg). This was an unmistakable plus when aircraft were propelled by engines whose power was at best marginal. He was also blessed with a natural talent for flying and an abundance of courage—though many people attributed this to alcohol. Reports at the time suggested that he was "bibulous" or that "he carried about him an aura of alcohol," and that he usually indulged in a few belts before taking off for one of his exhibition flights. Whether or not this was true, he became the first pilot to introduce

OFFICIAL SOUVENIR
PROGRAM
BIG AVIATION MEET & AIRSHIP FLIGHTS

10¢

MINORU PARK
VANCOUVER, B. C.
March 25-26-28, 1910
AUSPICES
Vancouver Aviation Committee

Harry Ginter in the Strobel dirigible, Queens Park, New Westminster, 1909. These early exhibition flights drew large crowds and were treated as a festive occasions.

A hot-air balloon ascent in Vancouver's Stanley Park, circa 1906.

Charles Hamilton, centre, flanked by his mechanic and his manager, at Minoru Park, March 25, 1910, before take-off on the first exhibition of a heavier-than-air flight in B.C.

Hamilton's Curtiss biplane before take-off and in flight. A crowd of 3500 watched this exhibition and it was reported under front-page headlines in all the local newspapers.

stunts in his performances. Before then, simply flying an aircraft and landing it qualified one for the title of dare-devil. Soon, however, spectators began to tire of merely watching a machine fly, and Charlie Hamilton gave them the renewed excitement they craved.

In his Canadian debut, as with many of these early demonstration flights, Hamilton took off from a race track: the Minoru Park track in Richmond. Finding a surface smooth enough for the unsprung, bicycle-wheel undercarriages of those days was not easy and a race track usually provided an acceptable surface. Besides which, it invariably had a grandstand from which spectators could marvel in comfort and, no doubt, secretly hope for something as dramatic as a crash — possibly even a death — material for an anecdote that would grow with the telling over the years.

Most people thought that if the engine stopped the machine would crash; the idea of gliding was still only vaguely comprehended. One of Hamilton's first and very successful stunts was to climb to some 1,500 feet (460 m) above the exhibition ground and cut his engine. Then he would dive steeply, pulling out, as the newspapers invariably claimed, at the last possible moment before landing. Spectators, convinced that he was diving to destruction, displayed gratifying reactions. Strong men shouted in dismay and, all over the grounds, if the newspapers are to be believed, young women fainted. On some occasions pilots emulating Hamilton did fail to pull out, but there were ample incentives to take risks because exhibitions were very rewarding financially. A pilot could earn as much as $10,000 for two or three flights of ten or fifteen minutes' duration.

In this case, although the 3,500 spectators who turned out were denied the ultimate drama of a crash, there was plenty to excite them. As the Vancouver *Daily News-Advertiser* reported, Hamilton's first flight that day ended in a minor mishap:

He had been up in the air about ten minutes, flying in fine style, and was coming towards the grandstand, when something went wrong with his steering gear. His machine took a curve towards the middle of the field, and landed with a sharp list to one side, spurting up a cloud of dirt and ripping the tire from one of the gliding wheels. Some injury was also done to one of the planes [wings], which struck the earth, but the aviator himself landed fresh and uninjured.[4]

The accident resulted in a two-hour delay while the damage was repaired, and the crowd grew restive; but then

... the aviator justified his reputation for courage of the kind seen only in men who play with the clouds. Making such repairs as he could within the period of his spectators' patience and with his machine still incomplete, the engine was again started, the propeller again buzzed, sending the coats of his assistants flying with the swift revolutions as they held the machine to the earth. Vaulting into his seat Hamilton gave the front planes the slant which could catch the air, and then like a giant sea gull the machine rose to the accompaniment of deafening cheers.[5]

On the day after this account was published, Hamilton made a much more significant flight. He took off and followed the north shore of the Fraser River until he reached New Westminster, 10 miles (16 km) away, returning safely to the race track after 30 minutes in the air. Two days later, he took on a racehorse, a local favourite called Prince Brutus, in a one-mile race. Unfortunately, he spotted the horse too much of a handicap, allowing it and its rider, Curley Lewis, a start of five-eighths of the course.[6] Hamilton lost, much one suspects, to the delight of the reactionaries in the audience.

To people in the Greater Vancouver area, the advent of the aeroplane was clearly a major event. There seem to have been two reactions to the experience: one aesthetic; the other pragmatic. The former was an intriguing response: a sense of beauty which, though often expressed in overblown prose, emerges as a more than superficial perception:

Like a huge bird with outstretched wings, rushing to the defence of her brood, the biplane came sweeping down the track upon its tiny wheels and in front of the grandstand the aviator caused it to rise. When the amber colored machine stands upon the ground with its power shut off, it looks benign in a cumbersome sort of way, but as soon as it leaves the earth it seems to have entered its natural element. Its ascent, as controlled by Mr. Hamilton, is as gradual and graceful as the rise of an unstartled pheasant and its every move is marked by flashing swiftness and by beautiful design.[7]

Virtually all journalists at the time commented on the grace and beauty of Hamilton's Curtiss biplane when it was flying. The pragmatic reaction was just as obvious. The purpose of these exhibition flights was to make money, and the money had to come from spectators. Thus, to transport the public to Minoru Park in Richmond, a distance of several miles from downtown Vancouver, the B.C. Electric Railway Company added to its normal schedule of trains a number of flat cars equipped with seats, as well as several observation cars borrowed from the

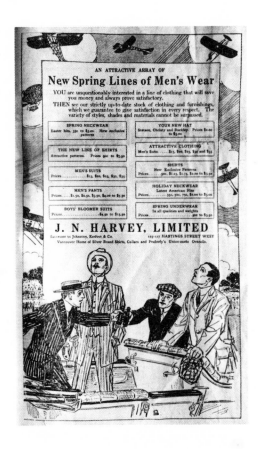

Canadian Pacific Railway. And although Hamilton's budget apparently did not allow for paid advertising, his forthcoming demonstration was accorded ample newspaper space. There was even an advertisement for Ghirardelli's Ground Chocolate in the Vancouver newspapers, featuring a fearless aviator, his tie swept back in the wind (though judging by the controls, the machine was obviously a Wright biplane); and another for the latest fashions in clothing, surrounded by a border of different aircraft in flight. There were indications that hopes ran high for the future of aviation in other quarters. British Columbia was enjoying a powerful real estate boom at the time, and the *Daily News-Advertiser* reflected the spirit of free enterprise flourishing in the Lower Mainland:

Something unusual in advertisements is to be found in another column of this issue. It advertises flying machines for sale. The fact that airships are now a practical success, as much at least as the automobile was in its earlier stages, has been demonstrated, and the flights to be given at Minoru Park during the next few days will show practically how easy it is to make a flight, once the mechanism of the machine is understood.

Stancliffe & Co., of this City, invite inquiries regarding biplanes, and it is not improbable that the enterprising real estate men who are making money will invest in at least one to convey customers in the latest style to the scene of purchase.[8]

Yet in spite of this, and the fact that people flocked to see an aircraft flying in those days, few of them seem to have regarded aviation as anything but an attractive trick or stunt. Proof of this attitude came later that same year when William W. Gibson, working in almost total isolation from other aviators, designed and built his own aircraft, the *Twin-plane*; and then, because there were no suitable ones available in British Columbia, he emulated the Wright brothers and designed his own engine.

Chapter Two

British Columbia's First Aircraft

*"...with a machine that resembles
very closely a western hayrack."*

THE CALGARY *Daily Herald*

While most concede priority to the Wright brothers, there is a claim that a British Columbian achieved heavier-than-air controlled flight in a steam-powered helicopter in 1903. His name was Lou Gagnon, a miner at the Nickel Plate Mine in Rossland. His claim was investigated some 30 years after the event by Father Freney—a journalist for ten years before he became a priest—and found to be persuasive but not conclusive.

It appears to be a hybrid helicopter-autogyro. Apparently the main rotor had fixed pitch and there was no mechanism to tilt the disk. Steering (and presumably counteraction of torque from the main rotor) was achieved by a pivoting vane (rudder) mounted behind a conventional propeller. Fore-and-aft control was achieved by moving forward or back in the fuselage (no mention of gyroscopic effect). Nor is there any mention of lateral control. Nonetheless, witnesses claimed it was only pilot error that caused the crash, after a two- to three-minute flight behind the great Northern Hotel, that virtually demolished the machine and seriously injured Lou Gagnon.

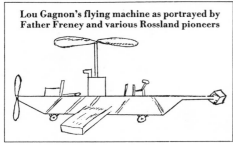

Lou Gagnon's flying machine as portrayed by Father Freney and various Rossland pioneers

RICHARD COOPER

William Wallace Gibson began his aviation career as a boy in the 1880s by flying kites over the Saskatchewan prairies. He constructed his own, constantly seeking to improve stability and flying characteristics. As a young man, he moved to the village of Balgonie, 15 miles east of Regina and, by 1905, he had established himself as a businessman with his own hardware store. He made a reasonable living and continued his flying experiments. From kites he moved on to model gliders and, eventually to a model aeroplane driven by a pusher propeller, in turn driven by the spring of a window blind. It was moderately successful. By this time, the summer of 1904, news of the Wright brothers' accomplishments had begun to filter through, even to the Saskatchewan prairies, and Gibson was hooked. He decided to build a full-sized aeroplane, but some years were to elapse before he had either the leisure or the money to make the attempt. In the hopes of achieving these requirements, he became a contractor, accepting a "contract to build a 20-mile stretch for the Grand Trunk Pacific Railway,"[1] and almost lost his shirt on the venture. He decided to cut his losses and move to Victoria in the autumn of 1906, where he set about making his fortune by investing what little capital he had left in a gold mine. Unlike so many others, he hit something like a jackpot, selling his share of the mine the following year for $10,000.[2]

With what must have seemed at the time a large amount of money in the bank, he went back to his experiments, flying larger powered models from the hilltop in Victoria's Beacon Hill Park. Then he finally set about building his first real aeroplane.[3] Gibson's approach was in sharp contrast to the two successful North-American types of the time: the Wright and Curtiss biplanes. He started with a rectangular wooden frame, braced with wires and fitted with turnbuckles and springs to provide the correct tension. His wings, placed one behind the other, were 20 feet (6 m) in span and tapered from eight feet (2.4 m) in the centre to about four feet (1.2 m) at the tips. The remarkable thing about the wings was that they had the shape later designers called "gull wing." They sloped down from a peak in the middle for about three feet (0.9 m), then slanted up again towards the tips. This provided a feature that later, once again, came to be called dihedral, and which provided a measure of lateral stability. The wings could also, on the ground, be moved backwards or forwards on the frame so that the correct centre of pressure—and hence fore and aft balance—could be achieved.

He had submitted his design for an engine to Hutchinson Brothers, a machine shop in Victoria, asking them to build it. They were sceptical but agreed to take on the work. It was to be a six-cylinder, in-line, air-cooled, two-cycle engine. The crankshaft was turned by Gill Brothers of New York, and the aluminum crankcase was moulded in Seattle.[4] Everything else was produced and assembled in Victoria. When the airframe was completed in 1910, the engine was mounted below the level of the wings, and directly between them. It drove two propellers, one in front and one at the rear. They were contra-rotating, thus obviating any problems with torque. A front elevator and a rudder at the rear completed a thoughtful and successful design.

It was a splendid accomplishment for which Gibson earned far too little recognition. What his efforts did evoke was derision. He carried out nearly all his experimenting in strict secrecy to try to avoid the jeers of his contemporaries, but the newspapers inevitably discovered when his attempt to fly the *Twin-plane* was to take place. As a Victoria *Daily Times* journalist described it:

After having worked on his invention for years, William Wallace Gibson . . . has at last succeeded in bringing his aeroplane to that state of perfection which enabled him to make a flight this week in the neighborhood of Mount Tolmie [some five miles (8 km) north of downtown Victoria].

The flying machine was seen at dusk Tuesday night in the neighborhood of Dean's farm, where it ascended and was guided successfully for some distance, and then came to the ground again.

Mr. Gibson has worked on the machine for about two years, and a few days ago he had it moved to a tent erected in the fields of Dean's farm, where he has been making his trial flights as secretly as possible in the endeavor to reach perfection before publicly announcing his success....

After the first flight was made successfully, Mr. Gibson took to flying in the morning, and yesterday morning the machine, after ascending, came to the ground again, where the concussion broke one of the wheels. The aeroplane is, therefore, disabled temporarily while a new wheel is being constructed.[5]

Two weeks later, the wheel replaced, Gibson took off again from farmer Dean's field after a run of only 50 feet (15 m). Unfortunately, when he had flown some 200 feet (61 m), he tried to counteract drift with his rudimentary rudder control (two small wooden yokes attached to the rudder control cables were slipped over his arms). He leaned on the wrong one and swung straight towards a sturdy oak tree. He shut off power and landed immediately but rolled into the tree, seriously damaging his machine.

Gibson was philosophical about the accident:

In discussing the flight, Mr. Gibson said he was under the disadvantage of having to learn the art of aviation by experience, there being no "flying schools" in British Columbia. His flights have demonstrated to his satisfaction that the machine is all that is required and all that is necessary to demonstrate it is practice in "airmanship."[6]

In 1911, influenced by Sir Hiram Maxim's book, *Artificial and Natural Flight*, Gibson accepted Maxim's theory that wings of a narrower chord were more efficient than the wings he had designed for the *Twin-plane*—fortunately, he rejected Maxim's curious conviction that, like a ship, an aircraft would be naturally stable and would need no lateral control. So Gibson set about designing his second machine, the *Multi-plane*, using numerous narrow wings of shaped spruce. In place of a stick to control only the elevator, he had a wheel on the central column. The whole column moved fore and aft to operate the elevator; the wheel turned left or right to operate the ailerons—which were attached to the machine by leather hinges. The single rudder at the rear was "operated by a rope controlled by the airman's feet."[7]

This time, anxious to get away from trees, he conducted his experi-

A replica of William Wallace Gibson's *Twin-plane* built by the National Aviation Museum in Ottawa.

The original engine designed and assembled by Gibson to power his *Twin-plane* and, later, his *Multi-plane*.

Gibson (right foreground, in bowler hat) provides a demonstration of the strength of construction of his *Multi-plane*. Twelve adults are standing on the aircraft.

UNIVERSITY OF TORONTO PRESS

RBCM

William Wallace Gibson, circa 1910. By turns a shopkeeper, railway construction contractor and a mining promoter, he became the first man in Canada not only to design, construct and fly his own aircraft, but to design and assemble the engine as well.

A sceptical reporter from the Calgary *Daily Herald* described Gibson's *Multi-plane* as "...a machine that resembles very closely a western hayrack. PABC

VICTORIA, B.C.
1889.

This lithographic print, a precursor to aerial photography, was published by the Victoria *Daily Colonist* in 1889 and demonstrates how small Victoria was then. It had been a white community less than half a century. Even so, there had been a remarkable transformation from the Hudson's Bay trading post of 1846. Spurred by the Fraser River and Cariboo gold rushes of 1858, and the Yukon gold rush in 1898, Victoria had become a city. By 1910, Francis Rattenbury's Legislative Buildings had replaced the old ones—known with a mixture of irony and affection as "The Bird-cages"—and they were followed by the majestic Empress Hotel. The horse and the pack board had been replaced in large part by the street car and the automobile. Then, in 1910, W. W. Gibson brought the air age to Victoria; and in May 1911, Charles Walsh demonstrated that it was here to stay.

PABC

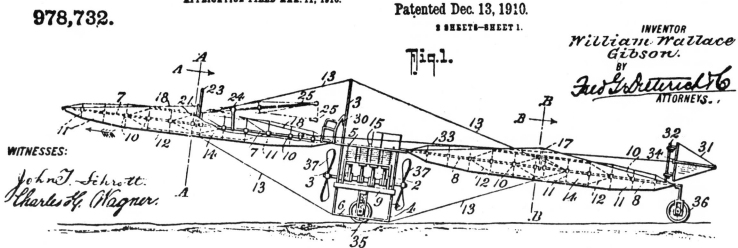

W. W. GIBSON.
FLYING MACHINE.
APPLICATION FILED MAR. 11, 1910.

978,732.

Patented Dec. 13, 1910.
2 SHEETS—SHEET 1.

Fig.1.

INVENTOR
William Wallace
Gibson.
BY
Fred G. Dieterich & Co
ATTORNEYS.

The original patent drawings for Gibson's *Twin-plane*, 1910.   RBCM

The innovative but unsuccessful design of the McMullen and Templeton tractor biplane at Minoru Park in 1911. A more powerful engine might have made all the difference.   PABC

ments in the wide open fields of Ladner, not far from Minoru Park, at the ranch belonging to Thomas Paterson, Lieutenant-Governor of British Columbia:

A Canadian aeroplane, invented by a Canadian, manufactured by a Canadian and operated by a Canadian, made its initial flight at the Paterson Ranch in...Ladner yesterday afternoon. It was not much of a flight, but there is every indication of the invention being a decided success.[8]

The *Daily Colonist* article goes on to forecast "Trips to New Westminster and Vancouver [and] in the near future...before the summer is over the inventor expects to fly from the Delta across the Gulf of Georgia to Victoria." Unfortunately, none of this came to pass because the weather had turned against Gibson. Rain kept the fields too soggy for flying, and continuing humidity began, after six weeks, to cause the aircraft to deteriorate. Once again he moved; this time to Kamloops, where the weather was more suitable. The Kamloops *Inland Sentinel* gave him front-page coverage:

"Kamloops never saw a show like this before." This was the comment of W. W. Gibson, the world famous aviator who is fitting up his flying machine at Alexandra park today. He is making ready for the flights which are to be given on Dominion day [July 1, 1911], Saturday at 3 o'clock.[9]

The almost braggart opening statement is in curious contrast to Gibson's earlier reticence and secrecy, and after this report there was nothing more in the newspaper about Gibson or his *Multi-plane*. Frank Ellis, who met Gibson in his later years, explains why. "He set up his plane in the exhibition grounds...but was pestered by a crooked promoter who tried to inveigle him into advertising the flights." It seems likely that the boastful statement attributed to Gibson by the journalist was, in fact, made by the promoter, because "Gibson left Kamloops...before any tests had been attempted."[10] This time he moved to the farm of a friend on the outskirts of Calgary, where he enlisted the help of a friend, Alex Jaap, as test pilot—and where, once again, the local newspaper, the *Daily Herald*, extended him a front-page welcome:

With a machine that resembles very closely a western hay rack and looks like a huge cage of widely spaced wooden slats braced with wires, two Canadian aviators are making short flights every afternoon....Their names are Gibson and Japp [*sic*].
Terah T. Maroney, an aviator from Great Falls, Montana, who has been studying

aerial navigation for years, accompanied the *Herald* representative out to the ranch to see the Gibson machine yesterday and pronounced it as unique. He examined it carefully and stated that it looked like an invention with a wonderful future.[11]

Gibson's contribution to flying ended on August 11, 1911, when Jaap, after several successful flights, chose a bad spot to land. He let his speed drop until it was too late to abort the landing and discovered that the ground was "...honey-combed with hundreds of badger holes.... His only chance of escape was to drop obliquely into the swampy ground of a nearby coulee. When the machine swooped down into the soft soil the wheels stuck in the mud and the terrific momentum literally tore the aeroplane to pieces."[12] Jaap escaped with a few bruises. Gibson announced his intention to rebuild, but apparently he was running out of money and eventually decided to abandon aviation and turn back to a business career — a successful one.

The next flying experiments in British Columbia also took place in 1911, when two brothers, William and Winston Templeton, and their cousin, William McMullen, built an aircraft based on Curtiss' design but with some modifications. The first indication is tucked away at the bottom of an inside page of the *Colonist* on September 24, 1910:

The Western Motor and Supply company has received an order from Messrs. McMullen & Templeton of Vancouver for the construction of a forty horse-power engine for an aeroplane built by them at Fairview, Vancouver. The engine, of the Humber type, is the first one to be ordered from the Western Motor & Supply company, which holds the agency for the supply of engines and aeroplanes. The machine built by the Vancouver men is of the Glen[n] Curtis[s] type, with some additional features added by the builders.[13]

The most significant "additional feature" was that the Templeton-McMullen machine had its engine and propeller in front of the pilot instead of behind him (the more or less universal practice with biplanes in those days). Apart from that, it was very much like a Curtiss, "with ailerons extending 2 feet [0.6 m] out on each end of the mainplanes... and the ailerons control is by shifting the balance of the seat."[14] An elevator was mounted at the front and a rudder at the rear. The only other departure was the mounting of vertical canvas screens between the upper and lower wings, just inside the ailerons. This was a feature adopted by a number of European designers at the time to minimize sideslipping.

Airship Built in Vancouver

Messrs. Templeton Brothers and McMullen, of Vancouver, B. C., Inventors and Constructors of Their Own Aeroplane.

The aeroplane business is the next to join our city as a commercial enterprise. The Templeton Brothers and W. McMullen, all energetic young business men and inventors of this city, are about to make their debut here in a machine of their own design and construction — planes instead of in the back. This will insure safety inasmuch as in case of an accident the engine will not fall on the driver, but will reach the ground ahead of him. The machine is 28 feet in length, with ailerons extending 2 feet out on each end between the

The newspaper report is confusing. It talks of the Western Motor and Supply Company receiving an order for the "construction" of an engine; then it goes on to say that the company holds the agency for the "supply" of engines. According to Frank Ellis, the Templeton-McMullen biplane was powered by a "three-cylinder, air-cooled, English-made Humber motor of the Anzani type."[15] This sounds much more credible; it is hard to believe that a company in Victoria was capable of constructing aircraft engines in 1911 — particularly since Gibson's engine, produced by Hutchinson Brothers only a few months previously, was the first aircraft engine to be constructed in the whole of Canada. But whether made in England or Victoria, photographs show that it was an Anzani type — a "fan" engine (precursor to the radial), and events proved that its 35 horsepower was insufficient to provide sustained flight. Although the designers accomplished a number of short hops at the Minoru Park race track in Richmond, they were unable to duplicate Hamilton's exploits. The machine was eventually damaged when it ran into a fence. It was then dismantled and stored on the Vancouver waterfront, where it was destroyed a few weeks later by a fire in a boat shed.

Chapter Three

Comedy and Accomplishment

*"...a mad rush from his machine
as though it were haunted."*

THE VANCOUVER *Daily Province*

Meanwhile, in April, 1911, three American pilots appeared in Richmond to give what was promised as a spectacular exhibition at Minoru Park. It was billed as a "Grand Easter Holiday Carnival of Flying-Machines," featuring Jack De Pries and the Manning brothers. Things did not go well for them. What was described as a large and enthusiastic crowd began to lose its enthusiasm because the first demonstration by Jack De Pries, advertised for 3 p.m., failed to get underway until 4:45. Then, after a take-off run of nearly 300 feet (91 m), in what was described as the "big eighty-horse-power machine,"[1] the aircraft finally became airborne only to swerve and ram the fence, scattering spectators in all directions. Fortunately, no one was injured, but the aeroplane was damaged and incapable of flying again that day.

However, a second, "smaller machine, with a forty-horse power motor,"[2] was wheeled out and this time De Pries accomplished a little more. After another long run, he managed to take off, cleared the fence and remained airborne for some 500 feet (152 m) before landing in the adjacent field. That ended the first day's grand exhibitions.

The second day was no more impressive. After another long take-off run, De Pries eventually became airborne and set off in the direction of Steveston, a few miles to the south. This time, he managed to stay in the air for about two miles (3.2 km), landing heavily in a field, damaging the machine and suffering a severe crack on the head in the process. Sunday's *Colonist* reported that "Jack De Pries . . . was probably fatally injured today while endeavoring to effect a landing after making a short flight. The biplane landed heavily, and De Pries was struck on the head with the engine. It is thought the base of his head has been fractured. The victim is in a comatose state."[3] Happily, Monday's *Province* was able to report that he was not seriously injured: "Jack De Pries, the 'Bird man,' has recovered from the concussion of the brain he was alleged to have suffered on Saturday. . . . In making a descent near Minoru Park, De Pries struck his head against a metal rod and bruised his scalp. The Sunday morning paper had his life hanging in the balance, but today it was announced that no fracture had occurred, though the skin was bruised."[4]

On the 18th, the final day of the "Carnival," it was the Mannings' turn. Browne Manning, flying the 40-horsepower machine, just managed to get airborne before landing again and hitting the fence. A second attempt duplicated the first and the *Province* was sardonic about his misfortunes:

Cold feet was a common complaint with the aviators at Minoru Park yesterday. Aerial navigation, the dream of the prime romancer of our boyhood days was nearly brought into vivid realization when Brownie Manning, of Manning Bros., in an attempt to break the height record for aeroplanes, rose about four feet from the ground, and then afraid that he really was going up, he altered his planes and made a quick return to terra firma, ran into a fence and damaged one of his wings, ending by nearly making a record of another kind—a mad rush from his machine as though it were haunted. . . .[5]

Unfortunately, the exhibition had been heavily advertised: the newspapers estimated the crowds on the first day at between 7,000 and 12,000 people. Yet none of the three principals seem to have had any real experience as pilots. De Pries claimed he had made over 1,200 flights without mishap.[6] Another journalist casts some doubt on this claim. Describing De Pries' second flight on the first day, April 14, he reported that "He headed westward right into the teeth of a nice little ten-mile breeze that was blowing. His management of his machine for the short time he was in the air, however, did not compare at all favorably with that of Hamilton . . . the only aviator who has ever previously flown at Minoru. The aeroplane tilted and dived in a very erratic manner. . . ."[7] De Pries' claim of 1,200 flights becomes even

more dubious when, in reply to a reporter's question about why he landed so quickly after this flight, he replied:

"I found a forty-mile current up there."

"Can't you fly in a forty-mile wind?" the reporter asked.

"Yes, if the wind is in the rear of the machine."[8]

This response raises more questions than it answers. A downwind take-off, with a 40-mph wind blowing, would have been something to see. Perhaps the kindest thing one can say about the "Grand Easter Holiday Carnival of Flying-Machines" is that it did little to further the cause of aviation in British Columbia.

The next exhibition a month later, this time in Victoria's Willows Park race track, was more successful, though here again there were hints of dissatisfaction. On May 30, the Victoria *Daily Times* (page 2), reported that a well-known American pilot, Fred. J. Wiseman, was bringing his Curtiss-Farman biplane from Oregon to demonstrate at Willows Park that extended flights were possible. In the event, the pilot turned out to be the lesser-known Charles F. Walsh, who made an uneventful 15-minute flight on his first attempt. On his second, as Victoria's *Colonist* reported, he provided some excitement:

In dodging through the trees one of his planes struck the branch of a tree and cut it off [the branch, not the wing] with the cleanness of a razor. He brought the twig back with him and will keep it as a souvenir. In travelling past the grandstand he took an apple from his pocket [the *Times* reporter claimed it was a potato] and threw it at the judge's box, striking the corner, which illustrates that the aeroplane might be destructively useful when employed for military purposes.[9]

Some time was to elapse before the military were persuaded to share the reporter's view. Walsh flew again, two satisfactory flights of some 15 minutes' duration on the 31st. There was some disappointment when an announced race with an automobile was cancelled ". . . because the B.C. Agricultural Association, so it was said, would not allow an auto on the track."[10] In addition, there were hints of sarcasm because promised passenger rides failed to materialize. "He had well advertised that one and two passenger flights were to be made yesterday afternoon, and the excuse given . . . was that the wind was not right for taking up passengers. There was no wind, and the weather was exactly similar to the previous day, when Walsh said it was fine for taking passengers but blamed the oil purchased in Victoria for his failure to succeed."[11] On

June 1, unhappily because it had been declared a school holiday so that children could watch the exhibition, a strong wind prevented any more flying. Walsh sensibly refused to succumb to the pressures that ended in John Bryant's fatal crash in Victoria two years later.

The next aviation celebrity to appear on the British Columbia scene was William M. Stark, a native of Vancouver. He was a young man of independent means who, like Glenn Curtiss, had started his career with bicycles and motorcycles. In 1901, he claimed the distinction of being the first person in Vancouver to drive an automobile with an internal-combustion engine, and became a car dealer.[12] Early in 1912 he set off to learn to fly at Glenn Curtiss' flying training school in San Diego, California. Curtiss had produced, with his pusher biplane, one of the most successful aircraft in North America at that time, and he was doing well by training newcomers to fly and then leasing them a machine. The pilot who leased the machine would pay 60 percent of his earnings to Curtiss and repairs and maintenance would be a shared cost on the same basis.[13] Billy Stark proved himself an apt pupil, learning not only how to fly, but how to repair his aircraft and maintain its engine. He became the first Canadian pilot who was taught to fly, rather than learning by haphazard way of trial and error.

Stark promptly accepted the lease deal and had his Curtiss biplane shipped back to Vancouver where, on April 13, 1912, he flew in Canada for the first time. This was a private exhibition, and only "Three score friends of William Stark were . . . thrilled at Minoru Park when Vancouver's first aviator gave a splendid demonstration in a Curtiss biplane. . . . At a height of six or seven hundred feet [180-210 m] from the ground he flew miles up and down the river at a speed which approximated a mile a minute. He was up just short of a quarter of an hour . . . and must have covered twelve to fourteen miles [19-22.5 km] through the air."[14] While this may not sound too remarkable, Billy Stark had to overcome the scepticism engendered by the De Pries-Manning fiasco the year before. He wanted to demonstrate that both he and his machine really were capable of flying.

A week later, he made three successful flights that earned rave reviews from the journalists, even though space in the newspapers was still largely pre-empted by news of the sinking of the *Titanic*. Unfortunately for Stark, spectators remained sceptical and only 700 of them watched his performance. Then, on April 24, this time from a larger field near Minoru Park, he took Jim Hewitt, the *Province*'s sports editor, up with him, making Hewitt the first passenger to fly in western Canada. As Hewitt described it:

A trip up one of the express elevators of a modern skyscraper can give one more thrills than a journey with Billy Stark. The ascent was made so evenly and so gradually that the peculiar falling-away sensation which is experienced in the elevator was altogether lacking. The forward movement was responsible for this no doubt. Once in the air the strong rush of the wind kept me so busy hanging onto the rigging to prevent being swept out of the machine backwards that I had no occasion to worry about falling. My only fear was that I might be blown out into space. We dashed through the air at a pace which approximated, as the aviator informed me afterwards, about forty miles an hour [64 km/h], and the feeling was somewhat similar to that which would be experienced on the cowcatcher of an express locomotive travelling at top speed against a head-on gale. The descent was for all the world like the drop of an elevator, but even then it was not so perceptible as the descent of one of those speedy express lifts.[15]

That same afternoon, Billy's Stark's, wife, Olive, became the first woman aeroplane passenger in Canada. She sat beside her husband on a plank attached to the lower wing of his Curtiss, bundled up against the cold, looking at once proud and apprehensive.

Stark's Curtiss biplane, like all aircraft of the time, was light enough to be fragile — a contrivance of bamboo, spruce struts, wire and fabric. The engine was a 75-horsepower, water-cooled V-8, fuelled by a tank mounted above it to afford gravity feed. For strength the airframe relied on wires, accurately tensioned with turnbuckles. It did not take much of an accident to reduce the machine to a tangle of splintered wood and canvas. Its structural integrity was to be tested shortly.

Spectators were still reluctant to make the long trek from downtown Vancouver to Minoru Park. Unfortunately, there were no really suitable locations to be found near the city, so Stark decided to try the exhibition race track at Hastings Park. It was surrounded on three sides by majestic fir and cedar trees so that, regardless of the wind direction, both take-offs and approaches for landings had to be made out over the waters of Burrard Inlet. To make it even more unattractive, the clearing was still studded with tree stumps.

Nevertheless, on May 4, Stark took off in front of a large crowd for an exhibition flight. It lasted for five minutes and ended with a successful

Jack Manning, left, with his brother Browne posing
with their aircraft in front of the grandstand at Minoru
Park, 1911.

VANCOUVER *WORLD*

The Manning brothers, Jack and Browne, on
either side of Jack De Pries the day before their Easter
exhibition flights—performances so brief and precarious
they provoked sardonic reports in the local press.

VANCOUVER *DAILY NEWS-ADVERTISER*

William, "Billy" Stark in his biplane with a young woman who may or may not have flown with him. His wife, Olive, did fly with him to become the first woman passenger in Canada on April 24, 1912. After the Manning-De Pries fiasco the previous year, Stark had to prove himself — and he did, with a polished exhibition of flying skill.

Billy Stark, with reporter Jim Hewitt of the Vancouver *Province* as passenger. Hewitt described the experience as "somewhat similar to riding on the cowcatcher of an express locomotive."

PABC

Stark's Curtiss pusher biplane being prepared for an exhibition flight in front of the Minoru Park grandstand, April 12, 1912.

PABC

On April 10, 1912, Billy Stark became the 110th pilot licenced by the *Fédération Aéronautique Internationale.*

RBCM

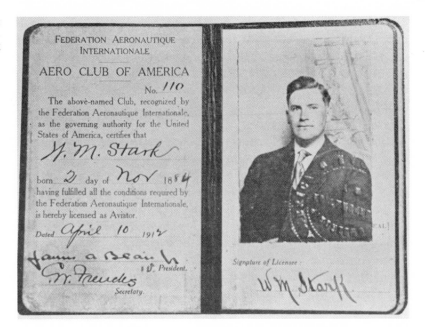

Phil Parmalee and Clifford Turpin's tractor biplane at Hastings Park, Vancouver, before their exhibition flights and the demonstration parachute drops by ''Professor'' Charles Saunders in 1912.

VANCOUVER PUBLIC LIBRARY

landing, even though Stark had to land downwind, an extremely difficult and dangerous thing to do in his lightweight aircraft. He made a second successful flight, but his third, and final one for the day, was more eventful. After flying towards Moodyville, about ten miles (16 km) east of Vancouver, for several minutes, he turned to fly back along the North Shore, executed some figure eights and settled down into his approach, still downwind.

If he hadn't already learned it, what happened next must have taught Billy Stark to anticipate the unexpected. Numerous instances of spectators dashing out in front of an aircraft when it was about to land had been recorded, but this time it was cows. Yet a newspaper reporter seems to have found nothing unusual about the situation: "A herd of cows grazing in the enclosure took fright as he neared the ground and one of them ran directly in front of the machine."[16] Stark had to open the throttle and pull up over it. By now he was obviously going to overshoot the landing, but the surrounding trees were too tall to clear, so he had to cut the engine and land, knowing that he must run into the fence.

"Two assistants, J. Perry, the machinist, and J. Watson, an auto driver, grabbed the machine in an effort to stop it and suffered the unique experience of being run over by an aeroplane."[17] Neither was seriously hurt, and Stark leaped from his seat in time to avoid injury; but his aircraft was damaged and he had to abandon his intention to take up a passenger that afternoon.

Three weeks after this courageous performance, Stark put on another exhibition in Willows Park, Victoria, as part of the May 24 Victoria Day celebrations. He was in the air for 20 minutes but, on landing, his rudimentary front-wheel brake failed to stop him before he reached a fence and his machine was damaged. Repairs were completed by the following day and he repeated the demonstration, this time without incident.

While Stark was performing in Victoria, two American pilots, Phil Parmalee and Clifford Turpin had followed his example; they were giving an exhibition at Hastings Park in Vancouver. Both had been members of the Wright exhibition team until the end of 1911, when they became independents.[18] Using a tractor biplane, somewhat similar to the McMullen-Templeton machine, but evidently with a more

powerful engine,[19] they provided a most successful programme. Not only did they make several impressive flights, but also performed British Columbia's first parachute drop from an aeroplane. Professor Charles Saunders,[20] dropped by Parmalee from 1,000 feet (305 m) over Burrard Inlet, landed safely on the North Shore. Unfortunately, we are not told what Saunders was a professor of, but we are told that he was dressed in red tights and his drop is graphically described in the Vancouver *World*:

Parmalee circled and turned inshore...at a height of about 1,000 feet [305 m]....
Finally Saunders could be seen hanging by his hands clear below the aeroplane. Then Parmalee throttled down the engine a trifle, for the hum of the exhaust perceptibly decreased, and at a signal from Saunders, Parmalee tilted the aeroplane upward, almost at an angle of 45 degrees for a few seconds. This not only decreased the speed of fully 40 miles an hour [64 km/h], at which they were traveling, but it allowed Saunders to drop off into space, grasping the ring of his frail parachute, on the action of which during the next few seconds depended his life.

Straight as a plummet the streak of red below the long streak of white dropped for fully one hundred feet [30 m]. Then, with a couple of preliminary flutters, the rushing air entered the extending ring of the parachute and it swelled like a huge umbrella.[21]

Saunders landed safely on the soft mud of a beach, where he was nearly mobbed by enthusiastic spectators. He had made numerous parachute drops from balloons, but this was his first from an aeroplane; and it was Parmalee's first experience of dropping a parachutist. They repeated the performance the following day. This time the landing was made right in the Park.

Shortly after this most successful exhibition, both pilots came to grief. Turpin was injured in a crash at the Meadows race track in Seattle five days later. An amateur photographer had sprinted out in front of him just as he was landing. Turpin swerved to avoid him and his wing caught on an iron post which swung him into the grandstand.[22] A spectator was killed and fifteen others injured. And, only two days after that, Parmalee was killed in a crash at North Yakima, Washington. He was flying in a strong and gusty wind. Something on his machine broke and he crashed from a height of 400 feet (122 m) into an apple orchard and died on impact.[23]

After this display, the birdmen, as they were invariably called by the journalists of the time, began to move inland to communities where no one had ever seen an aeroplane. Fittingly, it was British Columbia's own Billy Stark who set off to challenge the menacing mountains.

Nelson, B.C., was built on the side of a mountain, as Weldon Cook discovered when he arrived with his "hydro-aeroplane" in 1914. Note the grandstand on the barge behind the sternwheeler SS *Moyie*.

DAVID THOMPSON LIBRARY

Chapter Four

Beyond the Mountains and Over the Strait

*". . . to the aviator mountains loom
up as a hideous death-trap."*

WALTER EDWARDS

Before World War I, pilots never attempted to fly their aircraft from one meeting to the next. The machines were dismantled, crated and shipped by rail, or occasionally by sternwheeler, and then assembled for the exhibition. Little notice was taken of the mechanics who performed this task; the pilot received all the attention and the accolades when a successful flight was made. So it was in this case. On Dominion Day, July 1, 1912, Billy Stark was booked to give an exhibition in Armstrong in the north Okanagan Valley, the first such flight in the interior of the province. When one recalls that in 1912 Armstrong was a small rural community, and that travelling was far less convenient than it is today, the reported crowd of 4,000 people gives an indication of how much excitement these exhibition flights generated. It is interesting, too, to learn that Stark earned $1,500 for this demonstration, and that he did not disappoint his audience. The Armstrong *Advertiser* reported that

The chief attraction, doubtless, was the aeroplane flight by aviator W. M. Stark, a thing never before attempted in a mountainous district in America by any aviator in any machine...and the flight here by Mr. Stark was watched by other flyers all over the world with interest, who were anxious to learn the result of attempting such a flight in a region where gusty and badly broken air currents prevail.[1]

The wind, in fact, did give him some problems. The reporter

estimated it as a "forty mile [64 km/h] gale" and, after flying some four miles [6.4 km] down Otter Lake Valley to the south, Stark swung round in a wide circle and flew back. Then, "passing over the town he went north at about ninety-five miles an hour [153 km/h] and made a wide turn just south of Enderby, coming back on the west side of the Valley against the wind."[2] Unwilling to try a downwind landing, and unable to land into wind because the tall Agricultural Hall was in the way, he landed in a nearby field. The following day, when he went to fly the machine back to the exhibition grounds, he experienced engine problems caused by heavy rain the previous night. Thinking he had solved the problem, he took off, but when he reached a height of some 60 feet (18 m) the engine began missing again. He landed immediately and, "a tire on one of the wheels was punctured and one of the stay braces on a wing splintered."[3] The machine was returned rather ignominiously to Armstrong on a dray and shipped back to Vancouver the following day. But there was no hint of dissatisfaction; on the contrary, the Okanagan Valley community were delighted with their first view of an aeroplane in flight.

Stark was also booked to fly at the annual fruit fair in Nelson in September 1912 but, because of an accident in Portland, Oregon, he passed the contract on to his friend, Walter Edwards, an American pilot. The Nelson *Daily News* reported on September 20 that "the aeroplane has arrived and the airman is on his way." The machine, a Curtiss biplane, had been shipped in crates from Spokane by freight train (and, according to some reports, on the sternwheeler *Moyie*), and Edwards arrived with his manager on the 22nd. For the next week both the annual fair, and Edwards in particular, received almost daily front-page coverage. But Edwards was dismayed. He had not realized that he would be flying in a valley between steep mountains; and, in any case, the fair-ground from which he had to fly was surrounded by power and telephone wires, as well as fences. "Had I known the lay of the land at Nelson, I would never have agreed to my manager signing the contract to fly here," he told a reporter. "To the average tourist, the beautiful mountains are a scene of joy, but to the aviator mountains loom up as a hideous death-trap."

His skill, as it turned out, was equal to his courage and he put on a brave and creditable performance. On the 25th he made a 12-minute

flight, keeping well out over the lake to avoid the turbulence of the sidehills. The following day, after another impressive flight in a cold and gusty wind, he had to make three attempts before landing. Then, on the third, he touched down with too much speed and had to emulate Billy Stark, jumping out of his seat and hanging on to the struts supporting the forward elevator in an attempt to stop the machine. He was dragged along, but managed to slow it down so that very little damage was done when it hit the fence, and he was not injured. On September 27, the weather relented and he flew comfortably. On his third circuit of about three miles, he "caused no little consternation by landing on the C.P.R. flats. . . . When the engine first stopped it was thought he had fallen into the lake but after about five minutes suspense the welcome hum of the motor was heard and shortly afterwards the biplane was seen making for the fair grounds." In spite of Edwards' denial, the journalist who interviewed him afterwards was convinced Edwards had made a bet that he would stop at the flats to pick up a passenger — and that the passenger had lost his nerve and refused.

Mainly because of the flying exhibition, attendance at the fair was "fully five thousand above any previous year." Walter Edwards had given the community of Nelson good value for their money.[4]

These first flights were as significant and exciting as, for an obvious example, the first landing on the moon was to a later generation. At least two residents of Nelson could still recall them vividly after a passage of more than 75 years. Laura Donaldson was born in 1907. She remembers, as a five-year-old, travelling from her home at Crawford Bay to Nelson on a sternwheeler to have her teeth attended to. In the middle of what was no doubt her ordeal, the unfamiliar sound of an aeroplane, as well as shouts of excitement from the street below, rang out. The dentist dropped his instruments, scooped his patient out of the chair and ran down into the street with her. Laura's friends in Crawford Bay were filled with envy when, after returning home, she described what it was like to see an aeroplane flying.

Russ Fletcher was born in 1898 and he recalls playing hookey from school for two days to watch the first flights. As a 14-year-old he retains a much more detailed impression. He was able to describe the shoulder-operated aileron controls of the Curtiss-type pusher. In addition, he remembered that the stern of the machine was tied to a large butcher's

On Dominion Day, 1912, 4000 people turned out at the field adjacent to the Agricultural Hall in Armstrong to watch Billy Stark give the first demonstration flight in the Interior.

Walter Edwards' Curtiss-type biplane at the fair ground in Nelson before his exhibition flights, September 25-27, 1912.

R. WALMSLEY, COURTESY HENRY STEVENSON

We are fortunate that there was a good photographer to record Edward's flights out of Nelson fair grounds. Following his courageous display, the Nelson *News* reported that attendance at the annual fall fair was "fully five thousand above any previous year."

BOB EMORY, COURTESY HENRY STEVENSON

Nelson, matured even more rapidly than Victoria. It turned from a cluster of shacks in 1887, to a community of 800 by 1893. It owed its origin to construction workers for the CPR, who discovered considerable mineralization when they blasted rock cuts through the Kootenay mountains. The discovery brought a steady flow of prospectors. In 1887, two of them stumbled across a rich silver load on Toad Mountain, some five miles from what was to become Nelson, named after the incumbent Lieutenant-Governor.

The discoveries were rich enough to warrant a large smelter and, for several years, Nelson was a boom town. When the mines began to falter, agriculture and logging became the backbone of the economy. The benches along Kootenay Lake proved ideal for fruit growing. Timber was abundant and easy to transport on the lake.

While the larger centres like Vancouver and Victoria had race tracks, the smaller, interior communities invariably had fair grounds, and participated in regattas on the lakes. Nelson's fair ground—later called a baseball park—was the only practical location for the early aviation exhibitions. It was small, surrounded by buildings and hydro wires, but it had to do. The only alternative was the river flood plain, known as the CPR Flats, and here there was no enclosure; consequently, spectators would not have to pay to get close to the aircraft—something everyone wanted.

Another view of Edwards' aircraft at the Nelson fair grounds. This photograph provides a clear picture of rigging and construction details — and also illustrates that oil companies missed no opportunity to advertise their product.

HENRY STEVENSON

The popular exhibition team of Alys and John Bryant with their aircraft in Vancouver, July 1913. Although they were married, Alys still used her maiden name of McKey.

UNIVERSITY OF TORONTO PRESS

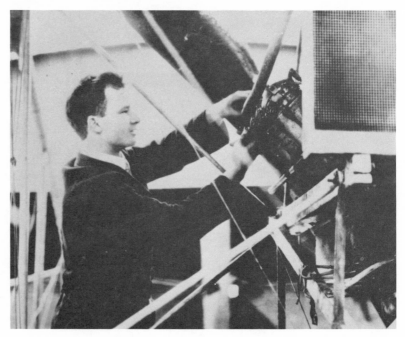

Removing the engine of John Bryant's aircraft from a roof in Victoria's Chinatown after his fatal crash. His wife never flew again after the accident.

VICTORIA *DAILY TIMES*

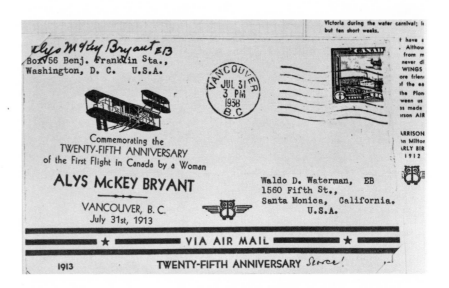

Weldon Cooke's "hydro-aeroplane" at the dock in Nelson, July 14, 1914. This was the last exhibition flight in B.C. before World War I. The photograph has been retouched to delete lettering on the boathouse behind the machine because the letters merged with details of the rigging.

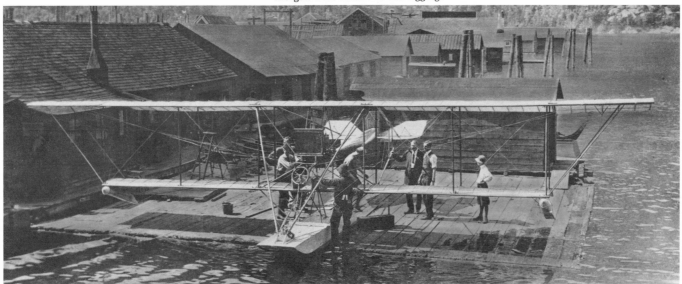

J. HARVEY, COURTESY HENRY STEVENSON

Weldon Cooke in flight over Nelson, 1914.

An unusual and little-advertised exhibition flight over Kelowna, circa 1914.

In August, Cooke had his aircraft shipped to Kelowna. He flew for one day during Regatta week, after which he was gounded by engine trouble. A month later, he was killed in a crash in Pueblo, California.

spring scale, which in turn was attached to a fence post. At take-off, the throttle was opened until the scale indicated there was sufficient thrust for take-off; whereupon, a helper cut the rope in front of the scales with a pair of large shears.[5]

Among the more popular of the early exhibition pilots was the husband-and-wife team of Californians John M. and Alys Bryant, who flew over Richmond at the end of July, 1913, and over Victoria in August. Their manager was F. A. Bennett, the same Bennett who had managed Walter Edwards' flights in Nelson the previous year. The site once again was Minoru Park race track, the aircraft a Curtiss-type pusher biplane. John flew on the morning of July 31, establishing "A new northwest record of 5100 feet" (1555 m).[6] To conclude his demonstration, Bryant throttled back at 2,500 feet (762 m), then dived steeply and, without using his engine again, landed almost exactly where he had taken off. At the time this was considered a very daring manoeuvre. In the afternoon Alys, who was still using her maiden name of McKey, took off and made the first flight in Canada piloted by a woman. This provoked a mixture of admiration, astonishment and, no doubt, some disapproval — women were not supposed to have either the skill or the courage for this sort of thing.

After their performance in Vancouver, the machine was shipped to Victoria to take part in that city's carnival week celebrations. They operated out of Willows race track. Alys made the first attempt to fly over the city on August 5, but the wind was "too boisterous" and she turned back.[7] The following day, John succeeded in flying over the city. Later that afternoon, he flew his machine to Cadboro Bay and landed on the beach, where he converted from wheels to a single pontoon, or float. Taking off and landing on water was a relatively new development; it added another element of novelty. As well, Victoria's inner harbour provided an excellent amphitheatre for spectators to watch the demonstration.

The next morning, August 6, he took off from the water at Cadboro Bay and, in spite of a strong, turbulent wind, he reached downtown Victoria, about eight miles (13 km) away, 20 minutes later, landed in the harbour and "turned into the opening of the wharf behind the G.T.P. [Grand Trunk Pacific], sidling gently in with the tips of his wings almost touching the wharf side."[8] He was greeted by a cheering throng of spectators.

Unfortunately, by the time he was ready to take off again, the wind was gusting even more vigorously. Although reluctant, John was under pressure because of his contract to fly again, and he took off, climbed to about 800 feet (244 m) and circled back over the city. This time the wind was too much for the machine. One wing collapsed and the aircraft crashed onto the roof of a building near the waterfront. The *Daily Colonist* described the accident:

> The daring airman, after twice attempting to bring his machine into the wind and at the same time descend towards the harbour, whence he had arisen five minutes before, dashed down like a plummet as his aircraft became helpless. When the plane [wing] collapsed Bryant was between 350 and 400 feet [110-120 m] from the earth. Bearing him securely attached to the seat, the machine fell almost perpendicularly, alighting upon the roof of the two-story structure at the northwest corner of Theatre Alley and Cormorant Street. With a crash that could be heard for several blocks the hydroplane dashed upon the roof. Bryant was underneath, the craft having overturned in its descent through the air.[9]

John Bryant died shortly after rescuers reached him on the rooftop, the first aviation casualty in Canada; his wife never flew again.

Gerry Wellburn, the distinguished philatelist and founder of the British Columbia Forest Museum in Duncan, witnessed this distressing moment in aviation history. Then thirteen years old, he had bicycled with a friend to a slight prominence at what is now the corner of Douglas and Southgate streets — the northwest corner of Beacon Hill Park. He recalls that it was a windy day and that Bryant had hesitated for some time before taking off. Gerry watched the aircraft climb from the harbour and fly north along Government Street. When the machine began its plunge towards the rooftops, he and his companion jumped on their bikes and pedalled furiously towards the scene; they arrived within three or four minutes of the crash. In Theatre Alley, which is now one of the alleyways in Victoria's Chinatown, they found part of one wing. Gerry kept a piece of the fabric as a souvenir.

By the end of 1913, exhibition flying was past its heyday; the novelty was beginning to wear off as the sight of aircraft in the sky became increasingly familiar. There were, however, two more exhibition flights in B.C. in 1914. The first was given by Billy Stark, in Chilliwack, some 55 miles (90 km) east of Vancouver, flying his trusty Curtiss pusher at the July 1 Dominion Day Fair. This time he was accorded only one paragraph in the local newspaper, the Chilliwack *Progress*, and it was couched in familiar terms. The headline was FLIGHTS OF BIRDMAN AND SPORTS ATTRACT THOUSANDS.

...At 8 o'clock [in the evening] he made another flight, a beautiful one, soaring away to the south and over the town at the rate of 60 miles [96.5 km/h] an hour. It was a graceful sight to see the daring aviator rise to the flight and soaring through the air like a huge bird and alighting in almost the identical spot from which he had ascended. A large crowd witnessed it and applauded loudly.[10]

To prove that generalizations are dangerous, the second exhibition that year was not greeted with a yawn. On the contrary, there was much excitement. The pilot was Weldon B. Cooke. He flew during the first Chahko-Mika[11] celebration held in Nelson on July 14-18, and provided novelty with his Curtiss-type "hydro-aeroplane," a single float configuration with tubular pontoons on the wing tips. The Nelson *Daily News* reported the event in almost as much detail as it had Edwards' visit two years previously:

Almost punctually on his scheduled time of 2 o'clock, Mr. Cooke cranked up his machine and left the float at the rowing club. He skimmed gracefully over the water out past the end of the city wharf, turned down the river and in a few yards rising with the grace of a bird. Ascending higher and higher, he continued down the river until he reached the vicinity of Grohman Creek where he commenced the return journey, passing over the city and continuing well past one-mile point.[12]

The following day "he experienced the worst winds in his career. His first attempt took him about 50 feet [12.5 m] in the air then he was forced to land. On his second try that day the wind carried his plane into the wharf, but without serious damage to his machine. On his third run he made a very short run."[13] He flew again on the 16th, sat out the weather on the 17th and put on a good show on the final day, when: "He made repeated flights up the arm of the lake and several low passes over the crowds. As a final salute Cooke stopped his engine while at a great height and 'volplaned' [glided] to the water amid greetings from the crowd."[14]

A month after these demonstration flights, Cooke had his machine shipped to Kelowna on Okanagan Lake, where he flew it for one day during Regatta week. Trouble with his six-cylinder, water-cooled, in-line Roberts engine prevented any further flights; then, like Parmalee, he was killed in a crash a few weeks after returning to the United States. It seems that, although Cooke was an accomplished pilot, he did not take maintenance very seriously. An inspection, after the fatal crash in September in Pueblo, Colorado, revealed that one of the wooden engine bearers was cracked through its entire length where bolt holes were drilled, one aileron had a broken rib, a control wire had been repaired with a piece of common haywire and the fuel tank had been "repaired" with a wooden plug.[15]

The report of a broken rib in the aileron is intriguing because a close inspection of the photograph taken at the Nelson wharf reveals no sign of the familiar Curtiss inter-plane ailerons; instead, Cooke, who built the aircraft himself in Sandusky, Ohio, the previous year, seems to have installed ailerons to the trailing edges of the upper wings — the photographs taken when he was on Okanagan Lake seem to suggest this. If so, it was a rash thing to do, because the Wright brothers considered this an infringement of their jealously guarded wing-warping patent, and Curtiss had deliberately mounted his ailerons between the upper and lower wings in an attempt to avoid this charge.

Chapter Five

What Had Been Learned?

*"... it was just like you'd been
shackled all your life and you suddenly
tore off your shackles."*

BECKWITH HAVENS

Cooke's flights ended the era of exhibition flying in British Columbia
until after World War I, which makes this a good time to pause and
trace very briefly the development of this brand-new technology in its
first decade. The Wright brothers solved the initial problems in 1903.
Before then, many people had conducted trial-and-error experiments
with limited success. What distinguished the Wrights was their patient,
scientific approach. They began by testing the possibilities of flight with
gliders on the sand dunes near Kitty Hawk, North Carolina. Having
succeeded with gliders, they set about the accomplishment of powered
flight, as Gibson was to do later, by designing and producing their own
engine. They adopted the pusher configuration, with the engine at the
rear of the wings but, to avoid problems with torque, they mounted two
propellers, driven by sprockets and chains from the crankshaft, and
rotating in opposite directions. One of the chains was simply twisted
into a figure eight to provide contra-rotation. In addition, they had
constructed a small but effective wind tunnel to help them find the most
efficient profile for their wings. Then, patiently, they set about solving
the problems of control.

By 1909, their original *Flyer* of 1903 had evolved into what was
considered the most successful aircraft in the world. Nevertheless, it

61

had several shortcomings and quickly lost its supremacy. To the Wrights, the question of vertical control seemed straightforward: they used two large horizontal flaps, or elevators (called horizontal rudders at the time), mounted on a boom in front of the machine, activated by a push rod. The elevators swivelled on pivot points, at first placed half-way between the leading and trailing edges; but this made the elevators too responsive and later the pivot points were moved forward, providing a more satisfactory balance. By pulling a control column back, the Wrights raised the leading edges of the elevators. Wind pressure against them pushed the nose up. Pushing the control column forward had the reverse effect. This was an incomplete solution and most contemporary accounts suggest that the Wright biplanes tended to forge an undulating path through the air, rather than flying straight and level. By 1909, they had moved one of the biplane, front-mounted elevators and installed it as a fixed stabilizer on a tail boom. A year later, and evidently with some reluctance, they moved the elevator system to the rear. The front-mounted elevators were controlled by a vertical lever on the pilot's left hand, moving fore and aft.

Fortunately, the Wrights had not been influenced by Hiram Maxim's theory of natural lateral stability (in fact, they had consciously avoided natural stability), but their solution to the problem of lateral control was, once again, only a partial one. With an ingenious system of wires and pulleys, they warped the outer edges of their wings. If, say, the right wings dropped, their control would pull down the trailing edges of the right wings and, because the two wings with their inter-plane struts were like a flexible box, this would raise the leading edges. Simultaneously, the reverse would occur on the left wings. This had the same effect as ailerons, and provided lateral control. The big drawback to their system was that the wings, because they had to be flexible, lacked the strength required for speed and the stress of rapid manoeuvres. A further disadvantage was that wing-warping was operated by another control column, on the right-hand side of the pilot, moving fore and aft.

The question of directional control was eventually ironed out on their gliders. Beginning with no vertical surface, they discovered that the machine tended to yaw, or sideslip. This was remedied by fitting a vertical fin on a tail boom. Although the fixed fin offered an improve-ment as far as yaw was concerned, the Wrights still had trouble

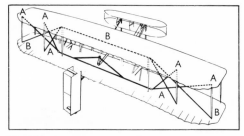

The Wright-wing-warping system.

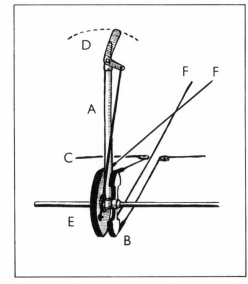

The Orville Wright sub-system of controls, 1909.

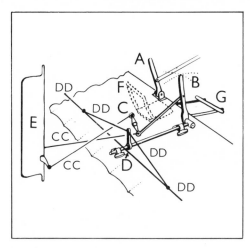

The Wilber Wright sub-system of controls.

executing turns, because, when they sought to straighten out again, wing-warping increased the angle of attack of the low wing, and also increased the drag; thus, without a movable vertical rudder to bring the nose up, the lower wing stalled (thus losing its lift altogether) and the machine went into what came to be known as a spin. "The problem was finally solved by changing to a movable vertical surface. This surface was coupled to the wing warping in such a way that the rudder worked with the lateral controls to start the turn."[1] This, too, was a partial solution. Eventually, they provided separate controls: one for the two rudders on the 1909 machine, and another for wing warping. The rudders were operated by a small, articulating lever attached to the top of the wing-warping control.

The pilot of a Wright machine sat in front of the engine and propellers, on the lower wing, between two control columns. The early Wright machines were equipped with skids as an undercarriage; it was some time before they switched to wheels. To take off, the pilot would start the engine—which, on the early machines, ran at only one speed—later they had a foot control to switch the magneto on and off—and the machine would gather momentum, assisted by a catapult device. Then, when flying speed had been reached, the pilot would pull back on the left-hand column. The first conscious decision he had to make, therefore, was which of the two columns he had to pull back on. At the same time he had to operate the rudder control on top of the right-hand stick. Next, if a wing dropped, he had to remember which stick to use, and remember, too, whether he had to pull the right-hand stick back or push it forward. In short, it required considerable practice and complete concentration to fly the Wright biplane, and it was a long time before these movements became instinctive. This problem was so significant that the Wrights built a simulator on which their exhibition pilots practised lateral control by the hour.[2]

To complicate matters further, when dual controls were introduced for instruction in 1911 they produced two kinds of pilots. Historian Thomas Ray explains why:

The rear elevators of the Wright machine were controlled by one of two vertical sticks located on the outer side of the two pilots' seats. The elevator stick nosed the plane downward when pushed forward and upward when pulled back. When banking for turns, the elevator lever was pulled back to compensate for any loss of altitude—the

The *Scientific American* had been sceptical about aviation's accomplishments until Curtiss' triumph at the Rheims Air Meet in 1909. Now they began to give aviation excellent coverage, as this illustration demonstrates.

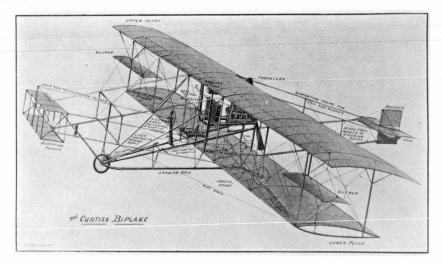

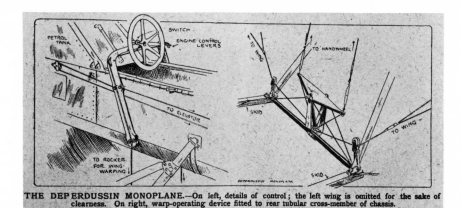

THE DEPERDUSSIN MONOPLANE.—On left, details of control; the left wing is omitted for the sake of clearness. On right, warp-operating device fitted to rear tubular cross-member of chassis.

The Deperdussin control system.

FLIGHT

As this 1910 cover illustrates, in spite of its scepticism, the journal was quicker than most to foresee the potential value of aircraft as military weapons.

Sometimes the pressure was just too much! In fact, the apparently demented gentleman is demonstrating his newly-invented crash helmet to an appreciative audience.

FLIGHT

A beautifully detailed drawing of the Wright biplane. *SCIENTIFIC AMERICAN*

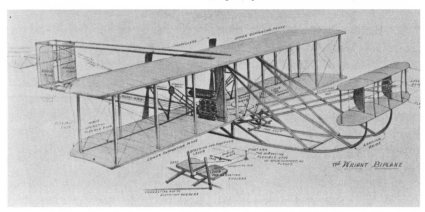

angle of a piece of string dangling freely indicated whether or not the turn was too steep for safety. Generally, the elevator stick as well as the wing-warping and rudder control stick had to be manipulated continuously to maintain level flight. A pedal connected to the magneto controlled the power output during each flight.

Since the Wright plane had only one wing-warping and rudder control lever between the two pilots' seats, each Wright pilot learned to steer the Wright plane with either his right or left hand, depending on which of the two seats he occupied during his training period.[3]

The first competition to the Wrights' domination of aviation in North America came from a group of remarkably talented designers assembled by Alexander Graham Bell, the by-then wealthy inventor of the telephone, who had been experimenting with kites and decided to move into the realm of powered flight. In fact, it was Dr. Bell's wife, Mabel, who put up the financing for this group, which called itself the Aerial Experiment Association (A.E.A.). The group was composed of two Canadian engineers, Frederick W. (Casey) Baldwin and John A. D. McCurdy; a member of the United States Army, Lieutenant Thomas Selfridge; and another American, Glenn H. Curtiss.

Curtiss, like the Wright brothers, had started his career making and repairing bicycles. He had graduated to motorcycles and became one of the most successful manufacturers. In 1904 he established the world speed record on one of his motorcycles at Ormond Beach in Florida, travelling at more than 60 mph (96.5 km/h), and went on to set several more, "culminating in his establishing a world speed record of 136.3 m.p.h. [219.3 km/h] at Ormond Beach in 1907."[4] By 1908, his engines were in demand for dirigibles, and it was for this expertise that he was invited to join the A.E.A. at a salary of $5,000 a year.

Dr. Bell had his summer home at Baddeck, Nova Scotia, and all the group's experimental flying was done either there or near the Curtiss machine shop in Hammondsport, N.Y. The group adopted a plan in which each member would become the design chief of an experimental aircraft. Their successes with the *Red Wing*, the *White Wing*, the *June Bug*, and the *Silver Dart* — the first aircraft to be flown by a Canadian, John McCurdy, in Canada — have been amply recorded.[5] For our present purposes, it was the evolution of the Curtiss-designed *June Bug* that is important.

By the end of 1908, Curtiss was progressively moving away from the A.E.A. to design and build his own aircraft. The first of these he called the *Gold Bug*, built in 1909 and, a little later, renamed the *Golden Flyer*. In many ways the *Gold Bug* was similar to the Wright machines, a pusher-driven biplane with a rudder at the rear, but with front-and-rear elevators — the front activated by a push rod, the rear with pulleys and wires — from a central control column. By moving the control column back, the leading edge of the front flap was raised. Wind pressure against it pushed the nose up. The leading edge of the rear flap was simultaneously lowered, pushing the tail down. Like the Wrights' solution to the problem, this was an incomplete one. But the big differences between the two machines were in the engine (an eight-cylinder, water-cooled engine generating 40 horsepower, as opposed to the 20 horsepower the Wright engine was capable of at the time), the use of a single propeller and the use of ailerons instead of wing-warping. The ailerons were mounted between the outer edges of the two wings and operated differentially, giving positive lateral control and allowing a much more rigid, and thus stronger, wing construction.

Even more important was the configuration of the pilot's controls. Now the pilot sat with a central control column between his knees, operating the elevators. On top of this control column was a wheel that activated the vertical rudder at the stern. Finally, the ailerons were operated by two yokes which fitted against the upper arms of the pilot. All of this meant that the controls acted with natural, reflexive movements. If the pilot wanted to go up he pulled back on the control column; if he wanted to go down, he pushed forward. If he wanted to turn horizontally, he turned the wheel in the direction he wanted to go. If a gust of wind caused one wing to drop, he simply leaned in the other direction to raise it.[6]

And when dual controls were installed on the Curtiss machine, they presented no problems: "The steering wheel was hinged on the control post so that it could be shifted and locked in front of either of the two pilots' seats. In addition, two pairs of shoulder yokes were provided so either pilot could operate the aileron controls."[7]

Because of these natural controls, the Curtiss aeroplanes gradually outstripped the Wrights in the era of exhibition flying. Although the Wrights, who had patented their wing warping technique, claimed that Curtiss' ailerons infringed their patent — the tangled litigation dragged on for more than a decade — Curtiss began to manufacture aircraft in his Hammondsport plant and became the most successful aircraft designer in North America for many years to come. One of the unexpected outcomes was that exhibition pilots could grip the central control column between their knees, hold their hands up in the air and control the machine by leaning one way or the other. "Look Ma, no hands!" was like magic to spectators, and Lincoln Beachey became famous for this "stunt." For the record, the aileron concept had been used by Esnault-Pelterie on a glider in France in 1904, and by the celebrated Brazilian pilot Santos-Dumont in 1906, once again in France.[8]

The next big step forward in controls came by accident in 1911. At the time, all Curtiss biplanes had an elevator mounted on a boom in front of the machine, as well as one on the tail. Two of Curtiss' exhibition pilots, Lincoln Beachey and Beckwith Havens, were flying at an exhibition. As Havens describes the development:

Lincoln Beachey was flying one day and hit a fence and broke his front controls. Well, there was a lot of money riding on this date and Beachey was out after it. So even though he didn't have any front control he flew anyway. He did some wonderful flying! So I thought, "There's something about this — he couldn't fly that much better than anyone else. I'll take my front control off, too."[9]

Havens' mechanic was reluctant to do this without permission from Curtiss. In the end, a day or two later, he agreed only if Havens would try out the machine before exhibition flying started for the day. "So I did," Havens records, "and it was just like you'd been shackled all your life and you suddenly tore off your shackles. Oh, it could fly! It was a mistake having those two controls, one in front and one in back, because the two controls were just fighting each other."[10]

Thereafter, it became virtually universal practice to mount a single elevator on the tailplane. The next change was to move the ailerons from between the wings and mount them on the trailing edges of the wings themselves. The system of controls adopted by the Frenchman Deperdussin for his monoplanes had become popular in Europe. An article in the British journal *Flight* described it in 1911. "The control is extremely neat, and the movements are more or less natural. A wheel, mounted in the centre of an inverted U-shaped sweep of wood, is rotated for the correction of lateral balance, while a to-and-fro motion controls the elevation. Steering is effected by the usual form of pivoted foot lever."[11] This system was later adopted — without the U-shaped sweep—by Curtiss for his JN series, until he finally settled for a stick and rudder pedals on the JN-4. Louis Blériot, conqueror of the English Channel, is generally credited with the adoption of the control configuration that has a central control column operating the elevators with a fore-and-aft movement, the ailerons with a lateral movement—and foot pedals to operate the rudder. Both of these latter systems have lasted until the present day.

The first decade of flying had been one of great excitement, considerable wealth to some, death to others. After the problems of controls had been solved, propellers and engines were the biggest headache for early designers and pilots. Countless shapes of propeller were tried in an attempt to improve their efficiency; and few engines would operate for very long before overheating. Time, and many experimental modifications solved these problems—propellers became more effective, engines more reliable and more powerful—and then, just as people were beginning to think of aircraft for other uses besides exhibitions, World War I broke out in Europe, and aviation emerged from its fragile beginnings into an era of rapidly evolving and more reliable technology.

Wartime brought urgent pressure for progress in aircraft design and construction. Geoffrey de Havilland's BE 2C illustrates how quickly designers and manufacturers responded. This photograph is of a BE 2C, restored by the National Aviation Museum, Ottawa, in 1964.

Britain's Maurice-Farman "Shorthorn," one of the most effective of the early designs in World War I.

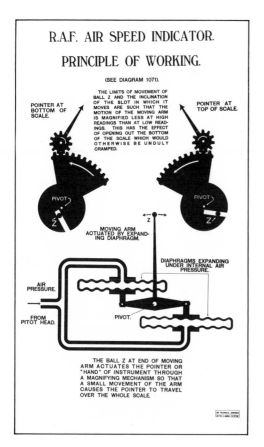

R.A.F. AIR SPEED INDICATOR.

PRINCIPLE OF WORKING.

(SEE DIAGRAM 1071).

THE LIMITS OF MOVEMENT OF BALL Z AND THE INCLINATION OF THE SLOT IN WHICH IT MOVES ARE SUCH THAT THE MOTION OF THE MOVING ARM IS MAGNIFIED LESS AT HIGH READINGS THAN AT LOW READINGS. THIS HAS THE EFFECT OF OPENING OUT THE BOTTOM OF THE SCALE WHICH WOULD OTHERWISE BE UNDULY CRAMPED.

POINTER AT BOTTOM OF SCALE.

POINTER AT TOP OF SCALE.

PIVOT

PIVOT

Z

Z'

MOVING ARM ACTUATED BY EXPANDING DIAPHRAGM.

DIAPHRAGMS EXPANDING UNDER INTERNAL AIR PRESSURE.

AIR PRESSURE.

FROM PITOT HEAD.

PIVOT.

THE BALL Z AT END OF MOVING ARM ACTUATES THE POINTER OR "HAND" OF INSTRUMENT THROUGH A MAGNIFYING MECHANISM SO THAT A SMALL MOVEMENT OF THE ARM CAUSES THE POINTER TO TRAVEL OVER THE WHOLE SCALE.

Chapter Six

The War in Europe

"... feared that the sound of aero engines would frighten their horses."

BRITISH MILITARY COMMANDER

World War I inevitably accelerated the pace of progress in aviation technology. Under the pressures of competition for technical as well as physical superiority inevitable in military conflict, more money was available for designers to test their ideas and improve their engineering techniques. The other legacy, a lasting one, was to provide a sizeable pool of trained personnel when peace did come. Virtually all the commercial pilots and mechanics in Canada in the post-World War I era had seen military service; many of them were still referred to by their rank several years after the war ended. A brief survey will help to set the scene.

When war broke out in Europe in 1914 the concept of empire was still very much a reality in Canada and there was no shortage of volunteers to join the militia and, later, the Canadian Expeditionary Force (CEF). When it came to flying, however, the only avenue for service was with the British Royal Flying Corps (RFC) or the Royal Naval Air Service (RNAS). Earlier, there had been two "blips" on the Canadian military aviation screen, but neither developed beyond that. In the first, the Canadian members of the by-then defunct Aerial Experiment Association, McCurdy and Baldwin, formed the Canadian Aerodrome Company, and were trying to make an impression on the Department of Militia and Defence. Because the *Silver Dart*, which had first flown in Hammondsport, N.Y., in December 1908, had received considerable coverage in the newspapers, there was some patriotic interest in generating a Canadian aviation corps. "The Governor General had officially drawn the attention of the British Government to the flying being done at Baddeck. Such services 'should be retained for Empire,'"[1] he suggested. And "Dr. Bell did his best to give the two young men a boost by speaking to the Canadian Club in Ottawa on March 17, 1909, before an audience that included the Duke of Connaught, then Governor General, and the Minister of Finance."[2]

Encouraged by Major G. S. Maunsell, the Department's Director of Engineering Services, an unflagging proponent of the value of aircraft to the military, the Department invited McCurdy and Baldwin "to conduct flying trials" at Petawawa, Ontario, in 1909. Conditions at Petawawa were far from ideal; the soil was soft and sandy. Four short flights were accomplished with the *Silver Dart* before McCurdy "struck the edge of a sandy knoll" while landing with the sun in his eyes, and the machine was severely damaged.

McCurdy and Baldwin now produced *Baddeck I*, their new company's first aircraft. It was untested and, in front of a large audience of military brass, it succeeded in making one short flight of about 100 yards (91 m) before a faulty engine switch ended this run. The high-ranking officers left to return to Ottawa, but the following day *Baddeck I* made its second flight. "Again, after running about two hundred yards [183 m], McCurdy lifted the nose and the aeroplane climbed very gradually. Unfortunately, after flying another hundred yards and gaining speed, the aircraft suddenly nosed up, climbed to thirty feet [9 m], stalled, and fell to the ground, landing hard on its after section. McCurdy was only slightly bruised, but his machine was badly damaged."[3]

That was the end of the trials, and the end of the Canadian Aerodrome Company's hopes of selling its aircraft to the Canadian military.

The second "blip" occurred in 1914, and can only be described as one of the many aberrations of the mercurial Sam Hughes, Minister of Militia. In the words of S. F. Wise, the official historian of the RCAF:

...early in September two men arrived at Valcartier, Que, where the 1st Contingent of the Canadian Expeditionary Force was preparing to sail for overseas and where Hughes himself had gone to supervise activities. Sam Hughes—who up to now had shown himself to be "not favourable to aircraft"—impetuously granted both of them commissions, authorized the purchase of a secondhand aeroplane, and so improvised a flying corps which sailed with the 1st Contingent. The two airmen, with the ranks given them by Hughes, were Lieutenant W. F. N. Sharpe of Prescott, Ont., and Captain E. L. Janney of Galt, Ont.[4]

Janney was "appointed provisional Commander of the Canadian Aviation Corps . . . and authorized to purchase one bi-plane, with necessary accessories, entailing an expenditure of not more than $5,000.00."[5] Janney purchased a Burgess-Dunne in Marblehead, Massachusetts, ". . . a tailless, swept-wing float-plane with a pusher propeller and two seats positioned in tandem in an open nacelle mounted on the lower wing."[6] Powered by a 100-horsepower Curtiss OX engine, it was a remarkably stable aircraft and there is evidence to suggest that Janney's decision to purchase this particular machine would have been supported by some distinguished aviation authorities. The prototype Burgess-Dunne was flown for the first time by test pilot Clifford Webster in March 1914. By May, the machine had aroused so much interest, and praise, in aviation circles that a committee of the Aero Club of America was struck to observe and report on its performance and flying characteristics.

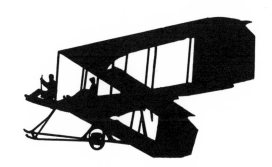

The tests were flown by Clifford Webster and lasted from about 11:00 A.M. to 4:30 P.M. The wind was quite strong, but this only allowed the plane to show off to advantage.

The report of the committee appeared in *Flying* for June 1914 and was enthusiastic to a degree seldom encountered apart from advertising copy. Webster had demonstrated that the Burgess-Dunne could be put in almost any position and, by itself, recover and continue flight on an even keel.[7]

Unfortunately, though, this was the same machine Janney had purchased, so that by September it was in need of a thorough overhaul, for which Janney could not afford the time. Instead, after a hasty and superficial overhaul, the aircraft was crated and shipped to Isle La Motte on Lake Champlain, Vermont, where it was assembled by the company's mechanics. From there, Webster flew with Janney as far as Sorel, Quebec, where they landed to refuel. A crowd had gathered on the wharf, and they expected to be welcomed as intrepid airmen. Instead, as they tied up, they realized that "their reception was to be a hostile one. The Chief of Police was the first to speak: his words were, 'You're under arrest.' He ordered Janney to hand over the pistol he was carrying and with the jeering crowd following behind, he marched the two men off to the local police station about a block away." They were suspected of being on a mission "... to bomb the Parliament Buildings at Ottawa for German sympathizers in the States."[8] A telephone call to Ottawa brought their release and, after refuelling, they left a disappointed Police Chief on the wharf and took off again.

Then, a few miles past Three Rivers, the engine started to act up. They landed to check it, decided, reluctantly on Webster's part, that it would do, took off again and flew a little further towards Quebec City before the engine packed up altogether and they had to put down on the water. They were towed ashore to the village of Deschaillons. Here, according to S. F. Wise, "the aircraft was loaded aboard a transport" to finish its journey to Quebec City.[9] According to Frank Ellis, the engine needed major repairs and Webster had to phone "his company at Marblehead, requesting that spare parts and mechanics be sent to Deschaillons as soon as possible." When the machine was serviceable again, they suffered more tribulations with a water-logged float before finally completing the trip to Quebec City by air.[10] Ellis' version is supported by H. A. Farr, who should have been in a position to know (see below).[11] Either way, the machine arrived in time to be embarked with the 1st Contingent of the CEF.

By this time, a third member had been added to the Canadian Aviation Corps. Harry A. Farr of West Vancouver became its first and only mechanic, with the rank of Staff Sergeant.[12] But then, having made his impulsive gesture, Sam Hughes apparently lost interest in his newly-established Aviation Corps. When it arrived in Britain, the Burgess-Dunne aircraft, in poor condition to start with, and further damaged in transit, was apparently shipped off to be stored at the Central Flying School at Upavon. Janney and Farr were discharged; Sharpe was transferred to an RFC squadron at Shoreham, where he was killed when he crashed on his first solo flight. By May 1915, the Canadian Aviation Corps had been disbanded.[13]

With this single exception, because neither the Royal Flying Corps, nor the Royal Naval Air Service was prepared to fund flight training in Canada, would-be pilots had only two options: either they had to enlist in the regular military forces and hope for a transfer on their arrival in Britain; or they had to pay for their own flying training before they could be accepted. The latter was usually an expensive proposition

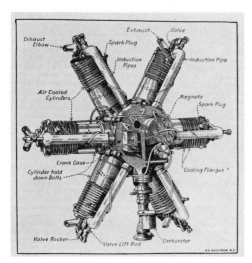

Schematic of an Anzani radial engine.

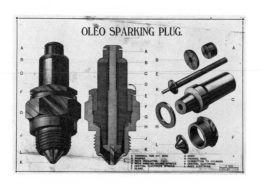

because most of them had to go to one of the flying training schools in the United States. In addition to the tuition fees, they had to support themselves for the several months it took to earn their licence. The most authoritative was the certificate issued by the *Fédération Aéronautique Internationale*. In the U.S. this was granted under the auspices of the Aero Club of America; in Canada by the Aero Club of Canada; and in Britain by the Royal Aero Club. Canada, not surprisingly considering its resources at the time, balked at the cost of forming a Flying Corps; and when one was formed in this country, it was not a Canadian but an Imperial Flying Corps, as we shall see.

The British, meanwhile, had made a slow start in aviation. Compared to France and Germany, they had little in the way of British-made aircraft and, with the notable exception of Claude Graham-White, the flamboyant S. F. Cody and Lieutenant J. W. Dunne (the same Dunne who had designed the Burgess-Dunne biplane), few practising pilots and designers.* The military, while vaguely perceiving the advantages an aeroplane might provide in reconnaissance, "feared that the sound of aero engines would frighten their horses";[14] and, as Major Maunsell had explained to the Canadian Militia Council in 1909, the British War Office's philosophy in aviation was "to encourage experiments, but to buy nothing."[15]

However, since 1908, the British Army had been experimenting with balloons (as had the Americans and the Prussians much earlier), mainly for artillery spotting, and established an organization called the Imperial Balloon Factory in Farnborough. Towards the end of 1910, the Balloon Factory was renamed the Royal Aircraft Factory, and expanded to include aeroplane experiments. (In 1918, it was to be renamed for a third time, the Royal Aircraft Establishment, to avoid confusion with the newly-formed RAF.) Then, on April 1, 1911, the Army formed an "'Air Battalion of the Royal Engineers, to which will be entrusted the duty of creating a body of expert airmen.... The training and instruction of men in handling kites, balloons, aeroplanes, and other forms of aircraft will also devolve upon this battalion.'"[16] Finally, in 1911,

---

* However, a number of names destined for fame in aviation—A. V. Roe, Geoffrey de Havilland, T. O. M. Sopwith and Frederick Handley Page—were beginning to emerge; but they were handicapped by lack of funds and, surprisingly, the lack of an effective and reliable British aero engine.

A Vickers FB-5 "Gunbus."

DONALD CHAPMAN, COURTESY GEOFFREY ROWE

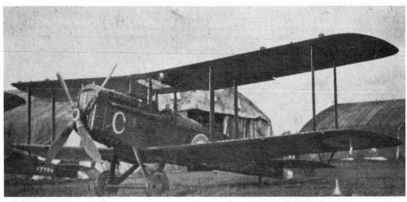

A DH4.   GORDON PETERS COLLECTION, RBCM

Another admirable restoration: an Avro 504K. This model, together with the Curtiss JN-4, were the Allies' two most successful and widely used training aircraft in World War I. Bob Bradford, left, and Paul Hartman at the Rockliffe air show, August 1968.

GEOFFREY ROWE

The Sopwith Camel was one of Britain's most successful fighter aircraft. This was an experimental F.1/1, with tapered wings and a 130-horsepower Clerget engine. It was abandoned because it proved no better than the standard Camel.

NATIONAL MUSEUMS OF CANADA, COURTESY GEOFFREY ROWE

The cockpit of a de Havilland DH9A. Although the number of instruments was increasing, blind-flying was still in the future.   RBCM

A Sopwith Camel taking off. This was probably a night fighter. The two forward firing machine guns were mounted on the upper wing so that the pilot would not be blinded by the gun flashes.

NATIONAL MUSEUMS OF CANADA, COURTESY GEOFFREY ROWE

spurred by developments on the Continent — the French had some 200 serviceable military aircraft, Britain 12 — the War Office decided to create a

...Royal Flying Corps to embrace "soldiers, sailors and civilians." No one would hold executive rank unless he were an expert flyer. The present Air Battalion would cease to exist and would be absorbed into the new corps. The headquarters would be at Netherton, on Salisbury Plain, and a large tract of land had been purchased for this purpose for the sum of £90,000.[17]

Clearly, the British War Office was as reluctant to spend money on training its aviators as was its Canadian counterpart. "To join the Royal Flying Corps, officers would first have to have the consent of the military authorities, be medically fit, and then obtain a Royal Aero Club Aviators Certificate. The cost of this, some £75, would have to be borne by the officer, but would be refunded if he was passed by and accepted into the R.F.C."[18]

By Royal Warrant, the RFC became an official entity on May 13, 1912, but then, as in Canada, an element of comic opera ensued. There were plenty of young men willing to pay for their flight training, but practically no suitable aircraft were available — the ultimate strength of the Corps was to be 131 aircraft — so, finally, despite its policy of "buy nothing," the government had a competition to select an aircraft. The trials took place on Salisbury Plain in August, 1912.

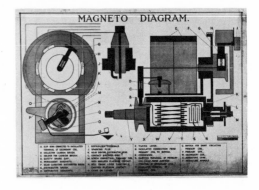

[They were] not an outstanding success. Twenty-five aircraft took part, almost a third of them French. The tests called for a series of flights to demonstrate climbing ability, top speed, load-carrying potentialities and operation from rough ground. The last mentioned test involved a landing and take-off in a ploughed field.

Entirely at the whim of the weather, the aircraft staggered through the tests with varying degrees of success. Among the contenders was the inimitable Cody, who had entered a huge aircraft nicknamed "The Cathedral" [the Cody V]. This was powered by an equally huge 120 horsepower Daimler engine.[19]

In fact, Cody's massive biplane was almost totally unsuitable for military use. It was more like a large kite than an aeroplane, and only its powerful engine kept it in contention. In the end, it was declared winner of the competition — even though it placed fifth on average in the various trials. "One can only conclude," writes historian J. M. Bruce, "that the judges must have been overly impressed by the unquestionably excellent field of view enjoyed by the Cody's crew and, perhaps, by the hand starter and the braking device, this last being an example of

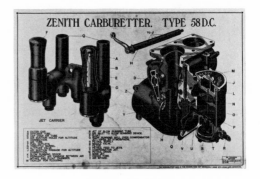

Neanderthal technology. It consisted of a chain wrapped round the landing skid to provide extra ground drag; this chain could be lifted by the pilot to permit take-off."[20]

Norris has a more plausible explanation:

Paradoxically, there was one other aircraft present which should obviously have been declared the outright winner. This was a B.E.2, designed by Geoffrey De Havilland and built at the Royal Aircraft Factory. But the factory had no authority to construct aircraft as it was purely an experimental establishment. It overcame this by "refurbishing" crashed aircraft. "Refurbishing" usually meant a completely new design by the gifted De Havilland. The designations applied to the aircraft continued this fiction. The letters "B.E.," for instance, stood for "Blériot Experimental" because the machine was, ostensibly, a reconstructed Blériot.[21]

If the British appear even more bumbling than usual in their approach to the use of aircraft as a military weapon, it is only fair to point out that in the United States, where the very first aeroplane flight was accomplished, the military were just as hesitant and ineffectual. For reasons inscrutable to anyone but a large military bureaucracy, aviation had become the responsibility of the Signal Corps, and the Corps possessed a motley collection of aircraft: six Wright pusher biplanes; three Curtiss pusher biplanes; two Burgess & Curtis (not Curtiss) pusher biplanes and one Burgess & Curtis H tractor biplane. Moreover, the Corps' big problem was that pilots trained on the Wrights could not fly the other aircraft — because they had the Curtiss control system — and vice versa. To make matters worse, the Wright machines suffered a series of accidents.

Between July 1913, when No. 11 was lost at Texas City, and February 1914, when Lt. Post died in No. 10, every machine of this type but No. 16 . . . was destroyed in an accident, usually killing the crew.[22]

As a consequence, the Chief Signal Officer appointed a board of enquiry. On February 24, 1914, the board recommended "that all pushers be removed from service." This meant that "Only No. 22 was left for training — one airplane, on the eve of the beginning of the First World War in Europe!"[23] By a curious coincidence, a similar, but less binding decision had been made in Britain in the summer of 1912 after two monoplanes had crashed, both with fatal results. In this case, although a committee of investigation concluded that both accidents had almost certainly been caused by pilot error, and "although the monoplane was exonerated, the feeling of revulsion remained. The Monoplane had been given a bad name and the early pilot was a superstitious fellow."[24] The consequence was that the British concentrated almost exclusively on the design of biplanes throughout World War I.

Nevertheless, if there had been an element of farce in Britain at the outset, the Royal Flying Corps soon dispelled it when war broke out. Then even the most reactionary army commander was forced to concede that aircraft were invaluable as a tool for reconnaissance — for monitoring enemy troop dispositions and movements. The next development was to try to stop the enemy from enjoying the same advantage. Aircraft were provided with armament — at first revolvers and rifles, then machine guns — and aerial warfare took on its own dimensions. Given these realities, the British government abandoned its parsimonious policy and began to recruit and train large numbers of pilots, observers and mechanics. At the same time, the race was on to produce faster, more powerful and more manoeuvrable machines. Inevitably, people began to think of machines capable of carrying bombs and, by doing so, becoming offensive as well as defensive weapons. All of this resulted in a vastly accelerated development of aircraft design and construction.

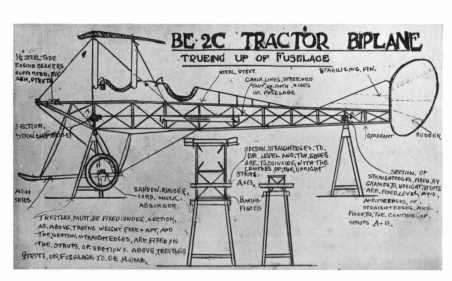

A drawing from the workbook of mechanic
L. Hill, RNAS, 1915.
CLARENCE HILBORN ESTATE

Chapter Seven

The War in Canada

"A Patriotic Undertaking For Defence"

BRITISH COLUMBIA AVIATION SCHOOL PROSPECTUS

Although military thinking was changing in Europe, back in Canada, there had been no change in attitude. While realizing that air power was now an important factor in the war, the Canadian government showed no inclination to become financially involved. Instead, two privately operated flying training schools opened in Canada in 1915. The first, and major one, was the Curtiss Aviation School, which began operations in May, 1915 at Long Branch near Toronto. At the same time a factory managed by John McCurdy, Curtiss Aeroplanes and Motors Limited, was established for the production of aircraft in Toronto. The factory produced Curtiss JN-3, two-seater tractor biplanes (which developed shortly afterwards into the JN-4), and which, together with the British Avro 500 series, were the most successful training machines of World War I.

The Curtiss Aviation School in Toronto was started with sufficient capital to build three impressive hangars at Long Branch. In addition, a flying boat base was established at Hanlon's Point, on the island facing Toronto harbour. Two hangars were erected and training commenced with a number of Curtiss two-seater flying boats, while the JNs were used for landplane training at Long Branch. Long Branch was Canada's first airfield and Hanlon's Point its first seaplane base.

In addition, the government paid for the training of eligible pilots "on the understanding that graduates would proceed overseas at government expense to become members of either the RNAS or the RFC."[1] The

Curtiss Aviation School in Toronto provided the RFC and the RNAS with many competent pilots, more than a few of whom went on to distinguished careers in aviation after the war ended.

The second private training school to open was in Vancouver. Its beginnings were far more humble than its Toronto counterpart as, unfortunately, was its contribution to both the war effort and aviation in general. The prime mover was Billy Stark, who had earned his spurs as an exhibition pilot in Vancouver and Armstrong in 1912, and Chilliwack in 1914. The Curtiss pusher Stark had brought to Canada from San Diego, where he was trained at the Curtiss school in 1912, was still in flying condition in 1915. He managed to persuade a group of patriotic businessmen to join him in the venture:

In the summer of 1915, he [Stark] and Judge "Jack" Schultz, together with W. E. Burns, met at Ye Old English Billiard Parlour, in Vancouver, and decided to start a flying school. Each member was to contribute $100 with which to buy a plane. Twenty-seven people agreed to join, but only 12 contributions were forthcoming. J. W. Pattison, J. H. Senkler, K.C., and H. O. Bell-Irving, Sr. were part of this group.

Further funds were raised by public subscription and the Club purchased Stark's plane for $2,500. Stark was appointed flying instructor at $25 a week. Pupils were to pay $200 towards expenses, and the Canadian Government agreed that graduated pilots would be given all assistance to go overseas to join the RNAS or the RFC. Imperial Oil donated 200 gallons [910 l] of gasoline and twenty gallons [90 l] of lubricating oil. An application was made to the Federation Aeronautique International[e] in France for official recognition and the issuance of a charter. This was granted and the Aero Club of British Columbia commenced operations as a flying training school at Minoru Park.[2]

Stark's duties as an instructor were arduous. His Curtiss was a single-seater; hence he had to sit on a plank on the leading edge of the lower wing, shouting instructions to his pupils while they practised taxiing up and down the field—a field that was far from smooth. After this rudimentary dual instruction, the pupils would travel solo, gradually increasing their speed until they were making short hops over the ground. Stark employed the technique he had learned from Curtiss at San Diego. He put a wooden block under the foot throttle to limit the pupil's speed. As the pupil became more adept, the block was shaved down until, finally, he was able to make longish flights within the bounds of the flying field. The problem now was that the field they were using was not long enough for this to be done safely, so they moved to a nearby farm in an area called Terra Nova on Sea Island, near the site that was eventually to become Vancouver International Airport.

The field had been prepared and a 30- by 40-foot (9 x 12 m) hangar erected at one end of the "runway." Now it was possible for the pupils to take off and circle the field. Things were going well. Between September and November, two pupils, M. E. Seymour and P. E. Smith graduated. They were examined and passed by Lieutenant Colonel C. J. Burke of the RFC who had come out from Britain to interview prospective Canadian candidates for the Corps. By November, however, the field had become waterlogged and a third move was necessary. This time they moved to a building belonging to the Royal Vancouver Yacht Club in Coal Harbour.

Billy Stark had had his machine fitted with a single pontoon the previous year and flown it as a hydroplane around Stanley Park in Vancouver. With the help of Henry and James Hoffar, who were boat builders, Stark's machine was once again converted to a floatplane and training resumed — but only in a desultory fashion because the weather was consistently inclement. On one of their occasional training sorties, with the pupil taxiing across the water at a good clip, and Stark on his piece of plank attached to the lower wing shouting instructions, the single pontoon hit a submerged log. Both men suffered a ducking, but fortunately they were uninjured and quickly picked up by a passing ferry.[3] However, Ken Molson and H. A. Taylor have a different version of what happened: "The float was waterlogged and the aircraft sank with Sidney Mowat, the lightest student, on board."[4] Either way, although the machine was salvaged, the damage was extensive.

This put an end to training in 1915. In the meantime, because both the students and the Club were rapidly running out of funds, "arrangements were made with the Commanding Officer of the 58th Battalion, then recruiting in Vancouver, to place them on the strength of his unit. This entitled them to draw pay and allowances, while still remaining actively connected with the Aero Club of British Columbia."[5] Seldom has military brass demonstrated such flexibility.

And then the Club was reorganized — a comprehensive and ambitious reorganization. Indeed, it was so ambitious that it aroused the interest of entrepreneurs south of the border:

That Vancouver has become better known as an aviation centre is evidenced today in a telegram received by J. W. Pattison, secretary of the Vancouver Aero Club [*sic*], in which an offer is made by the Berger School of Aviation [of Chicago] to furnish two

Wright planes and two instructors for the B.C. Aviation School Limited. The offer will not be considered for the reason that work is now progressing on a number of new machines for the local school at the plant of the Hamilton Aero Manufacturing Company limited, and will soon be ready to turn over to the B.C. Aviation School of this city.[6]

In fact, an American manufacturer had beaten the Berger School to the punch. Thomas Foster Hamilton, who later went on to produce the celebrated Hamilton Standard propellers, had set up the Hamilton Aero Manufacturing Company in Seattle as early as 1910. By 1915, he was constructing "a speedy tractor biplane — it is believed it will see service in Canada."[7] This machine never reached Vancouver. Instead, probably because of trade restrictions, and because Canada was at war and prospects of aircraft production looked very promising, Hamilton decided to form a subsidiary company in Vancouver and build his machines there. The Hamilton Aero Manufacturing Company was incorporated under the B.C. Companies Act (1910) on October 27, 1915,[8] and a small factory was opened on Fourth Avenue (though some sources place it on Front Street).

The reorganization, consequently, took the following format. The Aero Club of B.C. remained intact but, in addition, the B.C. Aviation School Limited (described on the cover of the prospectus as "A Patriotic Undertaking For Defence") was incorporated in association with the Hamilton Company. The agreement between the company and the school was set out at some length in the prospectus. Fortunately, a summary was provided:

The salient points of the arrangement are briefly as follows:

1. The B.C. Aviation School Limited is being formed with a capital of $50,000 divided into 5000 shares of $10.00 each with the object of establishing, maintaining and carrying on a School for the teaching of aviation and the operation of aircraft of all kinds and of all sciences, trades and vocations incidental thereto and its memorandum provides for the necessary powers of such an organization.

2. The Hamilton Company agrees to sell to the School four aeroplanes of kinds adapted for the teaching of aviation from start to finish. They are as follows:

    1 Roller Aeroplane valued at $2500.00.
    1 Flying Boat valued at $6500.00.
    1 Military Tractor valued at $10,000.00.
    1 Pusher type [military] valued at $9000.00.

The plans and specifications of these aeroplanes are completed and made part of the agreement.

3. Besides this the Hamilton Company covenants to repair and make fit for primary

school purposes the aeroplane held by the Aero Club under purchase agreement and also covenants to provide the mechanical and shop training required by the School for its pupils.

There was a good deal more detailed information about the objectives of the school and how it was to be financed and managed. The directors would be a mix of Aero Club members and Hamilton Aero executives: H. H. Stevens, M.P., G. H. Cowan, K.C., and J. H. Senkler, K.C. representing the Aero Club; T. F. Hamilton, President; G. C. Crux, Secretary; and W. E. Burns, Barrister, representing the Hamilton Company. Meanwhile, the Aero Club of B.C. was to expand its horizons:

The Aero Club of British Columbia is being incorporated under the Benevolent Societies Act and its scope being enlarged to include the following objects:

(1) To arrange for the examination of candidates and pass them for Royal Aero Club certificates.

(2) To assist the military authorities with information or work in the event of military aviation being established in this territory.

(3) To insure that civil flying in this territory is carried out under control and that harm to aviation is not done by irresponsible flying or flying to the danger of the public.[9]

Alas, it was nearly all castles in the air. Patriotic citizens did not flock to take up the $10.00 shares. Nevertheless, enough money was raised to purchase one of the four aircraft listed in the agreement. It was the "Military" tractor biplane. All 12 of the Aero Club students, after doing a little token drill with wooden rifles in the Cambie Street Armouries, made their way down to the factory and helped with the construction of the aircraft. Presumably, the "military" designation was a marketing ploy to appeal to patriotism. In fact, the machine was a two-bay, single-seater biplane powered by a 60-horsepower Maximotor engine.

It was tested by Hamilton at Minoru Park, probably in May 1916, but,

The aircraft was found unsatisfactory for the School's purposes and was modified to a two-seat machine. A second cockpit was added under the centre section, an extra bay was added to the wings, two small wheels were fitted at the front of the undercarriage skids, and the 75 hp Curtiss O engine from Stark's Curtiss pusher was installed.[10]

The new machine, and the B.C. Aviation School, then moved to Pitt Meadows, an agricultural area some 25 miles (40 km) along the Fraser Valley, to the east of Vancouver. Apart from the engine change, little

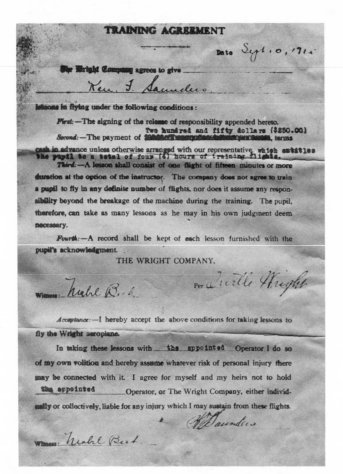

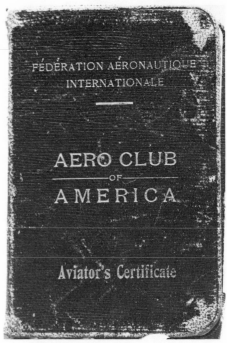

RBCM

Ken Saunders, like many would-be B.C. wartime pilots, borrowed money and took his flying training at one of the Wright brothers' Flight Training Schools: The Huffman Field in Dayton, Ohio. RBCM

Saunders earned international pilot's licence number 353, and the rank of Major, as well as the award of a DSO, as a military pilot. When he returned from Sweden in 1920, he was granted Canadian Commercial pilot's licence number 170, and went on to a distinguished career in civil aviation.

RBCM

has been said about how the Hamilton trainer performed but, although the pupils received considerable ground-school training, little flying was done. This may have had something to do with instructors. "Stark had severed his connection with the Aero Club in the winter of 1915, and two other pilots were engaged, both from the United States. Although they both came well recommended, neither Clarence Hilborn nor N. B. Robbins was at that time a licensed pilot."[11]

In those days, the fact that they did not have their certificates really did not imply lack of competence. Many pilots flew for two or three years without going through the formality. In any case, Ellis records that the Hamilton was "cracked up at Pitt Meadows, while under, or more probably while not under, the control of Charles Raynor. Since funds were at a low ebb, the accident brought to an end the active career of the school."[12] Molson and Taylor offer a slightly different report of this accident: "Later in the year the aircraft crashed after an engine failure while being flown by C. O. Rayner [sic], and the operation of the School stopped."[13]

The next aviation development in British Columbia involved the boatbuilding brothers, Henry and James Hoffar. From the beginning they had taken an interest in flying. They had provided storage for the Templeton-McMullan plane in their boathouse in 1911 (which, unfortunately, was destroyed when the boathouse caught fire), and they had converted Stark's Aero Club Curtiss into a single-pontoon floatplane when training had to be suspended at Terra Nova because the fields became too waterlogged. Now they decided to build an aircraft themselves. Molson and Taylor record that the general configuration of this machine was taken from an illustration of an Avro which the brothers had seen in a magazine. In fact, the British journal *Flight* published a series of articles on the Avro Biplane which discussed in some detail both materials and construction methods. In addition to photographs, there were plan and profile drawings with dimensions, and some "construction detail" drawings, as well as a profile of the Avro wing section,[14] and it was probably these that the Hoffars used; but they were a long way from working drawings, of course, and the Hoffars had to rely on their acquired knowledge of aviation and their cumulative experience as boatbuilders for the final outcome. They also had to convert the machine to a hydroplane, and their success was a consider-

$500.^{00}_{100}

Nesley October 7, 1916

550 days after date I promise
to Pay to
James Shephard _____ or Order
the sum of five hundred Dollars
with Interest @ 5%

Clarence L. Hilborn.

Received five Hundred
Dollars on account
James Shepherd

William Hilborn in a Sopwith fighter.

The Hilborn family in Quesnel, just before the brothers left to join up. William, top left; Clarence, top right.

The start of the long journey to Deseronto by BX (Barnard's Express) stage coach down the Cariboo Road, April 1917. The building in the rear is Anclers Post Office and roadhouse.

CLARENCE HILBORN ESTATE PHOTOS

William and Clarence.

Like so many young men at the time, the brothers Clarence L. and William C. Hilborn decided to join up in 1916. Both also decided to become pilots, and they followed the custom of the time by borrowing money and setting off from their hometown of Quesnel to sign up for service in the Royal Flying Corps in December with Captain Lord Innes-Ker, who was recruiting in Canada for the RFC. Their next move was to join the Hamilton Aviation School in Vancouver.

Receipts for fees paid by both brothers from the Hamilton School, dated October 16, 1916, and a recommendation from a firm of lawyers, are, unfortunately, the only evidence to turn up so far that they were connected with the School. Apart from a puzzling mention by Frank Ellis that Clarence Hilborn was hired as an instructor in 1917, neither of the brothers is mentioned in any list of the students, either trained or partly trained.

Towards the end of 1916, they apparently ran out of money and returned to Quesnel for the winter — an unusually severe one. Then, in the spring of 1917, they were instructed to report to Deseronto, Ontario, for flying training in the RFC, Canada. They graduated, and were granted commissions on August 19, 1917. After further training in England, Clarence was posted to 59 Squadron on the Western Front, and William to 66 Squadron on the Italian Front, where he served with Billy Barker.

Both had successful military careers: William shot down six enemy aircraft and was awarded the DFC on September 2, 1918, and Clarence was twice mentioned in dispatches. Unhappily, William was killed in action before the war ended, but Clarence returned to live in Vancouver until he died in 1978. (All of the photographs on pages 88-90 are from the Clarence Hilborn Estate.)

Cowan, Ritchie & Grant.
BARRISTERS, SOLICITORS, ETC.

TELEPHONE SEYMOUR 2450
                     2451

CABLE ADDRESS "COWANGRAN" VANCOUVER

GEO. H. COWAN. K.C.   GEO. A. GRANT.

827-836 ROGERS BUILDING.
470 GRANVILLE STREET

Vancouver, B.C.

28th December, 1916.

Captain Lord Innes-Ker,
        Hotel Vancouver,
            VANCOUVER.B.C.

Sir:

        We have much pleasure in recommending Clarence Laurent
Hilborn and William Carl Hilborn, brothers, for your acceptance
for the Cadet Wing of the Royal Flying Corps. We have had occasion
to see considerable of these boys in connection with the B. C.
Aviation School, and formed a high opinion of their abilities
and characters, and think that they will develop successfully in
the work.

                                Yours faithfully,

Certificate No. 8266

ROYAL FLYING CORPS.

(Officers.)

CENTRAL FLYING SCHOOL,

UPAVON, WILTS.,

15th October 1917.

GRADUATION CERTIFICATE.

THIS IS TO CERTIFY THAT 2/Lieut C. L. Hilborn

General List

has completed a *long in the Military Wing course at the Central Flying School, and is qualified
short
for service in the Royal Flying Corps.

L.A. Strange Lieut Colonel
                    and Commandant.

* Strike out word not applicable.

W7448—2137   4000   9/16   HWV(P750/1)   H16/859
1729—H4164   5000   5/17

William.

Clarence.

B.C. Aero Club students with Billy Stark's enduring Curtiss pusher on Lulu Island, 1915. Left to right, William McRae, Cyril Scott, Billy Stark, Philip Smith, Murton Seymour and Vick Phillips.

The Hamilton Aviation School's first aircraft at Pitt Meadows, 1915.

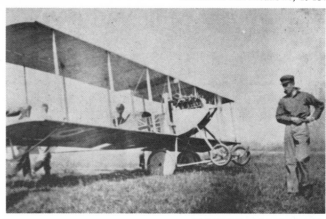

Murton Seymour, one of the first two graduates of the B.C. Aero Club, later went on to a distinguished civilian flying career. He was awarded the McKee Trophy in 1939 for the part he played in developing Canadian flying clubs.

The Hamilton biplane under construction at the Hamilton Aero Manufacturing Company plant with president Thomas Hamilton and all the students of the Aero Club. Left to right: Frank Smith, M. B. Wright, J. P. Crawford, C. O. Raynor, M. A. Seymour, T. F. Hamilton, Philip Smith, W. E. Damer, W. G. McRae, J. S. Haight, A. G. Hodgson and C. E. Perkins.

The Reveille.

The Hoffar brothers' first and successful attempt at aircraft construction, the H-1, taking off from Burrard Inlet, January, 1917.

A photograph of the Avro Biplane published in the British journal *Flight* in 1912. It was probably from this photograph and the accompanying two-view drawing that the Hoffars constructed the H-1.

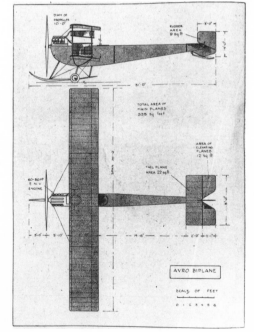

Henry Hoffar, circa 1918.

James Hoffar in the H-1 at the Coal Harbour dock beside the Company's boathouse, 1917.

James Hoffar, right. It may have been a damp fishing trip, but it was obviously a successful one.

James Hoffar, centre, aboard the SS *Princess Patricia*.

Because "the Fraser was an unruly river, and in those days often froze over, Admiral Baynes late in 1858 had H.M.S. *Plumper* survey Burrard Inlet, and chose English Bay's south shore (Jericho Beach) and the extreme head of the inlet as naval anchorages.... The Admiral wanted coal, as well as anchorages. The *Plumper* returned in June and dug two tons of 'very good quality' from exposed seams on the shore, about the present north foot of Bute Street:" hence, Coal Harbour. It was from the Hoffars' boathouse that Victor Bishop set off to fly to English Bay.

School of Military Aeronautics
E. House. Toronto University

Practical flying dual & solo
X. C. F. S. Camp Rathbun
Deseronto. Ont

June 30/17
Advanced course in flying and
military aeronautics.
Officers Mess. Camp Borden.

Date and Hour	Wind Direction and Velocity	Machine Type and No.	Passenger	Time	Height	Course	Remarks
11/10/17 6.55 AM 7.35	W	BE2E 4432	solo	40	6000	circled aerodrome	1 ldg.
11/10/17 5.45 5.30	W	4432	solo	25	2500	"	1 "
12/10/17 10.50 11.45	W	1333	solo	55	4000	about, east of "	1 " Photos.
15/10/17 7.15 8.55	S.W.	1333		1.40	4000	Home Batt west of Grantham	1 " Puffs.
16/10/17 2.30 12.30	SW	RE8 4601	Capt. Readman	20	2.500	south of aerodrome & return	1 " instruction on RE8
16/10/17 4.00 4.25	SW	4601	solo	25	2.000	circled aerodrome.	1 " O.K.
16/10/17 6.00 6.20	SW	BE2E 1333	solo	20	1500 and 2000	about "	2 " Night landings O.K.
16/10/17 3.40 3.55	SW	RE8 4601	solo	15	3000	" "	1 " Axel bent on safe of runway ldg.
						Total time flown week ending Oct. 17. /17	5 hrs 0 MIN.
						" " " " dual	.20 "
						" " " " solo	4 hrs 40 "
						" " " to date. solo	52 - 58 "
						" " " in air to date. dual and solo	60 - 18 "
						Tests passed Aa bombs. Spund strips & panneau Art. obs. photos. Height & Formation	

T. Leigh-Mallory Lt.

Pages from Clarence Hilborn's Flying Log Book.

Date and Hour	Wind Direction and Velocity	Machine Type and No.	Passenger	Time	Height
11/6/17 4.45 PM	SW - S	JN4A C. 540	Instructor Dr Sedgwick	Min. Ldg 15 - 1	
12/6/17 4.50 AM	S.	" 546	"	40 - 2	
13/6/17 10.17 AM	S.S.E Bumpy	" 546	"	8 - 3	
14/6/17 9.50 AM	W Fair	" 549	"	65 - 14	
15/6/17 5.35 AM	West Slightly Bumpy	" 549	"	31 - 8	
				159 MIN. 28 Ldgs.	

A student's misjudged approach.
Accidents were inevitable in the haste to provide
fighting pilots for the Western Front after the Battle
of the Somme—though few, perhaps, were as embarrassingly
visible as this one at Camp Borden.

Machine Type and No.	Passenger	Time	Height	Vert Galant Course	Note April 21. 1918 Remarks # 3
RE8.				Mentioned in Field Dispatches	May 4. 1918 Communique # 5
C 2241	Lt W.H. Leighton	.10	8000	Fanvillers. Cadas. V. Galat.	To view aerodrome.
C 2241	" "	3.10	4000	Huburterne — etc	277SB on R14049 100 rds fired.
C 2241	" "	1.50	6000	Fonquillers.	6 bombs harassed on Puisieux 250 rds fired from 1000 Forced down at Pommier
C 2241	Sgt. Godwin	.20	1000	Brauval etc	ENG. TEST Satis.
C 2241	Lt Thomson	.40	1000	" Donllers.	" " "
C 2241	" "	.50	1500	" "	6 Bombs on Trenches at K38d.
C 2241	" "	2.15	1-6000	Huburterne. Mailla Mailly	AA v. active 199SB on HBL 923520
C 2241	" Leighton	3.30	1-5000	dispatches Fonquivillers	100 Rds. 7 oKs. 150 Rds 4 bombs on K 29b.
C 2241	" "	3.15	15000	" "	Front quiet 4 bombs on K24b Eng trouble
C 2241	" "	1.55	3000	" "	1,2 seater EA over Fonquillers on patrol.
C 2241	" "	1.10	5000	" "	Cons'dr SHELLING by EAB. Very
C 2241	" "	.25	1000	Brauval — Donllers.	Satis. ENO TEST.
C 2241	" Thompson	.30	1500	Donllers. Brauval.	Satis Flip.
C 2241	" Bridge	1.25	2000	Heburterne etc.	Patrol. 2 NFs 194 SB on L21. Unsucc.
C 2241	" "	1.05	4-5000	COMM#5 MENTIONED IN Dispatches	194 SB on HB. ∧21 Succ. NF. L36671. acc.a.
C 2241	" "	3.30	4-5000		
C 2241	" James	1.15	8000	47th arra. Puisieux.	18 plates exposed.
Total flying time from			12·4·18 — 5·5·18		26 hrs. 05

Major Raymond Collishaw,
DSO and Bar, DSC and DFC,
of Nanaimo, B.C. was the
second-ranking Canadian ace in
World War I. RBCM

Major Donald R. MacLaren,
DSO, MC and Bar and DFC,
described as "one of the last
and greatest of the First World
War aces," in front of his
Sopwith fighter.

PUBLIC ARCHIVES CANADA

Another page from Clarence Hilborn's Flying Log Book while on operations on the Western Front in 1918.
He was Mentioned in Dispatches on April 21, 1918, and again on May 4.

able achievement. Designated the H-1, it was constructed of spruce and ash, braced with piano wire (although the wings were not internally braced). Both fuselage and wings were covered with unbleached cotton. The result, was a two-bay tractor biplane, with a single main float, two small floats at the wingtips, as well as one under the tail. Power was provided by a Roberts 6X engine, a six-cylinder, in-line, water-cooled two-stroke, offering 75 horsepower.[15] The Hoffar brothers now faced a problem shared by many builders of early aircraft: they had to learn how to fly it. Molson and Taylor have this version of what happened next:

Neither brother had flown but it was agreed that they should be able to get the feel of the controls by taxi-ing along the water and then should be able to rise, say ten feet off the water. James Hoffar won the toss and with him on board Henry towed the H-1 to the centre of Burrard Inlet. The aircraft was taxied away for about a mile and then turned and headed back towards Henry in the boat. By the time the aircraft was abreast of the boat it was clear of the water and was soon at about 100 feet [30 m]. . . . James made a flat turn near North Vancouver and headed back towards the boat, gradually losing altitude until he alighted on the water at full throttle about a hundred yards from the boat.[16]

Such instant expertise strains credibility. Even Charles Hamilton, who was regarded as a prodigy among quick learners, took some instruction from Glenn Curtiss before flying on his own;[17] he began his solo flying with short hops, and he had had considerable experience in the air as a dirigible pilot before stepping into an aeroplane for the first time.[18] The dates are confusing, too. Molson and Taylor report that "In 1915 Henry and James Hoffar . . . decided to build an aircraft" and, after describing the machine, say that "construction of the aircraft, which had to be fitted in between boat building, took about four months"; but they don't say whether or not they were consecutive months. Ellis has the start in the fall of 1916, with completion "by the early summer of 1917."[19]

The first mention of the H-1 in the newspapers found so far was a brief article in the Vancouver *World* on December 16, 1916 (p. 21). The caption read, "Vancouver Men Build Seaplane: Flying Test to be Given at English Bay During the Coming Week by an Expert"; then the article went on to report that three more seaplanes were to be constructed for the proposed flying training school; a number of students were waiting to sign up for the course; and W. Knox Martin of Seattle, who had an American aviation licence and six years of flying experience, was to be the instructor.

A second newspaper article, dated January 16, 1917, reported a "test" flight by Knox Martin the previous afternoon, and that "Jim Hoffar acted as mechanic and used the student's seat in the machine"; and, two paragraphs later: "This was the first trial flight and Knox Martin declared that the machine was one of the steadiest he had ever had the pleasure to pilot."[20]

Then, on January 22, the Vancouver *Province* (p. 12) carried a captioned photograph of the Hoffar machine half submerged, with its tail in the air. The caption reads: "Striking a submerged channel buoy in Coal harbor, the seaplane of the Hoffar school, which was to make an exhibition flight over English Bay yesterday afternoon, sustained damage to one of the pontoons and Aviator Knox Martin and his companion, Mr. J. B. Hoffar, had to abandon the flight and have the machine towed in with its tail in the air."

There is yet another conflicting report of these events, this one by Earl MacLeod who, at the time, was embarking on a distinguished flying career:

In the autumn of 1916, two brothers, Jim and Henry Hoffar, who had a marine engine business at Coal Harbour in Vancouver, commenced construction of a seaplane, and I contacted them. They were impressed by the fact that I was already accepted for service in the RNAS, and they agreed to qualify me as soon as their plane was completed, at a reduced charge of $400. They made arrangements for a flying instructor from South America by the name of Martin, to instruct both themselves and myself, and had a legal document drawn up to that end. Before the agreement was signed and the plane ready, I received a telegram that changed that plan. I may mention before continuing that the pilot, Martin, remained only a short time in Vancouver, departing before the plane was ready to be flown, and that Jim Hoffar unfortunately crashed it when he tried to fly it by himself.[21]

And finally, historian Frank Ellis, in a newspaper article in which he says that he had discussed these events with James Hoffar, some years before, has this description:

Jimmie Hoffar undertook to become pilot, first doing much taxiing about on the surface of Burrard Inlet, to familiarize himself with the controls. As the weeks passed and he became somewhat adept, he finally began making short hops in the air....[22]

The truth probably lies somewhere between these extremes because there is reasonably clear evidence that Jimmie Hoffar did learn to fly the

THE DAILY PROVINCE, VANC(

SEA PLANE ABANDONS FLIGHT WHEN IT HITS SUBMERGED BUOY

H-1 competently. On July 9, 1917, with a journalist, B. A. McKelvie, as passenger, he flew over downtown Vancouver:

Twenty years ago I sat with "Jimmie" Hoffar in the primer class at the old Mount Pleasant School. Last night I sat with "Jimmie" Hoffar in the carriage of the big seaplane he and his brother Henry constructed at their boat-building establishment at Coal Harbour, and soared with him over the city, inlet and Stanley Park at the rate of seventy miles an hour.[23]

Clearly, this was no tentative hop. They reached an altitude of about 2000 feet (over 600 m) and claimed the record of being the first aircraft to fly over downtown Vancouver (though the same claim had been made for Knox Martin in January). Apparently, the H-1 was rapidly deteriorating by the end of 1917 and, after the engine and propeller were salvaged, the remains were "buried at sea."[24]

However, while the progress of aviation in British Columbia was, to put it kindly, tentative, elsewhere it was accelerating dramatically — particularly on the Western Front in Europe, and around Toronto in Canada. By the end of 1916, the battle of the Somme had brought about a profound change in the attitude of army commanders to aircraft. No longer were they worried about frightened horses; instead they were insistently demanding more aircraft to support their troops. In the words of historian Alan Sullivan:

The battle proceeded with unprecedented intensity, and with it a never-ending aerial warfare. Pilots were rushed from England with a few hours' solo work and absolutely no gunnery practice, to find themselves instantly in the thick of the combat. It is, therefore, not astonishing that the wastage of our fighting men ran up to twenty-five per cent. per month.

The filling up of the Royal Flying Corps combatant strength was made additionally difficult, as the Corps could no longer draw from regimental officers now needed for the coming offensive by which it was proposed to relieve the tremendous pressure on the French at Verdun.

It is true that the strength of the Force was, in anticipation, more than doubled during the three weeks which preceded the Somme, but this largely exhausted the available supplies of fighting personnel.

How reasonable, therefore, that the established success of Canadian pilots, and the fact that in Canada lay an almost untapped reservoir of future strength, should turn the eyes of the War Office to that Dominion. Double operations were planned for the Spring of 1917. The need was instant and imperative.[25]

In World War I, the Canadian government displayed none of the reluctance to become involved, nor the anxiety about Canadian autonomy, demonstrated so clearly by Prime Minister Mackenzie King,

Among the many Victorians who learned to fly with the RFC, Canada, was Alex t. Stewart, seen here both in front of, and in the cockpit, of a Curtiss JN-4 during training at Mohawk, Ontario. Stewart, son of a former Mayor of Victoria, had been on the staff of the *Daily Colonist*. He sent articles to the newspaper describing his experiences as a cadet in training.

A. T. STEWART ESTATE PHOTOS

particularly in the early days of World War II. The response was prompt and remarkable for its efficiency and scope. The British War Office authorized the formation of the Royal Flying Corps, Canada, in December 1916. By the end of January 1917, contracts had been let for the construction of the first two training fields, one on the outskirts of Camp Borden, the other at Long Branch, "some nine miles west of Toronto, where was formed the first flying unit of the Royal Flying Corps, Canada."[26] By this time, too, Curtiss JN-3 training aircraft had been ordered from the company's Buffalo plant, and construction had begun on a factory for the newly-incorporated company, Canadian Aeroplanes Limited, a factory that covered an area of six acres. Here, the production of aircraft moved from the empirical to a much more scientific basis. Ribs, spars and longerons which had formerly been painstakingly hand-carved were now produced on machinery to shape them and assembled with accurate jigs to align them. The piano wire used for bracing, both within the wings and for interplane strength would

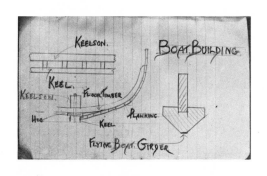

... live up to a pull of a ton and a half, and control wires will stand the same test. So accurate are these latter that in the process of their manufacture the heated metal is drawn through a forming die made of an aperture in a diamond.

The propeller ... is five-ply white oak, glued, compressed and formed up by machinery that is almost human—and took its origin from a lathe designed by Peter the Great to make gun stocks. It is a far cry from Russia to Toronto, but the principle is identical.... The successor of Peter's lathe carves them, four at a time, to one thirty-second of their finished form, and the final touches and balancing are hand work.[27]

The factory eventually employed over 2000 workers and, in 21 months, produced 2900 aircraft. The majority were Curtiss JN-4 (Canucks)—built under licence and with some modifications and improvements over the American JN-4—as well as 30 F5 flying boats for the U.S. Navy. In 1918, the factory began production of the Avro trainer, but completed only two, while an additional 100 had been fabricated and were ready for assembly when the war ended.[28]

The Canadian modifications to the JN-4 included:

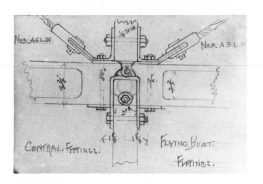

... a slight amount of skeletal and cosmetic surgery and some tinkering with the nervous system by which she was controlled. In this, ailerons were applied to the lower wings as well as to the upper. The Deperdussin controls were eliminated in favor of the stick type in both cockpits. There was a modification to the landing gear. The split trailing edge was substituted for the flattened-tubing type of wings.

The greatest initial changes were made to the empennage. For the Curtiss wood framework, the Canadians substituted one of steel tubing but continued to cover it with fabric.[29]

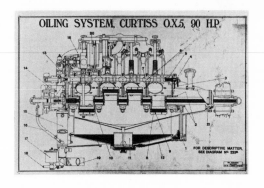

The initial plan was to form four training stations, each station to have one or more aerodromes—and each station to support five training squadrons. This was later revised to three stations.[30] The first was Camp Borden, where training was underway in March 1917, and which had five squadrons operating by the beginning of May. The second was at Deseronto, with aerodromes at Mohawk and Rathbun, which had five squadrons operating by the end of May; and the third was North Toronto, with aerodromes at Long Branch, Leaside and Armour Heights, which had three of its five squadrons operating by the end of May.[31] A squadron consisted of three flights of six training aircraft, or a total of 18 machines. Altogether, 3135 pilots were trained, of whom 2539 went overseas. By any standards, this was an astonishingly efficient and well-organized operation. But what happened next is more relevant to our interests in British Columbia.

In April 1917, when the United States entered the war, an agreement was reached between the U.S. Army Signal Corps and the RFC. American squadrons were to be trained in Canada in return for training in "snow-free Texas" for the RFC during the winter of 1917-18.[32]

In July 1917, the first detachment of 1500 Signal Corps airmen arrived at Leaside and were promptly distributed throughout the system. Meanwhile, the training Stations had been renamed as Wings: Camp Borden became 42 Wing, Deseronto, 43 wing and North Toronto, 44 Wing. In November 1917, 42 and 43 Wings were moved down to Texas to continue their training because, at the time, nobody thought it possible to fly under winter conditions. Fortunately, a decision was made to keep 44 Wing at North Toronto "to test the feasibility of training under Canadian winter conditions."[33]

Alan Sullivan, who wrote what amounted to an official RAF report on the whole operation, describes how this test turned out.

Prior to the operations of the Corps, it was generally assumed that the obstacles to intensive training in a snow-covered country were almost insuperable, but in the light of last winter's experience it is difficult to imagine the limit to which the aeroplane may not safely be used in the latitudes of the far north. Its apparent fragility, the exposure of the pilot, the fact that a large percentage of accidents occurred in making landings, and the mental picture of a machine floundering through snowdrifts in an attempt to rise, all

Evidently it was a hot summer in Ontario in 1918.   A. T. STEWART ESTATE

seemed to reduce the matter to an impossibility. To-day it has been demonstrated by the work of the 44th Wing of this unit that, with such provision as has already proved suitable, the aeroplane will rise from a snow surface more easily than from bare ground at temperatures far below zero, [and] land in spots inaccessible in summer time....

The process was one of return to aboriginal principles, in that there was adopted a method used by the North American Indian, since first he traversed the frozen waste. Experiments soon evidenced that undercarriage wheels were out of the question in snow more than six inches deep, and by the elimination of things that rotated and the adoption of things that slid, the aeroplane fell, so to speak, into line with the winter customs of the country.[34]

There is, of course, a delightful irony here: the first aircraft to fly, the Wright machine, had adopted the "aboriginal principle" by using skids rather than wheels. In fact, though, this was a very significant step forward for Canadian aviation. People had quickly seen the advantage of floats, or pontoons, for operations in a country with few fields to land in more than 50 miles (30 km) north of the U.S. border. But even this meant operating only when there was no snow on the ground or ice on the lakes and rivers. Now, the possibilities seemed endless to those who were seriously thinking about using aircraft — people like surveyors and exploration geologists. As we shall see, financing was slow to respond in commercial flying, but the military carried on from their wartime pioneering to lay the groundwork of the great bush flying days of the late 1920s and the 1930s.

Practice take-offs and landings came to be known as "touch and go." This one appears to have been more touch than go. The caption reads: "Nothin' much." Unfortunately, a few weeks later young Alex Stewart had a more serious accident which put an end to his flying career. After convalescence in Victoria, he was able to join the navy as a Wireless Telegraphy Officer.   A. T. STEWART ESTATE

Chapter Eight

After the War to End All Wars

"Hydroplane drops on roof of West-end house"

VANCOUVER *Daily Province*

For obvious reasons, little planning for a commercial future seems to have prevailed among the western allies during World War I. There was, however, at least one exception. The forest industry began, not only to think about use of aircraft, but was prepared to experiment with them. This is hardly surprising because the British Columbia forest industry had been galvanized by the demand for "aeroplane spruce" towards the end of the war. In fact, a provincial order-in-council in 1917 gave the Imperial Munitions Board authority to by-pass negotiations with lease holders for standing spruce and deal with "equitable compensation" later. As a result, the cut of first-grade spruce jumped from 116,000 board feet (49.15 m³) in January 1918 to 6,850,000 (2902 m³) by November.[1]

But the first use of aircraft in forestry goes back even further. British Columbia forestry historian John Parminter records that, as early as 1915, aerial forest fire patrols were

...made in the summer of 1915 in Wisconsin. A glowing report describing experiences there was published in the April 1916 issue of the only Canadian forestry magazine of the time, the *Canadian Forestry Journal*. The author stated that "the efficiency of an aeroplane in spotting forest fires is without doubt as practicable as any use to which it could be put," and that finding fires wasn't a problem so much as ascertaining their exact location.[2]

By 1918, the British Columbia Minister of Lands, T. D. Pattullo, was persuaded by "an air service veteran returned from the European front," to implement aerial forest fire patrols in B.C., and a lease contract was let by the Department of Lands to the Hoffar Motor Boat

105

Company, who apparently had already begun constructing their second aircraft, the H-2.

The Department of Lands aircraft was to be a flying boat, popularly referred to at the time as a "hydro-aeroplane," and based on a Glenn Curtiss design. Consideration had been given to obtaining a surplus machine from the Royal Air Force but this was not feasible.[3]

The H-2, an elegant and attractive aircraft, was a two-seater, pusher biplane, with small cylindrical floats below each wing tip. It was powered by a 100-horsepower Roberts 6X engine (both the engine and propeller had been retained when the H-1 was abandoned).[4] According to Parminter, the H-2 was test-flown for the Department "in late August, 1918, by Flight Commander Capt. W. H. MacKenzie of the Royal Air Force. He pronounced it to be a 'really excellent machine,' which 'will fly herself.' Without hesitation the Forest Branch signed a one year lease with an option to purchase...."[5] According to Molson and Taylor, it was test-flown by James Hoffar on September 3, and then handed over to the Forestry Department.[6] So there is some confusion about who first flew it, and about the date.[7] There was no confusion about the next development in this project. The Vancouver newspapers of September 4 carried banner headlines: "FLYING BOAT FALLS: FIRST PLANE CRASH IN CITY. Hydroplane Drops on the Roof of West-end House."

The H-2 had been taken up for another test flight, this time by Flight Lieutenant Victor A. Bishop. According to his diaries, which were meticulously maintained from 1917 to 1919 (the second of which contained a summary of his activities dating back to 1913), Bishop emigrated to Vancouver from England in 1913. On September 27, 1915, he joined the 72nd Battalion, Canadian Infantry (CEF). Arriving in France on August 18, 1916, he survived some of the heaviest trench warfare in World War I before returning to England at the end of April 1917, when he applied for a transfer to the RNAS. He was accepted on October 17 and posted to Vendome for training the following month.

His log book records that he received 7:15 hours of dual instruction on a Caudron before his first solo. After 27 hours and 43 minutes of instruction at Vendome, he was posted back to Calshot, in the south of England, as an armament flight instructor. Finally, with a little over 200 hours of flying time, he was granted three months' leave and returned to

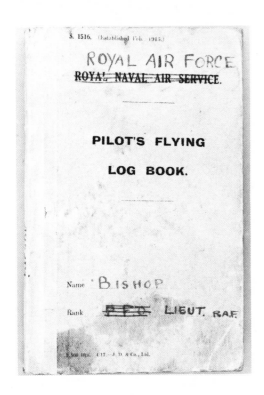

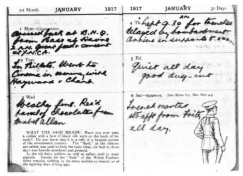

A page from Victor Bishop's Diary when he was serving as an infantryman on the Western Front.

V. A. BISHOP ESTATE

Vancouver in August, 1918. But for two 15-minute flights early in 1919, the last entry in his log book is a brief description of his Vancouver accident.[8]

Parminter gives a more detailed account of what happened:

Ascending at 3:00 PM from Coal Harbour, Bishop flew over the city, Burrard Inlet, and English Bay. While over False Creek at an altitude of 1,200 feet [366 m] the engine started to miss and the aviator considered heading for English Bay, then decided in favour of Coal Harbour and headed there. Before getting over the water the engine stopped altogether and the aircraft, at the wrong altitude and lacking enough forward speed to permit manoeuvering, went into a spinning nose dive.[9]

The Vancouver *Daily Province* reported that "Lieut. Bishop crashed into the roof of the home of Dr. J. C. Farrish, on Bute St. at Alberni St.... Rushed to hospital, the pilot was not seriously hurt, although he had crashed through the roof of the building and dropped into the bathroom."[10] In fact, according to relatives, Bishop actually fell into the bath and, in any case, he did suffer an injury to his back that plagued him for the rest of his life. Eventually, in the 1950s, he had to undergo an operation to relieve the pain of crushed vertebrae.

Nobody seems to have questioned why Bishop was asked to fly the H-2. Presumably, the assumption was that the Forestry officials had seized the opportunity to get a second opinion on the Hoffar machine. In fact, as his diary reveals, there was more to it than that. On September 3, 1918, he recorded that he "Drove Frank to warehouse then went to Hoffar's place. Saw Stewart [Forestry Dept] at Court House re seaplane proposition." Then, the following day:

In morning called at Court House and had interview with Caverhill. Offered me $225 a month to do Forest Patrols. Took up Hoffar machine at 2. Up for 20 minutes then engine stopped—got into spinning nose dive from 1200 feet and crashed into Dr. Farrish's house on Bute St. Rushed to Vancouver General. Extra "World" and "Province" issued—great sensation. Beyond couple of black eyes and bruises, hardly hurt myself. Visitors, flowers and fruit galore. Being treated like a hero.

However, he was not discharged from Vancouver General until September 16, and had to receive daily massage treatment for more than a month after his discharge. He was to discover in the years ahead that he had hurt himself. But the offer of a monthly salary to fly forestry patrols to a serving officer in the RAF (by then the RFC and the RNAS had been combined into the Royal Air Force) while the war was still in progress is puzzling. Presumably it must have been contingent on his discharge from the RAF.

The elegant but ill-fated Hoffar H-2 nearing completion, probably in late July or early August, 1918. Left Henry Hoffar, centre unidentified, right James Hoffar.

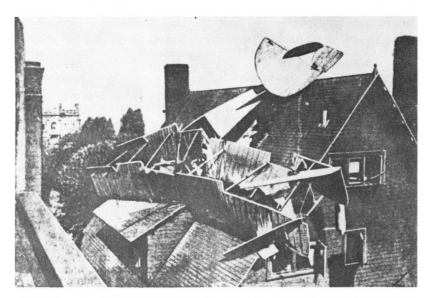

The H-2 on the roof of Dr. Farrish's house at the corner of Bute and Alberni streets, Vancouver, September 4, 1918. *POPULAR MECHANICS*

Flight Lieutenant Victor A. Bishop in 1918, just before he made his unrewarding test flight of the H-2. VICTOR BISHOP ESTATE

The Hoffar H-3. "The life of this aircraft proved to be quite short; while taking off on a projected flight to Victoria, we struck a deadhead off Burnaby Shoal and the ship was a total loss."
VANCOUVER CITY ARCHIVES

Meanwhile, the H-2 was a total write-off. The Minister of Lands, Duff Pattullo, while "expressing deep regret over the loss of the plane," also announced

...the cancellation of the aerial forest fire patrol program, and the swift demise of the proposed provincial air service. He said the government would make good the cost of the plane to the Hoffar firm....Given the multitude of uses to which an aircraft could be put when not needed for fire patrols, it was planned to have a new aircraft constructed as soon as possible. For reasons unknown, this remained undone and the honour of first discovery of a forest fire from the air in Canada was claimed by an air crew in Quebec on July 7, 1919.[11]

It is difficult to avoid a sense of frustration, and impossible not to both sympathize with and admire the Hoffars. Although the H-2, like the H-1, was derivative—it was based on a Curtiss design—all the indications were that it would have been a successful aircraft if the engine had not failed at such an inopportune moment; and effective forest-fire patrols as early as 1918 might well have made British Columbia a leader in Canadian commercial flying. The Hoffars, however, did not give up after this setback. Henry recalls their next venture:

The following year I designed the "H.3" flying boat which was checked during construction by Eddie Hubbard and Bill Boeing, and its structural features were reflected some years later in the Boeing B-1-E and Canadian Boeing 204.
    The "H-3" as shown in the photo was equipped with a six-cylinder, 150 hp Hall Scott engine. The life of this aircraft proved to be quite short; while taking off on a projected flight to Victoria, we struck a deadhead off Burnaby Shoal and the ship was a total loss. Fortunately our injuries were not severe.[12]

This ended the Hoffar brothers' aviation activities during World War I. Early in 1919, however, they became involved in another venture: United Aircraft of British Columbia, Limited.

As suggested earlier, when the war ended in 1918, there were few aircraft readily available for conversion to civilian use. In Canada, however, there was almost a glut of war surplus Curtiss JN-4s, the two-seat, American-built "Jennies," or Canadian-built "Canucks" (the most readily observed difference was that the Canuck had ailerons on both upper and lower wings; whereas the Jenny had them only on the upper wing). These could be bought in reasonably serviceable condition for what would now be called an "affordable" price.[13] Powered by a 90-horsepower, Curtiss OX-5 engine, the JN-4 was useful mainly for training or for barnstorming—giving aerobatic demonstrations and

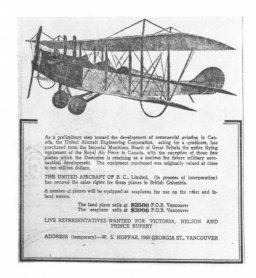

then persuading people to take rides at whatever price the traffic would bear. As well, it could carry some 200 lbs (80 kg) of mail in the front cockpit. The carrying of airmail was very much on people's minds at the time; first, because it promised a dependable income; and second, because it seemed by far the most suitable use for aircraft: passengers were still reluctant to risk their lives for the time-saving advantages of air transport.

Using these machines, large numbers of American airmen and a lesser number of Canadians, began to resurrect the exhibition flying of pre-war days almost as soon as the war ended. Most began as single teams of a pilot and mechanic who would tour the countryside, finding suitable farmers' fields from which to operate (hence the term "barnstorming"). The first task was to persuade the farmer to let them use his field. Not all were agreeable because if the crowds the airmen hoped to attract did appear, they usually trampled the farmer's crops and knocked his fences down; but the most potent persuader was the offer of a free flight. Nearly all farmers were beguiled by the sight of their own spread from where, so to speak, God normally looked.

Once over this hurdle, the barnstormers would fly over the nearby community and drop single-sheet flyers advertising the event. Usually they would offer a prize of a free ride to the first person to present them with a flyer. This always brought the children at the run, and often their parents as well. The exhibitions, to begin with, consisted of a display of aerobatics, followed by a session of rides. Sometimes a fixed fee was charged, perhaps $5.00, or $10.00 if it was an affluent-looking community; at others, the barnstormers gambled and offered rides at a dollar a minute. Pilots tended to dislike this one because few people could afford more than a very short ride, and this made for a tiring day. As well, they sometimes adopted the cent-a-pound tariff. The mechanic, with a bathroom scale, would weigh the passengers and charge them accordingly. Once again, pilots tended to be unenthusiastic about this scale of fees; first, because it meant short rides if a profit was to be made, which once again resulted in fatigue; and second, because it often brought out the local heavyweights, people weighing as much as 300 lbs (120 kg), to test the pilot's skill and nerve.

Before long, people became bored with watching loops and rolls, and something more spectacular was required to bring out the crowds. A new breed of airmen came into existence: the stunt men and, before very long, the stunt women. The first of these stunts was wing-walking, and began with the stunt man stepping out of his cockpit, usually the front one, and standing beside it on the wing while the pilot flew low over the crowds. Soon, the more intrepid moved out along the wing, holding on to the struts and even doing handstands between the wings. In some cases, a frame, which supported the stunt man in the small of his back, and to which he was strapped, was installed on top of the centre section of the upper wing. There he would stand while the pilot went through his repertoire of aerobatics. As competition grew to attract crowds, more gimmicks were added. A rope ladder was attached to the axle of the undercarriage. The stunt man would climb out of his cockpit onto the wing, down to the undercarriage axle and then down the stepladder to hang from the bottom rung by his knees or his ankles. When even this began to pall, young women were found to take the place of the men, and crowds for some reason found this more stimulating. Perhaps the ultimate in the stunt man's bag of tricks was to hang by his arms on the last rung of the stepladder beneath the aircraft and drop onto the roof of a moving car or train—sometimes onto the upper wing of another aircraft in flight.

Other crowd-pleasers were the parachutists. They started with single drops and then, following the example of Charles Hamilton, who had popularized this stunt in the years before World War I, performed multiple drops. The parachutist would step off the aircraft with three or four parachutes strapped to his body. After the first one had opened, he would cut it free, drop again before pulling the ripcord for the second one (or even, with some of the early parachutes, by opening a flap and pulling the parachute itself out), and so on. Considering that parachute technology was still in its infancy, this must have called for remarkable courage. The final development in the stunt era was for a number of crews to band together into a flying circus. One of the pilots would install a fuel tank on his undercarriage so that the engine would still have gravity feed when flying inverted. The result was another favourite with the crowds: formation flying, with the lead aircraft inverted. The flying circuses kept going into the late 1930s until, with the advent of increasing regulation, they found themselves more and more restricted and the fickle public quickly lost interest.

Chapter Nine

The Aerial League

"One of the most daring 'stunts' ever performed in the history of aviation..."

THE VANCOUVER *Daily Province*

In western Canada, the early post-war barnstorming was confined mainly to the prairies. Little was taking place in British Columbia, probably because pilots had to fly through or over the mountains to get from one venue to another—a daunting prospect with an ageing war-surplus JN-4. Yet, as an interesting contradiction, the first civilian stunt man to give a demonstration in Canada did so on a JN-4 (Can) flown by E. C. Hoy in Vancouver, B.C., in May 1919. Fuller *et al.*, give the date as May 31,[1] but on May 19 the Vancouver *Daily Province* published the following report (presumably of a rehearsal for the delayed aviation meet that finally took place on May 31):

One of the most daring "stunts" ever performed in the history of aviation was "pulled off" by J. H. Fieldhouse of New Westminster on Saturday while up in one of the Curtiss machines of the Aerial League of Canada with Capt. E. C. Hoy, D.F.C., at a height of 1500 feet [460 m]. Climbing out from the front cockpit of the machine, he made his way along the edge of the lower wing, dodging the many wires in his path, then turning, he climbed back into the seat again. Stepping out a second time he swung down by the edge of the wing and got his feet on the under carriage of the "bus," let go of the wings, and gripping the supports of the chassis sat on the cross-bar between the wheels. He returned to his seat by pulling himself over the edge of the wing and stepping into his seat.[2]

It is tempting to conclude that this successful venture led Ernest Hoy to think about the problem of finding a way through the mountains because, on August 7, 1919, he became the first person to fly, once again in a JN-4 (Can), from Vancouver to Calgary, and thus the first to conquer the physical and psychological barrier of the Rockies. The truth, however, as is so often the case, was more capricious and he won the opportunity to make history by chance rather than design; and there were other aviation "firsts" in B.C. before Hoy's accomplishment.

Late in the war, the Aerial League of Canada had materialized in Montreal and Toronto. The organization's objectives were quite simply to advance the cause of aviation in Canada. By 1919, branches had been set up in Vancouver and Victoria, and it was this organization that set the wheels in motion. On May 13, two members of the Aerial League accomplished a "first." The *Province* carried a long column on the achievement under the sub-heading, "Sixteen Miles of Open Water Are Crossed by Flyers":

Left Minoru Park at 4:23 p.m., arrived at Victoria at 5:45 p.m., dined at the Empress Hotel, left Victoria at 7:12 p.m., arriving at Minoru Park at 8:06, attended a meeting of the Aerial League of Canada and was made vice-president of the league all within six hours. Such was the experience of Capt. Alfred Eckley, and in doing so he established the record of being the first person to make the trip to Vancouver Island from the mainland by air . . . Capt. Eckley was accompanied by Capt. C. All [E. Hall].

His tour gives an interesting demonstration of the practicability of the airplane in the commercial world and may be regarded as the forerunner of a new era in business relations between Vancouver and Victoria. Actual time spent in the air was two hours and sixteen minutes — about one-half of the time it takes to make the trip by boat in one direction.[3]

Not to be outdone, the Victoria branch of the Aerial League went into action on May 18, when Lieutenant R. Rideout and Lieutenant H. Brown, in a JN-4 they called *Pathfinder*, flew from Victoria to Seattle. Leaving Willows field in Victoria at 11 a.m., they were delayed by a "strong head wind encountered over Port Townsend." The head wind left them short of gas, so they landed at Coupeville, about 60 miles (100 km) north of Seattle, where they stayed from 12:20 until 4:30 p.m. before completing the trip to land at the Jefferson Park golf links, Seattle, at 5:50 p.m.[4] (The Victoria *Colonist* had them landing at Beacon Hill Park in Seattle.[5]) They carried the obligatory letter of greetings from the Mayor of Victoria to the Mayor of Seattle, in this case inviting him to attend the Victory pageant to be held in Victoria on May 24.

Eddie Hubbard, of whom we shall hear more in a moment,

. . . went up . . . when they arrived late in the afternoon, leading the Pathfinder to the landing field.

Mr. W. E. Boeing, Seattle's aeroplane manufacturer, was on the field to meet the local boys, and it was one of his planes that Hubbard was flying.

Acting Mayor Lane was forced to refuse the invitation to return here [Victoria] in the Pathfinder, but will try to attend the celebration on Saturday.

As the weather continued unfavorable on Sunday night, the aviators decided to stay in Seattle for the night, and they received very hospitable treatment from the citizens.

The Pathfinder started for home at 11:22 on Monday morning, arriving here at 12:39, making a little better than sixty miles an hour [100 km/h].[6]

These "firsts," however, had been upstaged by an American first. The Vancouver *Daily World* reported that W. E. Boeing had left Seattle at noon on February 27 to fly to Vancouver, accompanied by his mechanic, Eddie Hubbard. In fact, Hubbard was the pilot and Boeing a passenger, and they were delayed by a snowstorm, which forced them to land at Anacortes. The following day, they made it to Coal Harbour by 1:15 p.m., delivering a sack of mail from Seattle to the Vancouver Post Office at 2:00 p.m.[7] This constituted the first international flight west of the Great Lakes. On March 3, Hubbard and Boeing left the Royal Vancouver Yacht Club at 12:30 p.m. with a sack of mail containing 60 letters from the Vancouver Post Office to be delivered to the Post Office in Seattle. They were intending to travel via Victoria,[8] but changed their minds, probably because of weather conditions. After landing to refuel in Edmonds, Washington, they flew directly to Seattle, arriving there three hours after leaving Vancouver. This constituted the first "official" international air mail flight. The following year, in 1920, Hubbard began a regular air mail service between Seattle and Victoria, "and for seven years . . . successfully flew the trip almost daily, summer and winter, in both the best and the worst weather the Pacific Coast had to offer."[9] Eddie Hubbard almost certainly pioneered the practice, when the visibility deteriorated, and the water was reasonably smooth, of touching down and taxiing at high speed on the "step," watching out for deadheads in his path. When the visibility improved, he would take to the air again. This technique has been employed ever since on the west coast by floatplane or flying boat pilots.

To return to the Aerial League, they had ambitious plans for the year. The May 23 issue of the *Province* announced an aerial meet at Minoru Park on the following day, Victoria Day. A total of six machines were to take part: one machine from the Victoria branch of the Aerial League; four from the Vancouver branch; and one belonging to the Vancouver

Aerial Transportation Company. All were Canadian Curtiss JN-4s and were to be flown by Lieutenant G. K. Trim,* Captain A. Eckley, Lieutenant "Miny" MacDonald, D.F.C., Captain E. C. Hoy, D.F.C., Captain George Dixon and Lieutenant E. Hall, who would demonstrate stunting, simulated dogfights and formation flying. As well, a description of what stunt man Fieldhouse was going to do, almost identical to the report published on May 19, was given. The final event was to be a race to New Westminster and return, and the prize was to be a considerable one: a brand new aeroplane "of the Canadian training plane type," donated by the Ericson Aeroplane Company Ltd. of Toronto.[10]

Meanwhile, spirits had been dampened by an accident at Minoru Park. Miss Edna Brown of the editorial staff of the *Daily World* had been invited by the Aerial League to fly over the city in one of their machines on May 21. No doubt the League was hoping for good publicity; instead, they suffered a setback because the machine, flown by Lieutenant G. H. Foy, crashed on its return to Minoru Park.

Lieut. Foy's story of the accident was that, as he was nearing the aerodrome his passenger must in some way have jammed the controls of the passenger seat of the J.N.-4 plane which was built for training purposes. Although he tore the heel from his boot in the endeavor to release the controls, Mr. Foy found this was impossible and therefore speeded up his plane to avoid a crash. The machine, however, nose dived from a height of about two hundred feet [60 m] and crashed to the ground.[11]

Foy "escaped with two broken ribs and some heavy contusions on his face," but the unfortunate Miss Brown suffered "from a broken ankle, deep cuts about the head and shock, fractured skull and other injuries." In fact, it turned out that her skull was not fractured, but her injuries were serious enough as it was.

A further setback ensued when the aerial meet on Victoria Day had to be postponed until the following Saturday, May 31, because of rain.

In spite of the rain some ten thousand people made their way out to the park by auto and train, and were greatly disappointed by the news that the meet would have to called off.... There were, however, about 2000 people who would not be turned away and stayed around the grounds and the grandstand in the hopes of seeing a "let-up" in the rain and a consequent "flip" by one of the planes. The rain did "let up" for a few minutes and the young pilots decided to reward the crowd for its trip to the park....

* Some sources give the spelling as Trimm.

Hoy, Hall and Trim managed to do some steep turns, and even a couple of loops, beneath the 1400-foot (430 m) cloud base. Their performance was rewarded "with a round of applause."[12]

The meet did finally take place on Saturday, May 31. A long and glowing report of its success was in the *Daily World* on June 2. The pilots representing the Vancouver branch of the League were MacDonald, Hoy, Dixon, Hall, Eckley, Trim and Foy (who obviously could not have been too seriously injured in the May 21 crash), as well as Lieutenant Jack Clemence of Victoria, who was flying *Pathfinder*. There was yet another description, identical to the two previous ones, of the heroics of stunt man J. H. Fieldhouse. Two highlights were, "an eight lap race at low altitude around the track.... This race went to Lieut. G. K. Trim, who out-distanced Captain Eckley by a narrow margin, but sufficient to get him the Panama hat that was offered for a prize"; and "the big race of the afternoon to New Westminster and back [which] started with four planes and was captured by the plane belonging to the Vancouver Aerial Transportation Company. This plane was piloted by Lieut. "Miny" MacDonald, D.F.C., and was a winner by almost a minute over the other planes competing in the race. It is understood that the prize for the race, a JN-4 plane, will be turned over to the aerial League here when it arrives from the east."[13]

It was, and it went on to become the first plane to cross the Canadian Rockies. Before then, though, the Victoria branch of the Aerial League held an aerial meet at Willows Park, now elevated by the newspapers to Willows Aerodrome.

Probably because it occurred so soon after the Vancouver meet, and possibly because the Winnipeg strike, with its accompanying "riots" was monopolizing the front pages, the newspapers gave only modest coverage. The *Daily Colonist* (June 10, 1919), carried a single column on page 12 which promised "Sensational flying of the most daring character," together with a large advertisement. Another, even larger advertisement the following day, the day of the meet, promised "Freak Flying, as practised by war pilots to relieve the monotony of every day flying."

In their report of the events on June 12, they headlined the news, LADIES TAKEN UP IN PLANE. "The first lady passenger ever carried by an

Ernest Hoy, pilot, with S. Thompson in front, at Minoru
Park, 1919. the Curtiss JN-4 (Can) became the workhorse
of post-World-War-I commercial flying.

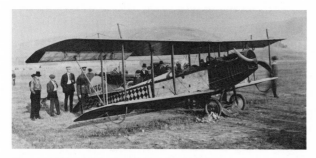

Ernest Hall in Vernon, August 5, 1919.

R. Rideout and W. H. Brown on the first flight from
Victoria to Seattle, May 18, 1919. This photograph, taken in
Seattle, may have been doctored: the aircraft seems out of
scale.

George Dixon, left, and Ernest Hoy just before the Aerial League meet at Minoru Park which took place eventually on May 31, 1919.

G. K. Trim, rear cockpit, made the first commercial flight from Vancouver to Victoria on June 27, 1919. According to the Victoria *Daily Times* he carried "J. N. Harvey as passenger and a small consignment of merchandise."

Eddie Hubbard and Bill Boeing, who is holding the mail bag of the first "official" international air mail flight between Seattle and Vancouver, February 1919.

UNIVERSITY OF TORONTO PRESS

120

Some of the participants in the Aerial League meet. The caption under this newspaper photograph reads: Left to right, H. E. Cook, E. C. Hall, J. Clemence, J. A. Longley, G. Dixon, E. C. Hoy, W. M. MacDonald, J. H. Fieldhouse—but there are ten people in it.

VANCOUVER *PROVINCE*

Lieutenant E. Hall, one of the pilots in the Vancouver Aerial League meet. Later, he appeared to involve himself in a race with Ernest Hoy to be the first to cross the Rockies. If it was a race, it ended in Creston when Hall's "...plane ran nose on into an automobile, and described an almost complete somersault."

VANCOUVER *PROVINCE*

Minoru Park from the air, taken during the Aerial League meet of May 31, 1919.

VANCOUVER PUBLIC LIBRARY

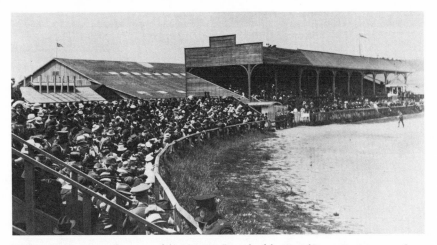

Willows Park race track, scene of the Victoria Branch of the Aerial League's air meet on June 12, 1919. In spite of the crowd in the stands, there were complaints about people who sat in their cars around the perimeter of the track to enjoy the spectacle free of charge.

PABC PHOTOS

George Dixon with a young passenger at Willows Park.

Ernest Hoy at the Willows Park meet with a passenger who may have been Miss Marie Sweeney, but who looks remarkably like the celebrated artist Emily Carr.

On September 23, G. K. Trim accomplished another first: he carried the first unofficial air mail from the Mayor of Grand Forks to Nelson residents George Horstead, manager of the Nelson Fair and to Frank Payne of the Nelson *Daily News*. For some reason he chose not to land on the CPR flats; instead he chose a small field. The aircraft had to be pushed back into the trees to gain every inch possible for take-off. It wasn't quite enough.

The JN-4 was salvaged and shipped back to Vancouver by railway flatcar for repairs.

Trim wading ashore after landing in the lake.

On September 28, 1919, W. H. Brown and mechanic C. Plant became the first crew to land in Duncan, where Brown gave an exhibition of aerobatics, followed by passenger trips the next day. Forty local residents were "...ecstatic about the experience."

JACK FLEETWOOD

Ernest Hall became the first pilot to land in Kamloops in August 1919.

COMINCO COLLECTION, RBCM

Ernest Hoy in Vancouver before his first flight across the Rockies to Calgary, August 4, 1919.

In 1919 the Hoffar brothers made this conversion of a JN-4 to a "seaplane". The single float with two wing-tip floats was not an entirely successful conversion because the OX-5 engine lacked the necessary power. Second from left, Henry Hoffar; right, James Hoffar.

aeroplane over Victoria went up yesterday afternoon. . . . Miss Gwendolyn Richards, sponsor of the Victoria plane Pathfinder, made the first flight. The honor of being the second lady passenger was auctioned, and Miss Marie Sweeney won the privilege." Miss Richards' pilot was George Dixon and, on instructions from Mrs. Richards, he refrained from any stunting. Miss Sweeney flew with Ernest Hoy and, if her mother was present, she made no such stipulation. "She had flown in California before, and asked to be stunted [a curious choice of words]. Captain Hoy certainly complied with her wish."

Because the Victoria branch had only the *Pathfinder*, Robert Rideout flew it, with Mr. Thompsett, President of the League as passenger, to Vancouver, to "complete arrangements for the meet here and to escort the Vancouver planes to Victoria to take part." When he took off from Minoru Park to return, "he got about fifteen feet [5 m] above the ground and was making a banking turn, when the fire extinguisher . . . evidently jarred from its place by the bump of the take off, fell in the way of the rudder bar, preventing its use. Control gone, Lieutenant Rideout had just time to shut off his engine when the plane sideslipped and the wing crashed into the ground." Neither of the occupants suffered more than minor bruises and contusions, and the Vancouver branch rolled out another machine to take back to Victoria. With Rideout leading, the three machines in V formation took one hour and 14 minutes to return to Willows field.

The programme in Victoria was almost a carbon copy of the one in Vancouver: aerobatics; formation flying; a race round the track; a performance by stunt man J. H. Fieldhouse; and, finally, a race to Sidney and back, won by Rideout. The *Colonist* reported that

. . . attendance at the aerial meet was good, there being several thousand people at the Willows. Also there were rows of cars along the roads surrounding the aerodrome, and Victorians, able to pay for expensive cars, got a good show without paying a cent. Aerial League officials went down the line of cars and made $10 by selling ten cent programmes. This gives some idea of the number of cheap guys, as they are officially known.

The Victoria *Times* carried only one short column in its June 12 issue, reporting that Bill Boeing and Eddie Hubbard of Seattle had visited the aerial meet in their seaplane. The reporter seemed particularly interested in one aspect of the aircraft:

This is the seaplane which is very popular with bridal couples in Seattle. It has two cockpits meant normally to carry two people, but the operators have found it quite easy to get a pair of newly-weds into the front seat, as they are not embarrassed at sitting close together. The plane is due back in Seattle about 5 o'clock this afternoon to take a bridal couple to Tacoma. The aerial honeymoon is becoming quite fashionable in Seattle owing to the added thrill.

The Victoria branch of the League then moved up to Nanaimo and Duncan. The August 21, 1919, issue of the Cowichan *Leader*, reported that

Residents were interesting in seeing the Pathfinder No. 2 pass north to Nanaimo on Saturday, August 17, about 2 P.M. It was observed returning again about 8 P.M. The distance is 75 miles [120 km] between Victoria and Nanaimo, and was covered in 54 minutes. The flying machine also carried a special mail. While on a weekend visit to Nanaimo, several local residents saw the maneuvers performed by this machine, including looping the loop, nose-diving, spiral falling, gliding, and many other stunts.

In the October 2 issue there was another report:

On Friday, Sept. 26th 1919, at 11:30 A.M., H.R.H. Prince of Wales officially opened the Cowichan Fall Fair, with its Victory Exhibition.

There was a whirr in the air as the Pathfinder 2 circled down and passed low over the cheering concourse. . . .

The 'plane spotted a fire at Hillcrest Lumber Co's mill. The value of aeroplanes in forest protection was thus abundantly demonstrated.

The following day, pilot W. H. Brown, accompanied by mechanic C. Plant, gave rides to more than 40 local residents. The names of all of them were recorded in the newspaper; and for each of them it was their first experience in the air. Unfortunately, there is no record of how much these rides cost; but, according to the reporter, those involved were ecstatic about the experience.

Historically, the Aerial League's next venture was by far the most significant. Prizes had been offered for a flight from Vancouver to Calgary by the Vancouver *Daily World*, the Calgary *Herald* and the Lethbridge *Herald*. The only stipulation was that the flight had to be completed in 18 hours. According to Frank Ellis, "Lots were drawn among those members of the Vancouver Branch of the Aerial League who had been war pilots [there were very few pilots around who had not], and the first name out of the hat was that of Captain Ernest C. Hoy, D.F.C."[14]

On his first attempt, Hoy took off from Minoru Park early on the morning of August 4.

There was not a light to be seen, and the interested spectators wondered how Captain Hoy could "take off" in the darkness. They soon discovered that he was not worrying about his "take off," for at exactly 3:40 o'clock he opened up his engine and the roar of the exhaust announced that the flight was on. As the machine rushed across the ground, all that could be seen was the flash of fire from the exhaust pipes. The plane itself was not visible, and the fire spitting from the exhaust was a wonderful sight.[15]

Mechanics are very seldom mentioned in these early reports. If they were heroes, they were certainly unsung ones, so it is interesting to find this time that they were, at the very end of the column in the *Daily World* of August 4:

Several friends of Captain Hoy witnessed his departure, including W. J. Imlay, Secretary of the Aerial League, J. H. Fieldhouse, who motored all the way from New Westminster to see the "take off," and Vincent Webb, representing The World. W. T. Jack, fitter and engineman, and George Sinclair, rigger, who have been working hard during the past few days getting the machine in shape for the flight, also witnessed the departure.[16]

Unfortunately Hoy only got as far as Chilliwack, some 55 miles (90 km) east along the Fraser Valley, where he was forced down by bad weather and planned to return to Vancouver that afternoon, hoping to make another start the following morning. His route was to have been Vancouver to Vernon, Vernon to Grand Forks, Grand Forks to Cranbrook, Cranbrook to Lethbridge and, finally, Lethbridge to Calgary. The only modification to the aircraft was the installation of a 12-gallon auxiliary gas tank. The flight had been well advertised, and the newspapers reported that a large crowd, which had congregated at Vernon to greet him, was disappointed when he failed to arrive. They were doubly disappointed because Lieutenant Trim was also "scheduled to give a flying exhibition in connection with Vernon's two rally days for the reception of all Okanagan Valley returned soldiers," and he, too, failed to get through.[17]

In fact, it was foggy in the Fraser Valley that afternoon, and Hoy did not return to Vancouver until August 6. There is no more mention of Trim, but "Lieut. Ernie Hall, flying the Vatco [Vancouver Aerial Transportation Company] plane in the interior, flew from Kamloops to Vernon yesterday in one hour and fifteen minutes, according to word reaching here last night. He made the trip through wind and rain storms." Finally, on the morning of August 7, Hoy got away from Minoru Park at 4:13 a.m. It was a bright, calm morning. "Dawn was just

Above—Close-up view of Captain E. C. Hoy and his machine. Below—Captain Hoy and his two mechanics, W. T. Jack, fitter and engine man, on left; George Sinclair, rigger, on right.

Start Drive Against American Profiteers

Government is Making Definite Efforts to Reduce High Cost of Living—Five Big Meat Packers Are to be Prosecuted—Export of Food Stuffs and Other Necessities May be Prohibited.

breaking as he passed over Chilliwack," and he climbed to 5,500 feet (1670 m) through the Coquihalla Pass, then on up to 6,500 feet (nearly 2000 m) as he "made use of a pass between Merritt and Vernon, which he had not known before."[18]

After a quick breakfast and refuelling in Vernon, he left at 8:19 and "passed over Kelowna at a height of 4500 feet [1370 m]. Reaching Penticton, he followed the Kettle Valley [railway] line to Midway, where he passed over Lieut. Hall, who had landed, and circled over him to show that he had recognized him."[19] Hoy landed in Grand Forks at 10:24, where, intriguingly, Hall "passed him." The Vernon *News* goes on to report: "Thence, onward, it seemed as if it were going to develop into a race between the two, although Hall was not in any way eligible for the prize being offered." We shall never know if Ernie Hall really was trying to upstage Hoy because he flew over him at Grand Forks, and, "As Hall passed out of sight at Grand Forks it was the last seen of him by Hoy, and, as matters turned out, it was the last lap of Hall's race, for, while taking-off at Creston his plane ran nose on into an automobile, and described an almost complete somersault. Hall escaped with some severe bruises, and the aircraft was shipped to Vancouver."[20]

Meanwhile, Hoy was making excellent time on his leg to Cranbrook. The weather was benign, though he encountered some turbulence in the afternoon. Leaving Grand Forks at 11:15, he reached Cranbrook without incident at 2:05 p.m. Now came the real challenge, the actual crossing of the Rockies. He took off from Cranbrook at 2:35 — his refuelling stops were getting shorter — and headed for the great barrier. Ellis describes this stage of the historic flight with the understanding of a man who had himself flown in the mountains in a light aircraft in the early days:

He soon found that it was not a case of flying over the mountains but between them, for he could not force his machine high enough to fly freely above them. When going through the Crawford Pass, he scraped by with only 150 feet [46 m] of clearance between the wheels of his plane and the rocks and treetops below. Try as he would, he was unable to make the Curtiss climb another foot. With her load, the Jenny had a top ceiling of 7,000 feet [2130 m], and the airman was forced to steer through passes where the surrounding peaks pierced the sky at much greater altitudes than he himself could gain. In such places, often confined, there were vicious up- and down-drafts, which the pilot was not aware of until he was into them. However, he reached Lethbridge safely at 6:22 p.m., and found almost the entire population waiting for him.[21]

Taking a little longer this time to refuel, Hoy left Lethbridge at 7:18. His arrival in Calgary evoked some graphic journalism: "Coming like an express train on schedule time out of a dusky haze of smoke and low-hanging clouds over the city of Calgary, Captain Ernest C. Hoy, D.F.C., in his JN4 airplane, swooped down into the Bowness landing field, seven miles west of the city, and touched ground at precisely 8:53 p.m. city time."[22] By then it was nearly dark, and he was guided in by rockets and flares set off by members of the Calgary Aero Club. The landing field was illuminated by the headlights of hundreds of cars belonging to some of the 5,000 spectators there to greet him. He had succeeded with a brave and significant achievement. The total elapsed time for the trip was 16 hours and 24 minutes, of which 12 hours and 24 minutes were flying time. This left just over four hours for refuelling and catching his breath. Hoy's elation when he reached Calgary must have been tempered with weariness.

On each leg of his flight, Hoy had carried letters and newspapers to be ceremonially handed over on landing. Calgary was no exception. After a well-earned rest of three days, he left at 9:50 a.m. for the return flight, this time by a more northerly route, via the Kicking Horse Pass to Golden; then on to Revelstoke and Kamloops or Vernon, depending on unspecified circumstances. It would be pleasant to be able to record that he landed back at Minoru Park to a triumphant reception. Unfortunately, that didn't happen. Things started well. The Golden *Star* reported that

The joyful cry of "Ship 'a-Hoy'" [the journalist must have been proud of that one] was heard in Golden Monday at 12:38 as the first glimpse was obtained of the biplane J.N.4, Capt. Ernest C. Hoy, D.F.C., proudly soaring in the sky over the mouth of the Kicking Horse Canyon.

It had been intended that the landing should be made on the ball ground inside the racecourse and when Capt. Hoy sighted the large white cross and smudges that had been prepared, he promptly circled over the spot.

But he decided that the space available was not sufficient, flew on over the town and made a satisfactory landing in a field on the property of Thomas King on the western outskirts.

Almost the entire population of Golden had gathered at the recreation grounds at 10 o'clock, the time scheduled for the arrival of Capt. Hoy and the majority patiently waited until he hove in sight.

Immediately it was realized that he had landed elsewhere the crowd hurried off in motor cars, on bicycles, in rigs and on foot to meet him.[23]

The trip from Calgary had taken two hours and 42 minutes. He had followed the CPR tracks, flying over Lake Louise and Field. Then, at 2:45, Hoy began his take-off run at Golden to head west for Revelstoke. Shortly after, he made a steep turn and

When about forty or fifty feet [12-15 m] up the plane side-slipped to the ground, striking the tip of the left wing, swinging around and burying its nose in the opposite direction.

Onlookers rushed to the rescue, but before anyone reached the plane, Capt. Hoy, to the great relief of all Goldenites, was seen to extricate himself from the wreck and to stand up and wave his hand.

Although severely shaken, his only injuries are a possible black eye and a bruised shoulder.[24]

A number of accounts record that Hoy was forced to swerve during his take off because two Indians ran across in front of him; yet, oddly enough, there is no mention of this in the newspapers. The journalist writing for the Golden *Star*, who interviewed Hoy immediately after the accident, reported that "He attributed his mishap partly to an unfavorable air current which he met just as he started to bank and he also expressed the opinion that the lighter air at this altitude prevented him from rising as quickly as he expected." In any event, the same journalist wrote a fitting epitaph to this venture:

The approach of the J.N.4 down the Kicking Horse Canyon was certainly a glorious and inspiring sight and the people of Golden, while deeply regretting the untoward interruption to an epoch-making flight, which must be recognized as a doubly successful crossing of the Rocky mountains, are proud of their participation in the event.[25]

The Prince George *Citizen* emphasized this fact: "Captain Hoy pulls down the honor of being the first aviator to fly both ways across the Rocky Mountains on the American continent."[26]

It was gutsy stuff, and nearly all British Columbians must have felt proud when they read about it.

Photo taken from the air of the Parliament Buildings at Ottawa, Ont.
(PHOTO COURTESY FAIRCHILD AERIAL SURVEYS)

Chapter Ten

The Air Board

"It was, admittedly, a 'temporary expedient'."

DWAYNE LOVEGROVE

While all the events described in the previous chapter made the news and attracted the attention they deserved, they were isolated steps, rather than consistent progress. On the west coast, it was left to the military to provide the first continuing commercial operations, and to understand this apparent paradox we will have to retrace our steps for a moment.

After much prompting by Britain, who had been urging the Dominions to form their own air units to serve with the RFC (after April 1918, the RAF), Canada finally created a Canadian Air Force (CAF). As Wing Commander Hitchins describes it:

Although the Armistice intervened... the Canadian authorities decided to proceed with the formation of a Canadian Air Force. Accordingly, on 20 November 1918, two squadrons were formed at Upper Heyford [U.K.], composed of Canadian pilots and observers who had served with the RAF and Canadian ground personnel who had been trained in RAF schools.... It was intended and expected that this embryo CAF would be transferred to Canada to serve as the nucleus of the Dominion's post-war air force....[1]

There was, however, a problem. The order-in-council that created the CAF also stipulated that the CAF was only "for the purpose of the present war." Consequently, after the war, "the CAF was quietly disbanded in England in January and February of 1920, having been abandoned by a country which wanted to forget everything military, even at possible future expense."[2]

The anti-military mood of the country was real, but so was the inclination of the Canadian government to give as little assistance as possible to the embryonic air industry. J. R. K. Main, who joined the Department of Transport in 1936 and became Director of Civil Aviation in 1958, sums up the political climate of the times:

It is not altogether surprising that officialdom showed little interest in establishing intercity air services after World War I. Two transcontinental railway systems and several shorter ones had been pulled back from the brink of bankruptcy and consolidated into the Canadian National Railways System in 1918. Intercity airline systems have almost invariably looked to profitable mail contracts as the first reliable means of sustenance; so have railways. The lack of enthusiasm for supporting a competitive system, to share the already inadequate source of revenue, can thus be understood.[3]

The truth is that few public transportation systems in our society really support themselves. It is sometimes claimed that the Canadian Pacific Railway is an exception; but the CPR was granted relatively huge land grants as an incentive to proceed with its construction phase and, by the time competition from the trucking industry began to make itself felt, these parcels of land had appreciated in value, thus the CPR was able to diversify and support its railway. Truck companies and bus lines sometimes claim to be independent, too; but in their case the enormous cost of road construction and maintenance is born by the taxpayer. The same applies to modern airlines: there is a vast support structure of radio and radar communications aids, as well as the network of airports, with their large and expensive runways, control towers and terminal buildings, all maintained or manned by public servants. Consequently, after World War I, the budding aviation industry had to compete with established transportation systems; and to do this, it first had to prove itself without government assistance.

Nevertheless, while "the War Measures Act [had] controlled flying activities during the war . . . after the war, the 'Aero Club of Canada' was officially designated by the Royal Flying Club [England]" as the responsible agency. There could not (or certainly should not) have been a vacuum, because "the International Convention for Air Navigation, signed in October 1919, held national governments, including Canada, responsible for the regulation of civil flying regulations."[4]

After two hours of debate, agreement was reached both that some form of civil control was necessary, as well as some semblance of an air force. Historian Dwayne Lovegrove describes the ensuing compromise, which was very much in the Canadian tradition:

What resulted was the Air Board Act, which was passed on 7 May 1919 [sic]. It was, admittedly, a "temporary expedient"; the government wanted a structure quickly set up in order to assume early control over the sudden increase of flying activities, including those now known as "barnstormers." It initially consisted of three branches: a Certificate Branch (later renamed the Controller of Civil Aviation), an Operations Branch, and a Secretariat.[5]

This is how Parliament dealt with the problem. On April 29, 1919, the Minister without Portfolio "Honourable A. K. MacLean (for the Minister of Naval Service) moved for leave to introduce Bill No. 80, to authorize the appointment of an Air Board for the control of aeronautics."[6] MacLean introduced the bill for second reading on May 5 and the debate, an admirably courteous and temperate one, followed.

Mr. Morphy began by objecting that the Minister's intention was to set up a "theoretical Board rather than a practical one."[7] In general terms, the Minister conceded that he was feeling his way with the legislation and that experience would probably prove the necessity for amendments. Nevertheless, he insisted that legislation was necessary: "It [aviation] is unknown to both the common law and the statute law. Consequently, nobody can legally engage in flying to-day . . . it is not within the right of any individual to fly in the air with aeroplanes or hydroplanes, or any other machine of the kind, although there is no statutory law which directly prohibits it."[8]

Next came an objection familiar in Canadian history. Mr. Ernest Lapointe and Mr. Lemieux questioned the authority of the federal government to control aviation within the borders of a province and suggested it would be contrary to the British North America Act. MacLean agreed that this would probably have to be decided in the courts. In spite of this, Lemieux was optimistic about the future of aviation: "Perhaps we would save enormous railway subsidies by organizing an aerial postal service."[9] MacLean was non-committal, as he was on the subject of a revived Canadian Air Force.

The debate wound down with consideration of the effect of aviation on property rights. In other words, would aircraft violate existing property rights by flying over private buildings. MacLean's answer was that he thought not, but that it would be up to the Air Board to address that problem by providing ". . . a regulation that no flying machine shall approach the ground, or approach a building, within a certain number of feet. I have heard the story frequently, and I assume it is a fact, of somebody when flying in the city of Vancouver entering a bedroom where a patient was being attended by a doctor; the machine and the pilot landing in the bedroom. We will seek to avoid the repetition of such a discourteous act. . . ."[10] Presumably, he was referring to the unfortunate Victor Bishop in the Hoffar H-2, who landed not in a bedroom, but in a bathtub.

The debate on second reading of the bill ended amicably when Mr. Beland asked "Is it contemplated to have a certain number of aeroplanes reserved for the exclusive use of ministers of the Crown?" and the Minister of Defence and Militia, Major-General Mewburn responded, "You would not want to see the ministers any more up in the air than they are now, would you?"[11]

The bill proceeded to its third reading on May 6 without further debate, and was given royal assent on June 6, 1919.[12] The Air Board, appointed by the government, had sweeping powers: to regulate and control aerial navigation over Canada; to make regulations for licensing pilots, aircraft and air stations; to enforce laws, rules and regulations for the safe and proper navigation of aircraft; and for the organization, discipline, efficiency and good government of officers and men employed under the Air Board.[13] In effect the Air Board was to provide "a Civil Aviation Branch for the control of commercial and civil flying, a Civil Operations Branch in charge of all non-military flying operations, and a Canadian Air Force primarily responsible for training rather than defence."[14]

There are some grounds for suggesting that the Air Board — and, less than a year later, the Canadian Air Force — came into existence for other reasons besides the ones already suggested; authorities had been prodded again. This prod came in the form of a gift of a large number of war-surplus aircraft from the British government that was probably not entirely welcomed by the Canadian government, and certainly not by the opposition.

When the Air Board Act passed in June, 1919, the House approved a budget of $250,000 for its first year's operation. Early in the 1920 session, the House approved the same sum in the Main Estimates for the

Air Service. Then, only a day or two before the session ended, on June 30, they slipped in two supplementary estimates: $850,000 for civil aviation and $800,000 for the CAF. The debate that followed, unlike the one after the second reading of the Air Board Act the previous year, was far from amiable.

Mr. Dennis led off for the opposition by demanding, "What is this item for?" Mr. Guthrie, speaking for the government, responded with a lengthy explanation. "It so happens that we have in Canada about twelve thousand of the most highly trained military air men, of whom we know, that are to be found in the world." In brief, the proposal was to recruit some 5000 of these airmen and to give them one month of training every year to retain ". . . their interest in, and sympathy with the work in case in the future it may develop for commercial and scientific or other purposes as well as for military operations." Guthrie then went on to reveal the extent of the "Imperial Gift." "I may say . . . that we have received from Great Britain a very extensive aeroplane outfit . . . the value of which, I think, amounts to between five and six million dollars." He told the House that bases for the use of these aircraft were to be opened across the country.[15] In time, these turned out to be at Dartmouth, Roberval, Ottawa, Morley and Vancouver, with Camp Borden as a training centre. In 1921, the Alberta base was moved from Morley to High River because "It was too near the mountains"; and two new bases, one at Victoria Beach, Manitoba, on the southeastern shore of Lake Winnipeg, and the other at Sioux Lookout, Ontario, were established.[16]

Guthrie ended his justification by saying that air routes were to be laid out across the country and that suitable "landing stations" would be provided on "Crown lands which will involve no expense. This is a modern development and we intend to keep up with other nations, and particularly with the United States and with Great Britain."[17]

Mackenzie King went into the attack with a lecture about the supplementary estimate. ". . . if the government was even considering these large outlays they ought to have submitted them in the Main and not in the Supplementary Estimates. It is not treating Parliament or the country fairly to put an item in the Main Estimates of something like $250,000 for the Air Service and then in the last two or three days of the session bring down a Supplementary item of $1,650,000."[18]

Guthrie, perhaps rather unwisely, claimed that no one had been able to estimate the cost of dealing with the gift aircraft until they arrived in May. Mr. McMaster asked when the government had decided to accept the gift, because, "The acceptance of [this] gift may entail very heavy responsibilities on the donee. I am very much afraid that the Government has accepted these airships without, so far as I know, taking the Canadian people into its confidence...." Mackenzie King suggested that "the British government has adopted the policy of getting rid of its surplus war material by presenting it to some of the overseas dominions." Mr. Guthrie disagreed. "I assume that the motives of the British Government in making this gift to Canada were absolutely proper."[19]

There was more in the same vein before the government prevailed and the House approved an appropriation of $1,100,000 for civil aviation and $800,000 for military aviation. As for the "Imperial Gift," which the government had known about before it created the Air Board in 1919, it consisted of "100 aircraft, together with all the necessary spares, stores and equipment...80 aeroplanes, 14 flying-boats, 12 non-rigid airships and six kite-balloons together with hangars, sheds, inflating plants, spare parts, armament, wireless instruments, cameras, technical equipment, vehicles and other material."[20] An additional 16 aircraft had been donated to the Canadian government as a replacement for the "gift" machines presented to Britain during the war. Then, to add to this largesse, the Americans, who had during the last months of the war operated an early form of what the RAF later called Coastal Command, made a donation to Canada. Based at Sydney and Dartmouth, Nova Scotia, they had flown anti-submarine patrols off the east coast. After the war, "When the U.S. Naval Flying Corps withdrew from Dartmouth and North Sydney it left behind, as a donation to the Canadian government, 12 Curtiss HS-2L flying boats, and 25 Liberty Engines...."[21]

It was an embarrassment of riches that could not be ignored, and the Air Board was able to go ahead with the establishment of a rather tentative Canadian Air Force.

And although the new CAF was supposed to be simply a training organization, it managed to do much more by "seconding trained personnel to the Air Board for its Civil Operations Branch,"[22] and this is where British Columbia comes back into the story. "The Canadian

Air Board established bases across Canada, and Vancouver's Jericho Beach was chosen as their west coast base. In February 1920, temporary canvas hangars were erected. British Columbia's wet climate soon proved to be too much for the canvas structures and they were soon replaced by others of wood and metal construction."[23] Earl L. MacLeod, whose initiation into military flying in World War I we have already examined, provides the best account of operations from this base, and this is how he first became involved.

On my return to British Columbia in the spring of 1919, I discovered that by this time flying was in my blood. I applied for and obtained an International Flying Licence that was recognized at that time in Canada, namely Federation Aeronautique Internationale Aviator's Certificate No. 486, dated 17 September 1919, issued to me by the Aero Club of Canada. As many other pilots no doubt did, I wrote letters to Government Departments, both Federal and Provincial, suggesting civilian uses for aircraft and offering my services.[24]

MacLeod's opportunity came very soon afterwards. An officer he had served with in Great Britain, Major J. W. Hobbs, who "had been promised . . . to be in charge of the base at Jericho Beach—or rather, on the west coast," came out late in 1919 to select this base. Before doing so, he had written to MacLeod, who was living in Chilliwack, asking MacLeod to meet him in Vancouver and assist him in making the choice. MacLeod's account continues:

I arranged with an ex-pilot by the name of MacDonald, who had a car, a real limousine, to take us around the area. He took us out to Port Moody and along the Fraser River— both sides—and Jericho Beach. We decided that Jericho Beach was most convenient in many ways for the purpose for which it was to be used: that is, to accommodate just a few flying boats for work with various government departments, including fishery and forestry and that kind of thing.[25]

If Major Hobbs had in fact been promised command of the Jericho Beach base, he was to be disappointed because the first Commanding Officer—or Station Superintendent—was Major MacLaurin, an ex-RNAS and -RAF officer who had been returned to Canada from England to form the proposed Canadian Naval Air Service, a proposal that had vanished like the first CAF when Armistice was declared. Wing Commander Hitchins' account of this genesis is slightly at odds with MacLeod's. "Major C. MacLaurin, who had been designated air station super-intendent, selected a suitable site for a seaplane station at Jericho Beach on part of the old Naval Reserve on English Bay. . . .[6]

Construction of the Air Board's Jericho Beach flying boat base in Vancouver, 1920.

E. L. MACLEOD ESTATE PHOTOS

Kenneth Moffat, Head of the Wireless Section at Jericho Beach, 1920. He must have been underemployed for some time because the base Superintendent decided to use carrier pigeons for communication while on operations.

Major Claire MacLaurin, first Superintendent
of the Jericho Beach Air Station, 1921.

Arrival and assembly of the first H Boat (Curtiss HS-2L) at Jericho Beach, 1920.

G-CYBA being assembled at Carney's Landing, on Shuswap Lake near Sicamous. It had been shipped from Vancouver by rail for the Base's first operation in the Interior by MacLaurin, October 1920.

E. L. MACLEOD ESTATE PHOTOS

In 1921, the Base's fleet was increased by the arrival of the larger, twin-engined Felixstowe F3 flying boat.

Launching an H Boat on the slipway in front of the hangar at Jericho Beach.

The Prince George *Citizen* gave
ample coverage to the U.S. Army Air
Service's First Alaska Air Expedition
in August 1920.

PRINCE GEORGE C

VOL. 5. NO. 9. PRINCE GEORGE, B.C., FRIDAY, AUGUST 6, 1920.

American Flying Expedition Lands at Prince George Monday---Mishap to Capt. Street's Plane

Machines 2, 3 and 4 Land on Monday Morning with Slight Accident to Machine No. 3.—Captain Street Delayed at Jasper by Fire in Engine, Reaches Prince George in Thunder Storm and Overran Field Into Stumpy Ground, Damaging Machine.

After some delay at Edmonton caused by the discovery of slight leaks in two of the petrol tanks of the machines engaged in the United States Army flying expedition from New York to Nome, the machines left Edmonton on Sunday last and flew to Jasper, making the 200 mile flight in 95 minutes. The machines left Jasper about 9:30 on Monday morning, their progress being reported by telegraph operators along the line as they progressed towards Prince George. Long before the machines arrived the local landing ground was thronged with people, who took up positions clear of the ground and who acted with every regard for the safety of the pilots on their arrival. Shortly before 11 o'clock the first machine was sighted coming over the Fraser River, near the bridge, flying at an altitude of about 2000 feet. The two other machines followed immediately.

The first machine to land was No. 2, piloted by First Lieutenant Clifford C. Nutt, second in command of the expedition, with Second Lieutenant Eric C. Nelson,

been excellent for the landings, but it was noted with alarm by the flying men and the crowds at the landing ground that the weather was very threatening, some

AIRMEN GUESTS OF HONOR LAST NIGHT

Ritts-Kifer Hall Scene of Dance in Honor of American Flying Expedition.

The Ritts-Kifer Hall was the scene of a pretty dance last night given in honor of the aviators of the U.S. Army engaged in the

SEARCH FOR OGLE CONTINUES IN WOODS

Some of Police Force After Murderer Return to City, But Many on His Trail.

The pursuit of the murderer, Orvil Ogle, in the Mud River district goes on. Indian police from Stony Creek have been added to

PRINCE GEORGE *CITIZEN*

The pilots of the Alaska Air Expedition
in front of one of their four DH4B biplanes.
Left to right: Capt. St. Clair Streett, 1st Lieut.
C. C. Knutt, 2nd Lieuts. R. C. Kirkpatrick,
E. H. Nelson, C. E. Crumrine. PABC

The Alaska Air Expedition at Whitehorse. Lower photograph offers a neat comparison between the old and the new. By dog team, the journey from Whitehorse to Dawson City would have taken some 30 days. The Air Expedition made it in an hour and thirty-five minutes. PABC

Another view of the DH9A at the Crowle ranch.

Air Commodore A. K. Tylee in front of his
DH9A at the Crowle ranch, just south of
Revelstoke, October 14, 1920. The plane,
piloted by Captain G. A. Thompson, had just
crossed the Rockies on the Air Board-CAF's
Trans-Canada Flight.

REVELSTOKE MUSEUM PHOTOS

In either case, Earl MacLeod was appointed for duty on the west coast by the Civil Service Commission as an Air Pilot Navigator on July 1, 1920, and

My first job at the base [as an Air Pilot Navigator] was the operating of our Cletrac tractor, clearing drift logs and debris from the beach in preparation for construction of temporary offices, cement apron, slipway, and two wooden canvas-covered Bessoneau-type hangars.[27]

And the first HS-2L, carrying the registration letters G-CYBA,* which had been dismantled and shipped across the country by rail, was put together again at the end of August, 1920, and test flown by MacLaurin on September 24. After further familiarization flights, an "experimental flight was made to Victoria in an attempt to interest Premier Oliver in the proposed seaplane service as he had previously criticized expenditure by the federal government for forestry patrol."[28] No hints are offered about the success of this "experiment."

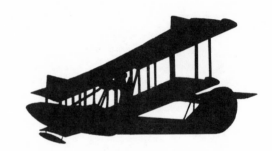

Towards the end of September, MacLaurin took off for the first operational flight. Accompanied by a Dominion entomologist, he flew to Slave River (Stave River) so that the entomologist "could inspect and photograph from the air swamp lands where the mosquito pest was believed to originate." A month after that, the aircraft "was dismantled and shipped to a siding near Sicamous (Carney's) where it was reassembled for a series of flights from Shuswap Lake as far west as Kamloops. On these flights MacLaurin was accompanied by a forestry officer (Mr. R. Cameron), as well as his photographer (C. J. Duncan) and mechanic (A. L. Hartridge)."[29] The Timberman (December 1920, p. 96) reported that "The first aerial photographs of timber limits in British Columbia for use of the department have been taken in the vicinity of Kamloops by Major C. MacLaurin, superintendent of the B.C. Air Station. The results have been very satisfactory." Clearly MacLaurin's efforts did make an impression on the right people because, a few months later, the journal, West Coast Lumberman (April 15, 1921, p. 43), reported that: "The provincial government has voted a sum of $20,000 for aerial reconnaissance and exploration work in connection with British Columbia's forests...."

MacLaurin completed what he had set out to do by November 15

* Canadian aircraft carried the British prefix G- to their registration letters until 1928; after which it was changed to the Canadian CF.

and, once again, the flying boat was dismantled and loaded onto a flat car for shipment to Vancouver. At this time, evidently, the crews felt that the HS-2L, with its Liberty engine, had neither the power nor the reliability for the kind of trans-mountain flying Ernest Hoy had accomplished the previous year. However, by 1921, they had the confidence to fly through the Fraser Canyon to Kamloops.

Before continuing with the story of the Jericho Beach operations, however, we shall have to break off to look at two other historic ventures in 1920: the U.S. Army Air Service's First Alaska Air Expedition, and the Air Board-CAF's Trans-Canada flight. The first was "to investigate the feasibility of establishing an air route into the far north."[30] It was composed of eight men to crew four de Havilland DH4B biplanes. The DH4 was a British design, but built in the United States and powered by a 400-horsepower American Liberty engine. Led by Captain St. Clair Streett, the expedition took off from Mitchell Field, New York on July 15. From the first, they encountered severe weather, as well as problems with engines.

It is not necessary for us to follow their laborious progress across the United States, but it took them 10 days to reach the Canadian border at Portal, North Dakota, flying on to land at Saskatoon. From there they flew to Edmonton on July 27, staying there until the 31st, when they tried to reach Jasper but were turned back by the weather. They made it to Jasper on the 31st, and left for Prince George on August 2.

As early as July 16, the Prince George *Citizen* carried a long article on the expedition. The Imperial Oil agent had laid in "a large quantity of gasoline and oil for the machines. The gasoline used is the special aviation spirit, refined for use in aeroplanes"; arrangements had been made with the Grand Trunk Pacific Railway for their agent in McBride to send a telegram when the aircraft passed and, "Mr. Feren, the company's agent here, has consented to have the roundhouse whistle blown a number of times to warn the public of the approach of the machines." The report included a diagram of the prepared landing ground, "situated on Central Avenue," which was a cleared and rolled field 300 yards (274 m) long and 100 yards (91 m) wide.

There was another long report the following week, July 23, cataloguing the slow progress across the United States and then, on August 6, most of the front page was taken up with a description of their

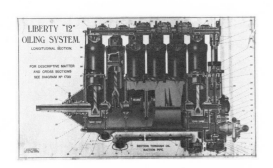

LIBERTY "12"
OILING SYSTEM.
LONGITUDINAL SECTION.

FOR DESCRIPTIVE MATTER
AND CROSS SECTIONS
SEE DIAGRAM N° 1733

SECTION THROUGH OIL
SUCTION PIPE.

landing in Prince George. The GTP telegram warning of their approach was received on the morning of Monday, August 2, and, "Long before the machines arrived the local landing ground was thronged with people."

Lieutenant Nutt was the first to land, and his "landing was very well judged." Next came Lieutenant Crumrine and his landing was "slightly marred by misjudgment of distance and speed, the pilot swinging his machine while it was running on the ground to prevent it overrunning the field, and owing to the softness of the ground one of the wheels sunk on the sharp turn, throwing the machine on its left wing tip." Frank Ellis describes the mishap as rather more serious: The machine, "went up on its nose in the bush at the end of the clearing. Long [Crumrine's passenger] went catapulting into the dense foliage, which broke his fall, so that he, at least, landed without injury."[31] In addition to a bent propeller, the left wing was damaged.

Meanwhile, the leader, Captain Streett, had had to return to Jasper shortly after take off with a burst oil pipe. By the time this had been repaired, and he had flown to Prince George, the light was failing and, as the Prince George *Citizen* reported, "it was noted with alarm by the flying men and the crowds at the landing ground that the weather was very threatening. . . . A heavy bank of black clouds crept over the sky from the southwest and before his machine was sighted flying out of the northeast, a thunder storm was in progress and rain was falling heavily." In spite of flares put out for him he, too, overshot the field and damaged one of his wings.

The expedition was to fly as a unit, so considerable time was lost in Prince George while the two damaged machines were repaired. Frank Ellis explains the sort of problems the expedition faced.

In the meantime, Captain Streett and Lieutenant Nutt had journeyed by train to Hazelton to size up the possible landing-grounds there. The outlook was melancholy beyond belief: such areas just did not exist. The only spot remotely suitable was on the farm of a Mr. Biern[e]s, and at the time it was a thriving field of oats! But the owner rose to the occasion and had a wide swathe cut through his standing crop, then harrowed and rolled the stubble to a semblance of a runway. Thus did British Columbia's first northern "air field" come into being.[32]

Streett and his expedition reached Hazelton without incident on August 13, and took off again the same day for Wrangell, Alaska. The ensuing journey to "furthest north," Nome, was a saga of bad weather and other misfortunes—but none of them serious enough to put an end to the expedition. "At 5:30 P.M. [August 23] they brought their four machines to a stop on the old parade grounds at Fort Davis on the very threshold of the Bering Sea. Four thousand five hundred miles of flying lay behind them, accomplished in 55 hours of flying time, over a period of 40 days."[33]

Their return journey was no less arduous. Leaving Nome three days later, they reached Fairbanks on August 31. They left Fairbanks for Dawson City on September 3, and reached Whitehorse the day after. Their next destination was Telegraph Creek, in northwestern British Columbia. The first attempt, on September 5, was aborted by bad weather. The second, on the 8th, was a little more successful, but only for one of them. According to Ellis, three pilots were forced to turn back; the fourth, Lieutenant Kirkpatrick, apparently had a slightly different agenda:

Kirkpatrick, becoming separated from the others, wound up four hours later at Wrangell. This was not due to miscalculation, on his part, however, but to very fine navigation under the worst conditions. On the journey north he had met a young lady at Wrangell and admiration had been mutual, so instead of turning back to White Horse with the others, Kirkpatrick turned the adverse flying conditions into a happy break which enabled him to reach Wrangell and renew acquaintance.[34]

The three aircraft at Whitehorse flew to Telegraph Creek on September 9, but the unfortunate Crumrine once again suffered severe damage to his aircraft, this time to the undercarriage. Repairs had been completed by the 16th, and were followed by two attempts to reach Hazelton on the 17th and 19th, both abortive because of weather. Kirkpatrick, on the other hand, managed to fly from Wrangell to Hazelton on September 16. The three aircraft at Whitehorse were delayed by weather until the 29th, by which time Kirkpatrick had flown, via Prince George, Jasper and Edmonton, to Saskatoon. The four machines were eventually reunited at Fargo, North Dakota, on October 11, and the flight finally ended at Mitchell Field on October 20.

Clearly, high-speed air transport had not yet arrived—they had taken 97 days, a little over three months, to cover 9,000 miles (14 480 km)—but the flight was a significant one because it proved that wheeled aircraft could operate over undeveloped country, and provided the obvious lesson that, if safe and suitable airfields had been available along the route, the elapsed time could have been dramatically reduced. Such luxuries were not provided until the 1930s, when, "...rough airstrips were established at several major points, notably Prince George, Whitehorse, McMurray and Aklavik. Grant McConachie organized Yukon Southern Air Transport which flew over most of the Northwest Territories"; and it wasn't until the early 1940s that construction began on suitable landing fields, complete with emergency lighting, radio aids and meteorological equipment at Prince George, Smithers, Grande Prairie, Fort St. John, Fort Nelson, Watson Lake and Whitehorse.[35]

The Air Board-CAF's Trans-Canada Flight, which had been suggested by Major MacLaurin when he was Acting Director of the proposed Canadian Naval Air Service, was similarly designed "to demonstrate the feasibility of such a flight from a commercial point of view; to prove the possibility of a fast trip from coast to coast without undue strain on the pilots or machines; and to serve as recruiting propaganda for The Canadian Air Force and to stimulate an interest in aviation by commercial firms and the public generally."[36] The trip was carefully planned. The aircraft were to be a Fairey seaplane, then being assembled by Canadian Vickers in Montreal, which was to fly from Halifax to Winnipeg; and from there on, three de Havilland DH9A's on wheels (part of the Imperial Gift to Canada) were to complete the trip to Vancouver. Plans included "ten places where mooring facilities would be laid out and ten more where night landing facilities would be provided. Stores of petrol and caster oil would be laid down at each landing-place...."[37] In addition, survey flights were to be carried out both on the eastern and western sections of the route. The eastern section would be under the control of Lieutenant-Colonel Robert Leckie, Director of Flying Operations for the Air Board; and the western under Air Commodore A. K. Tylee, Air Officer Commanding the CAF. To avoid the stigma of a military operation, all personnel wore civilian clothes.

The planners were confident, if not unrealistically optimistic: they were hoping to start the flight on September 27 — with a non-stop flight from Halifax to Winnipeg — and complete it in Vancouver by September 29, only 48 hours later. It took a good deal longer than that. To begin with, the Fairey seaplane proved unable to take off with a full load of fuel, and Lieutenant-Colonel Leckie, who was to fly the first leg, did not get away from Montreal to Halifax to start the first leg until September 29. After a series of mechanical problems, and delays caused by weather, Leckie finally took off from Halifax at 8:00 a.m. on October 7. The next news of him came in a telegram to Ottawa: "Regret to report forced landing 20 miles north of Saint John. Fairey machine crashed. I am arranging to continue flight in flying-boat from Halifax."

By this time, two flying boats were standing by to help: an HS-2L and a twin-engined Felixstowe F3. The HS-2L was at Halifax; the F3 at Rivière du Loup. After fighting his way through strong winds, Major Shearer in the HS-2L managed to reach the downed Fairey and picked up Leckie to fly him to Rivière du Loup. On the following morning, Leckie took off again in the F3 at 6:30, flying under a 300-foot (90-m) cloud base until he passed Montreal, where the weather finally improved. He landed on the river at Ottawa at 12:30 p.m., after a six-hour, non-stop flight.

The trip from Ottawa to Winnipeg was a good deal more encouraging. Even so, there were to be more delays. Leaving Ottawa at 8:45 a.m. on October 9, Leckie reached Sault Ste. Marie at 4:35 that afternoon, intending to take off again at midnight. By then, ground fog made the planned night departure impossible. He got away eventually at 7:30 a.m. on October 10, only to be delayed again for repairs to a leaking radiator at Kenora. Unable to continue until 8:15 p.m. for the last 155 miles (250 km) to Winnipeg, Leckie was now faced with a night landing at Winnipeg. He followed the Winnipeg River northwest to Lake Winnipeg; then turned south to follow the Red River to the city. A combination of darkness and ground fog forced him to put down on the river at Selkirk, some miles short of Winnipeg, at 10:45 p.m.

Captain Home-Hay, with Air Commodore Tylee as passenger, took off from Winnipeg for Calgary in the DH9A at 4:30 in the morning of October 11. With the CPR tracks to guide them, they made good progress until just after passing Regina, when engine trouble forced them back there for a landing. Captain G. A. Thompson, who later became a distinguished bush pilot, and who was waiting in Calgary with another DH9A to complete the flight to Vancouver, then flew back to Regina, picked up Tylee and returned to Calgary by 5:10 that evening.

Two more days were lost to weather while they waited to face the mountains.

"On October 13," according to Wing Commander Hitchins, "Thompson took off with Tylee,... passed over Sturdee, just east of Glacier, B.C., and at 1510 landed at the Crowle ranch four miles south of Revelstoke."[38] The Revelstoke *Review* (October 14, p. 1) gave the time as 2:10, but this was almost certainly a time-zone discrepancy. The newspaper reported that "The weather was not at all favorable, but the big plane was watched by hundreds of citizens as it made the circles previous to landing, which was accomplished successfully...."

"In Revelstoke," Hitchins continues, "the de Havilland was grounded by 'excessive fog' and 'weather most unfavourable for flight' until 1150 on the morning of Friday, the 15th. Good time (98 m.p.h. [158 k/ph]) was made then as far as Merritt, but fog in Coquihalla Pass forced Thompson to turn back when half-way through and he returned to Merritt to refuel and spend the night. The next day bad weather frustrated a second attempt to get through the pass. Finally, at 0940 on Sunday, the 17th, Thompson and Tylee took off from Merritt, passed over Agassiz an hour later, and landed at Minoru Park, Vancouver, at 1125 to complete the first flight across Canada 'A Mari Usque Ad Mare.'"[39]

From the Atlantic to the Pacific was a satisfying accomplishment, but it would be idle to hint that this venture had the significance of the first CPR train pulling into Port Moody in 1885. The 3,340 miles (5375 km) of the trip had taken a little over ten days—247 hours; whereas, the trip by train would have taken some 132 hours according to the then current schedule. Pro-rated, their progress was very comparable to that of the Alaska flight. Nevertheless, it was an important milestone at a time when many people were still inclined to regard aviation as a species of stunt.

As a sort of ironic footnote, Tylee, Leckie, Hobbs and Thompson, all of whom had taken part in the Trans-Canada Flight, decided to make sure they had crossed the entire country by setting off to fly from Vancouver to Victoria in an HS-2L. The Jericho Beach Station diary records that

After two and a half hours in the air the flying-boat forced-landed in the fog at Port Townsend, Wash, on Puget Sound, some 35 miles [56 km] south-east of its destination.

An hour later the party set out again, intending to fly due west to Port Angeles, a point almost directly across the strait from Victoria, but once again they had to put down at Friday Harbour, short of their objective. Unable to get the engine started again that day, the officers lay over until the morning of the 21st when a half-hour flight brought them safely, if by a somewhat circuitous route, to their original destination.[39]

The last sentence is slyly ironic. With the cream of the operational staff of the Air Board as crew, this wayward flight must surely have occasioned some hilarity among the base personnel. In any event, the Victoria *Daily Times* suggested as much in their caption describing the trip: TRANS-CANADA AIR FIGHT [*sic*] ENDS AT ESQUIMALT TO-DAY. " 'Comedy of Errors' Prevented Journey From Vancouver to Victoria Direct."[40] After which they went on to list how many important people had been waiting for two days to greet the distinguished crew.

The Base diary entry ends with the crisp comment that "Major MacLaurin travelled to Victoria by boat and flew his HS-2L back to Vancouver that afternoon."

K. F. Saunders, standing in front of an Avro 504 in Sweden, March 1920. He was demonstrating and attempting to sell British aircraft to the Swedes but found them more in favour of both the Germans and their aircraft.

RBCM

A JN-4 floatplane in Georgeson Bay, Active Pass, circa 1923. The S.S.*Adelaide* in the background.   GEORGE GEORGESAN, RBCM

Jericho Beach Air Station in the early 1920s.

E. L. MACLEOD ESTATE

Chapter Eleven

Jericho Beach:
The First Bush Flying

*"A suspicious parcel was dropped overboard
and there was a speedboat in the vicinity."*

EARL MacLEOD

The development of aviation in Canada after World War I was distinctively different from developments in Europe and the United States. To begin with, both Europe and the United States had large and relatively dense populations to encourage the prospect of passenger services, and their cities were relatively close together; whereas in Canada, the converse was true. Secondly, both Europe and the United States had large aircraft factories with the capability of a rapid production switch from purely military to passenger-carrying aircraft. In contrast, Canada had virtually nothing; even the Toronto factory had been liquidated as an economy measure as soon as the war ended.

As an example, in Britain, on May 24, 1919, "Avro Civil Aviation Service began operation of the first United Kingdom domestic air service when it started a daily Manchester-Southport-Blackpool service using Avro 504 and 536 single-engined biplanes."[1] By August 25 a "regular daily scheduled international commercial air service began... the operator was Aircraft Transport and Travel, and the route was between London and Paris."[2] This company became one of the four operators amalgamated to form Imperial Airways in 1924. The aircraft they used for these early scheduled runs were converted wartime bombers, which were large, powerful and available.

In Germany, the first air services were flown in "February, 1919, when Deutsche Luft-Reederie began regular operation between Berlin and Weimer, using mostly A.E.G. and L.V.G. single-engined monoplanes."[3] In Germany, too, the survivors of these early companies were merged into Deutsch Luft Hansa in 1926. Similar developments were taking place in France, Switzerland and Holland. However, in spite of their large population base, the private-sector airlines in Europe did not prosper and, in time, they were nearly all merged into large, state-subsidized airlines.

In the United States, commercial flying after World War I was almost exclusively developed by the Post Office — often in partnership with the military — starting in 1918 with a Washington-Philadelphia-New York airmail service. Eddie Hubbard, in his Boeing seaplane, provided the exception to the rule by inaugurating the first scheduled international airmail service in North America, between Seattle and Victoria, in October 1920; and he did so under contract, keeping the service running with remarkable skill and efficiency for seven years. By 1926, though, other "private companies began to operate mail services under contract to the U.S. Post Office and at least 11 routes were being flown by the end of the year, with passengers being carried on some of them."[4] In the United States, however, rather than merging into one large state-operated airline, eventually they merged into several large private-sector lines like United, TWA and Northwest Orient.

In Canada, too, operators turned hopeful eyes on the prospect of airmail services, but the Canadian Post Office did not emulate the American approach and, although there was much publicity over early efforts, airmail in Canada was fitful and slow to develop, as were attempts to provide scheduled passenger services. In the end, long distances, rugged topography and sparse population dictated that pioneer Canadian airmen would become celebrated for their bush flying.

The definition of bush flying is not easy to articulate, but for our purposes we can define it as flying in which the overwhelming majority of flights are into or out of unprepared landing areas. Canada in the 1920s was, and still is, richly endowed with these during the summer season — for a flying boat or a floatplane. Except for the prairies, the country was studded with lakes, often with rivers between them to afford a safe landing. And once the Royal Flying Corps, Canada, had demonstrated the value of skis on snow or ice in 1917-18, there was still an abundance of unprepared landing areas during winter months — but not for flying boats. For this reason, the west coast, where ice seldom endures for more than a few days, was an ideal area for flying boats and for bush flying; and so it proved for the civilian-oriented military pilots and mechanics at Jericho Beach.

Before then, there were one or two brief attempts to found private companies in British Columbia. The Vancouver Aerial Transportation Company tried in 1919, but quietly folded its wings in 1920. And in Victoria, W. H. Brown, in partnership with N. A. Goddard, founded Vancouver Island Aerial Service in 1920 by taking over the Aerial League's Curtiss JN-4, *Pathfinder*,[5] and commissioning "Messrs. Yarrows, Esquimalt," to convert it into a floatplane with twin pontoons.[6] But Brown, too, according to the Victoria *Daily Times*, almost literally faded away when flying alone between Alert Bay and Prince Rupert:

Flying the Curtiss seaplane of the Vancouver Island Aerial Service Ltd...Lieut. Harry Brown left Alert Bay for Prince Rupert on Monday evening last.... After flying north for one hour and a half, the Curtiss engine suddenly missed and the aviator was forced to land.[7]

The sea was relatively calm and Brown landed safely just off Nalau Island. Dusk descended before he could find what had caused the engine failure, and then the weather changed; within an hour a gale-force wind was blowing. The machine was driven on to a reef and broke up. As the reporter describes it,

The seaplane...was pounded to atoms with the pilot still in his post. The pontoons were the last to go, and Harry Brown stuck it out until the machine was sinking, and then jumped for the rocks. Missing the rocks the pilot fell into the water and was in some considerable danger of being severely pounded. However, making an effort he regained the shore, and watched his frail craft sink in pieces in some twenty feet [6 m] of water.

After sitting on a rocky ledge all night, because it was too dark to see, he spent some time exploring the small island. Finding it deserted,

Mr. Brown resolved to try the only course that would give him a chance to get free from the deserted island ... the pilot found a small log and paddled to sea on it in an effort to make the steamship route before exposure in the chilly waters or hunger overcame his strength.[8]

Harry Brown's courage and resourcefulness were rewarded. After paddling for several hours, he was spotted and rescued by the steamship

Hidden Inlet, bound from Alaska to Seattle; and although his partner, Goddard, told the newspapers that their company would buy another aircraft and continue their service, this does not seem to have come about; the company is not mentioned again in the newspapers.

Yet another commercial venture emerged in 1921. The Vancouver Island Aerial Transport Company was incorporated by J. R. Devereux of Victoria in July 1921. He had purchased the JN-4 (Can), G-CACO, from the Victoria branch of the Aerial League and based the machine in Comox, B.C. At that time, apparently, CACO was a floatplane; it was converted back to wheels the following January.[9] The March 21, 1922, issue of the Victoria *Daily Colonist* (p. 5) reported the end of this machine:

Local Machine Total Loss After Collision With Fence
on Sunday — Pilot and Wife Injured.

The engine failing when the machine was about 150 feet [46 m] above the ground just after having risen from the Willows fair grounds, the Curtiss aeroplane owned by the Aerial Transport Company, and piloted by Major Kenneth Saunders, D.S.O., who was accompanied by his wife, made a forced landing on Dalhousie Street, near Cadboro Bay Road about 4 o'clock Sunday afternoon [March 19], and was badly smashed through contact with a fence. Mrs. Saunders sustained a cut over the eye and suffered from shock, while her husband sustained scalp injury and a shaking up, but was not seriously hurt.

Here, as after Brown's mishap, there was a determination to continue operations. "The machine is rated as a total loss and a new one is to be secured by the company"; but there is no further mention of the company. For the two years before this accident Ken Saunders had been demonstrating and selling British aircraft in Sweden. After it, he went on to a distinguished career in Canadian aviation, but did little flying in British Columbia.

To return to Jericho, initially there were only three pilots on the base: Earl MacLeod, Claire MacLaurin and Bill Templeton — the same Templeton who, with his brother, Winston and their cousin, Bill McMullen, had built and tried to fly their own aircraft in Richmond in 1911; and who, when Vancouver Airport was opened in 1931, became its first manager, a post he was to hold for many years. In addition, there were Enid Henley, secretary-stenographer; Howard Hines, head of the Equipment Section; Clarence Duncan, head of the Air Photography Section; Kenneth Moffat, head of the Wireless Section; and Robert Coupland,

Shop Foreman. The remaining personnel, who either belonged to these Sections or were mechanics, were Charley Plant, A. L. Hartridge, Harry Bell, Frank Corp, Tommy Hill, (?) Slimmons, Alf Walker, John Nicholson, Harold Davenport, Norman Terry, Alex Dickie, Bill Tall, Bill Gear and Ted Cressy.[10]

Unfortunately, Templeton, who had contracted malaria "while flying in the Mediterranean area during the war," had a recurrence of the illness and had to give up flying. He was replaced as an Air Pilot Navigator in the summer of 1921 by W. H. Brown (apparently undeterred by his experience on and around Nalau Island), another ex-wartime pilot. As well, Major B. D. Hobbs—brother of the Joe Hobbs whom MacLeod had helped in the base selection—joined them the same year, but "... left quite soon to be the Station Superintendent of a new base that he was to establish at Victoria Beach, on Lake Winnipeg."[11]

Between them, these Jericho Beach pilots and their mechanics (shortly to be renamed Air Engineers) pioneered bush flying on the west coast, and one of the first operations—"peculiar to the Pacific Coast"—they found particularly satisfying: they began intercepting drug smugglers at sea. The method employed by the smugglers was to wrap the drugs in waterproof packages and drop them off incoming liners from the Orient, such as the CPR's Empresses, to be picked up by speedboats. Customs officers on board the liners had seen this happen but they were powerless to do anything about it until someone thought of using the HS-2Ls to meet the liners at sea:

When I flew Customs Officer Harry de Graves... on the first Customs patrol in 1921, we noticed that voracious seagulls circling the liner vied with one another to investigate en masse everything, large or small, dropped overboard, thereby ensuring that we could not fail to observe anything that might be jettisoned. On one later occasion, we in the aircraft were tested in respect to our effectiveness. A suspicious parcel was dropped overboard and there was a speedboat in the vicinity! We landed, picked up a well-packaged parcel, which we examined expectantly on completion of our escort patrol. We found the parcel well sealed, with many layers of waterproof wrapping, then several layers of other wrapping with nothing inside—a well-prepared dummy![12]

However, MacLeod goes on to point out that "... after our air patrol commenced, the price of underworld narcotics increased not only in Vancouver, but in Seattle, and that after a liner was allowed to arrive unescorted at any time a corresponding fluctuation occurred."[13] Another extension of this law enforcement role was to chase bootleggers. When

An H Boat taxiing briskly, location unknown.

An H Boat on a drug interception patrol over the *Empress of Russia*.

The air engineers at Jericho in 1921: Left to right, ? Clark, A. Dickie, H. Davenport, ? Slimmons and F.Corp.

Bill Templeton, manager for many years of the Vancouver Airport, demonstrates one of his responsibilities: cleaning up after a taxiing accident. A Stinson Reliant had collided with a Gypsy Moth.

PABC

Clarence Duncan, the Base's photographer, with an early camera installation in the H Boat.

E. L. MACLEOD ESTATE

Earl MacLeod clipping a message on the leg of a carrier pigeon before releasing it. Because radio equipment was considered too heavy—weighing as much as 150 lbs. (68 kg)—pigeons were used for communication in case of emergency.

E. L. MACLEOD ESTATE

Helicopter pioneers Alf Stringer,
left, and Carl Agar.

A Boeing flying boat spraying
insecticide in the early 1920s.

A more sophisticated installation of an Eastman camera in the H Boat. This installation made vertical aerial photography possible.

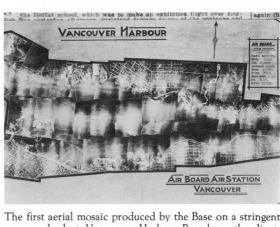

The first aerial mosaic produced by the Base on a stringent budget. Vancouver Harbour Board was the client.

Claire MacLaurin's HS-2L after the fatal accident off Point Grey, September 11, 1922.

wartime prohibition had been repealed, and the government set up liquor distribution from its own stores, with a hefty tax on the product, bootleggers "had developed a method of underpricing the Government stores with bootleg liquor, by bringing cargoes into Canada in bond, consigned to a bogus address in Mexico." Once cleared by customs in Vancouver, instead of heading for Mexico the cargo would be moved to remote inlets, broken up into manageable loads and distributed to "retailers" by speedboat.

In one of my own more memorable episodes in dealing with this situation, I carried Customs Officer Norman de Graves [brother of Harry] . . . on a flight in search of an ex-submarine chaser, S.S. 'Trucilla' cleared for Mexico and known to be in the liquor-running business. We spotted her in a snug cove on Jumbo Island, not far from West Point Lighthouse. By shutting off my engine and gauging my glide, we landed and were aboard before the crew, below deck, knew we were there. Mr. de Graves met the Captain and crew dramatically with drawn pistol when they appeared on deck! Several rifles were lying about the deck for protection, the Captain informed us, against hijackers! Mr. de Graves ordered the offending ship to Vancouver, remaining on board himself to see that it did so, and the owners were, in due course, fined.[14]

There was a strong element of competition between hunter and hunted in these sorties which the young pilots obviously found both stimulating and satisfying. The next sortie MacLeod describes, which occurred in 1924, had an element of sleuthing, as well; it concerned another form of bootlegging: illegal distilleries. In an interview with Paul Stoddart, MacLeod recalled that

One such scoff-law operation was discovered by Allan Hull, who was at the time commanding Jericho Beach [while] I was doing a two-year exchange of pilots with the RAF in England.

The customs department had learned that a certain scow would depart in tow from a berth in False Creek and return within the day with suspected consignments of illicit brew. The duration of each trip indicated that the suspected still must be within a radius of about 50 miles [80 km] from Vancouver. One day, it was observed that the outgoing empty scow had on board a white horse, and that the horse was not aboard when the scow returned. The problem then was to locate a white horse upcoast, in order to locate the still. I may say that any horse, let alone a white horse, up that part of the coast was unknown to those of us who regularly flew the route.

Allan Hull, with the customs officer as passenger, located the white horse at a secluded cove on Texada Island. Inspection of the cove revealed a large, thriving, industrial still, ingeniously concealed from view from the air by branches of trees that were pulled together over it by ropes and pulleys. The enterprising lawbreaker was convicted.[15]

While these entertaining patrols were being conducted, the crews were performing less glamorous tasks which were vital to the development of what came to be called bush flying. One has to remember that people did not automatically perceive the advantages aircraft might have for their jobs at hand; they had, in many cases, to be persuaded. Fortunately, MacLaurin and his crews had the sort of presence that does encourage people to try something new. They were clearly very competent people; confident but not cocky about the new skills they were demonstrating. One government agency to acknowledge this was the Forest Branch of the Ministry of Lands in its Annual Report for 1921.

The establishment by the Dominion Air Board of a seaplane base at Jericho Beach... gave the Branch an opportunity during the present season of trying out aeroplanes in forest-protection work....

Throughout the months of July and August a system of bi-weekly patrols was instituted. This patrol was carried out on Wednesdays and Sundays and consisted of a circuitous trip from Point Grey, following the Coast north of Bute Inlet...and returning by the east coast of Vancouver Island. The trip occupied about three hours of flying-time and meant that approximately 3,500,000 acres [1 144 000 ha] of territory was covered, and the forest officer in charge had a knowledge of all forest fires burning within that region....

In all, fifty-six flights were made, and the results were most satisfactory and show conclusively that the plane has possibilities as a complement to our ground force in forest protection, as well as being of considerable service in gathering general information rapidly and in supervision where time has to be considered.[16]

The dry prose of a bureaucratic report probably underestimates the delight that this development must have brought to a forest ranger who could now travel over large areas for which he was responsible with a minimum of discomfort and fatigue.

For the pilots and mechanics, however, there must have been some element of anxiety. One has to remember that the flying crews on these early operations had no radio communication. Once they left base they were out of touch. Although there was a Head of the Wireless Section on strength, MacLaurin evidently decided that they would not equip the HS-2Ls with radios because the airborne equipment at the time was both too bulky for the limited space and heavy enough to provide an unacceptable penalty. Instead, he solved the problem of communications early on by instituting a carrier-pigeon loft. In case, for instance, of a forced landing, a message could be clipped to the pigeon's leg and it would head for home. MacLeod recalls one such forced landing at "Secret Cove, not far from Horseshoe Bay; ... there was no communication to that part of British Columbia at that time; there was no road along the Sunshine Coast at all. I put a message on the leg of a pigeon and it got home surprisingly quickly. At any rate, the part that we asked for — the ignition part that had failed us — was brought to us within an hour-and-a-half by another plane from Jericho Beach."[17]

Another pioneering operation they undertook, in 1921, was

...the selection and establishment of Dominion Government Geodetic Survey triangulation stations across the high mountain ranges of southern British Columbia. These stations were placed at approximately 30-mile [50-km] intervals, so located that no visual obstruction existed between stations. Stations were completed that year at the highest point of Orcas Island; ... on one of the Golden Ears, at Alouette Lake — at that time it was called Lillooet Lake; on Amadis Mountain, at Cultus Lake; on Barr Mountain, at Walleach or Jones Lake; and we rendered assistance, too, at Pennask Lake and Okanagan Lake.[18]

The surveyor in charge of this operation, Fred Lambert, is quoted as estimating "...that in the one season as much was accomplished as would have required ten years by the old method." Of course, the surveyors still had to carry their equipment on their backs from the lakes to the mountain peaks, a slow and arduous process. As an interesting co-incidence, MacLeod lists some of the surveyors involved. The name of one of them was Agar. Just 27 years later Carl Agar who, with Alf Stringer and Barney Bent, founded Okanagan Helicopters, was proving to the provincial Topographic Survey that helicopters could go one better than fixed-wing aircraft by putting surveyors right on the peaks they selected for their sites.[19] Once again, this was found to increase productivity by a factor of at least ten.

The next task that came their way was one that was to continue indefinitely — one that all the Canadian Air Board bases across Canada embarked on at more or less the same time: aerial photography, with the eventual goal of mapping the entire country. At Jericho Beach, they were equipped with a new Eastman camera, specifically designed for vertical photography, and the hulls of the HS-2Ls had to be modified to accommodate it. As well, the machine-gun ring coaming in the front cockpit was removed to give the photographer more room to operate. Macleod and Duncan, the photographer, began this operation with a series of flights early in 1921: they photographed Vancouver harbour for the Harbour Board; the estuary of the Fraser River; a windfall area near Cowichan, on Vancouver Island; the top of Sumas Mountain, including Chadsey Lake; and a month later, produced the photographs to assemble a large mosaic of the Sumas-Nicomen Island area for the engineers of the Sumas Lake Reclamation Dyking Scheme. This project resulted in the draining of Sumas Lake in 1923, leaving "...tens of thousands of fish dried on the mud-and-sand lake bed, including many sturgeon weighing hundreds of pounds. Nearby farmers loaded large quantities of dead fish onto wagons for use as fertilizer."[20]

One of the constraints they worked under was that nearly all operations had to be self-supporting; in other words, the customer, whether a government agency or a private one, had to pay for the flying and, in the case of aerial photography, for the film and processing. Their first mosaic, for the Vancouver Harbour Board, was produced on a very tight budget.

When we made our first mosaic...we were allowed sufficient film to provide only a five per cent overlap;...five per cent, instead of the 60 per cent that is recognized as necessary for getting best results....

In our case, rough air, or side wind, or drift unfortunately adversely affected our very demanding precision flying on one of our first runs. When we pieced together the photographs for the mosaic, we discovered a small gap in the centre of Stanley Park. Our reputations at stake, we transferred a few trees from one of the prints of the Seymour Creek area to fill the gap satisfactorily. The Harbour Board informed us that the mosaic proved to be exceedingly useful to them.[21]

It is hard to exaggerate the part played by the Air Board-RCAF in the development of aerial photography and, later, photogrammetry (making maps from aerial photographs). Before their pioneering in this new science, much of the country was unmapped, so that travelling through or over it, let alone developing it, was extremely difficult and often hazardous. But most of this development took part east of the Rockies. This was simply because the HS-2Ls had a service ceiling of about 7,000 feet (2 000 m), which meant that few if any of the mountainous areas in B.C. could be photographed. For this reason, much of the mapping of the province had to wait until later.[22]

By 1921, the base had four HS-2Ls and one larger, twin-engined Felixstowe F3 flying boat, and Major MacLaurin was busy attempting to persuade people to use the service. The three primary industries — fisheries, agriculture and forestry — were his first targets.

In 1921, also, a variety of uses were made of our aircraft by the Fisheries Department, including research to determine whether fish eggs could be transported by air without affecting their fecundity; conveyance of fry for transplanting in out-of-the-way lakes and streams; and policing fishing grounds to deal with infringement of fishery regulations. Major MacLaurin had discussed such uses with the Inspector of Fisheries at Vancouver, Major J. A. Motherwell, and on 9 March, with myself as second pilot, had flown him, in our large F3 flying boat, for a demonstration inspection visit to the Dominion Government's Biological Station at Nanaimo. I made several flights in our HS-2L to the Department's Hatchery at Harrison Lake and to a Hatchery at Cultus Lake for the purpose of transporting fish eggs, etc. The research showed that the mortality rate of the fish eggs and fry, conveyed by air, was lower than by the old way of doing the job, i.e. by motor boat, canoe, packhorse, or by foot.[23]

Next, MacLaurin turned his attention to forestry; "fire-fighting, transportation of personnel, overcoming the mountain barriers, timber scaling from the air and so on. We blazed many a trail in the Forestry Service."[24] Persuading these agencies to use their aircraft was probably helped a good deal by the fact that nearly all their supervisors were ex-officers: "Major Leonard (Len) Andrews, ex-RAF... was the Provincial Forestry Supervisor in our Vancouver District, and employed our services in a diversity of ways."[25] They were indeed diverse. One of them, during the 1922 fire season which, according to MacLeod, was one of the worst in years,[26] was to carry a proclamation shutting down all the logging activities between the Queen Charlotte Sound-Rivers Inlet district south to Campbell River because of the fire hazard. Based at Alert Bay, on the northeast coast of Vancouver Island, MacLeod flew two forestry officials up and down the coast to every logging camp. To avoid wasting time beaching the aircraft, they would land and start shouting. Invariably this would bring a row boat out to see what trouble they were in. The unfortunate occupant of the rowboat would be left studying a proclamation telling him his operation was shut down, while the HS-2L took off for the next logging camp.

On July 28, they became actively involved in actual firefighting for the first time. Under the heading, "Flying Operations," the Forest Branch Report gave a lengthy account:

Possibly the most outstanding feat of the season was the transporting of fire-fighters to Buttle Lake in the centre of Vancouver Island.... To get into this lake with a crew of men would have required a two-day trip and the construction of about 14 miles of trail over a difficult country.... The big machine [the Felixstowe] and emergency fire-fighting equipment were wired for. The equipment consisted of a portable pump and set of tools. These were loaded together with 1,200 feet [365 m] of hose, a sixteen-man tent, six shovels, six mattocks, six axes, camp outfit, and provisions for six men for two weeks. Four fire-fighters were carried also.... The total load on this trip was 4,895 lb.

[2 220 kg]. Visibility was very poor, but the machine rose to a height of 1,000 feet [300 m] and hit across Vancouver Island to Buttle Lake. . . . The machine then returned to Campbell River and picked up three more fire-fighters. . . . [They] were landed at 4 in the afternoon [and] the fire was practically under control in the morning.[27]

On this operation MacLeod flew as co-pilot at MacLaurin, and while it sounds routine today, in 1921 it was an impressive performance; one that quickly brought to the people involved a keen appreciation of the savings in time and sheer, slogging hard work the use of aircraft afforded them. Moreover, the quick response prevented the fire from spreading to much larger areas and destroying more timber.

Before then, however, in May 1922, MacLeod had demonstrated another advantage. He worked with the federal Department of Agriculture to deal with white pine blister rust in the forests. This was affecting American, as well as Canadian forests, and a number of American researchers were involved. The defoliation of the trees was caused by a spore hosted, at one stage of its life-cycle, by *Ribes* shrubs — wild currents and gooseberries. The first hope was to destroy all such shrubs in the damaged pine forests; but the researchers discovered that, by taking sterile, sealed test tubes, coated on the inside with vaseline, and exposing them at various heights up to 10,000 feet (over 3000 m), then resealing them, they trapped spores at all levels tested. Clearly, this meant that the spores were not local; they could travel over mountains and for long distances, therefore, other solutions had to be sought. This operation took the base crews on some of their longest flights. MacLeod recalls one of them, starting on August 29, that took in Harrison Hot Springs, Alta Lake, Lillooet Lake, Fort Douglas (at the north end of Harrison Lake); then Harrison Hot Springs again before returning to Vancouver by September 2.

Things were going exceedingly well for the Jericho Beach base. Demands for their services were growing by leaps and bounds and, as they became more experienced in operating their flying boats, they began to relax and enjoy themselves. "It was something new," MacLeod reflected; "that's what made us so interested in what we were doing. They weren't paying us very much, but we did it because of our interest in flying."[28] Then, on September 11, 1922, "Our base was shocked and saddened beyond measure . . . when Major LacLaurin was killed in the crash of HS-2L G-CYEA, offshore from Point Grey."[29]

MacLaurin's accident caused the first two fatalities on the Base. Boats were quickly on the spot to attempt a rescue, but MacLaurin's body wasn't recovered until the following day (the post-mortem concluded he had drowned) and John Duncan died in hospital a few hours later.

E. L. MACLEOD ESTATE

MacLeod's H Boat on the Skeena River near Hazelton. He was there to carry out an airworthiness inspection of the Junkers JL-6 in the background.

Left to right, Tom Cowley, Earl Godfrey and Earl MacLeod.

E. L. MACLEOD ESTATE PHOTOS

Chapter Twelve

Success and Failure

*"...and we completed our season's flying on the
remaining eleven cylinders."*

EARL MacLEOD

MacLaurin's accident was at once tragic and perplexing. He had taken
off from Jericho Beach en route along the Fraser Valley to the Sumas
reclamation project with John Duncan, an engineer on the project, and
A. L. Hartridge, one of the Base mechanics. A few minutes later he
turned back, cut his engine and then suddenly nose-dived into shallow
water just offshore with such violence that the aircraft's back was
broken. Hartridge escaped with a sprained ankle and numerous bruises
and contusions, but Duncan was seriously injured and MacLaurin
presumably knocked unconscious. His body was not recovered until
the following day, and the post-mortem examination concluded that he
had drowned. John Duncan died of his injuries within hours of the
recovery of Claire MacLaurin's body.

Shortly after the HS-2L had gone down, pilots Tom Cowley and
Elmer Fullerton had taken off, accompanied by the shop foreman,
Robert Coupland, to see if they could help. They flew over the wreck
and, probably because it was in shallow water, and they saw that a boat
was in attendance, they returned to land at the Base, driving back to the
wreck site again in a car. Two days later, they were principal witnesses at
the inquest. Before then however, the Vancouver *Province* reported that
"All controls were in perfect condition. Though the machine took a
nose dive, the elevator wires which control the up and down movement
and are duplicated to ensure safety are intact and working freely."[1]

At the inquest, Hartridge said that he noticed soon after take-off that the radiator was boiling. He shouted to warn MacLaurin, and MacLaurin immediately turned back. Then Hartridge spotted a gasoline leak from the tank. Once again he shouted, and MacLaurin cut the engine.

The plunge, [Hartridge] stated, came almost without warning. He had turned to look at the leaking gasoline tank and when he looked back they were in a nose dive, pointing straight for the sea. Major MacLaurin had switched off his engine to make the descent in order to prevent fire, for the gasoline was leaking across the exhaust pipe.[2]

In the end, the coroner's jury found no cause for the accident; but Cowley and Fullerton, "The two pilots who gave evidence expressed their personal view that the accident was caused by the plane 'stalling.'"[3]

To speculate at this remove about what happened would be irrelevant, but it seems such a futile accident, made more poignant because Claire Maclaurin was well on his way to a distinguished flying career; and because his son, described in the newspapers as a handsome, flaxen-haired child, became an orphan. MacLaurin's young English war bride had died in 1918, shortly after their son was born.

However, life had to go on, and the accident does not seem to have had any effect on potential users of the air service. Squadron Leader A. E. (Earl) Godfrey "replaced MacLaurin as Superintendent at Jericho Beach on 18 October 1922 and continued as CO when the station became CAF Unit, Vancouver, on 25 November."[4] This change did not appear to have much effect on the operations at Jericho Beach; but, for administrative purposes, the Air Board no longer existed—it had become part of the new Department of National Defence which embraced all three services as well as the Air Board.

Then, in the summer of 1923, the federal Fisheries Department concluded that flying boats would provide an effective means for patrolling B.C. waters to guard against salmon poachers—particularly in the Prince Rupert area because that was the principal fishing district in the province at the time. When the decision was made, Earl MacLeod was acting in one of the other capacities of the Base pilots: an Aircraft Inspector. He had travelled to Hazelton by train to inspect an aircraft and grant, or withhold, an airworthiness certificate.

The machine he went to inspect had a distinctive history. Registered G-CADP, it was one of the two German-built Junkers JL-6,[5] all-metal monoplanes purchased in 1920 by Imperial Oil Limited to reach their new discovery well on Bear Island, soon to be called Norman Wells, on the Mackenzie River in the Northwest Territories. The two aircraft were christened by Mrs. McQueen, wife of the vice-president of the company. CADP became the "Vic" and CADQ became the "René."[6] Purchased in New York, the two machines were flown to Edmonton in the middle of winter by W. R. (Wop) May and George W. Gorman. Before they set off on what turned out to be an epic attempt to reach Norman Wells, Wop May left the company and was replaced by Elmer G. Fullerton, the pilot who gave evidence in the inquest into MacLaurin's death.[7]

Imperial Oil became discouraged by this early endeavour and abandoned their attempt to run an air service down the Mackenzie. CADP was flown from Imperial's base at Peace River Crossing to Edmonton and sat idle in a hangar until early in 1922, when it was purchased by L. S. Bell, president of the ponderously named Railway Employees' Investment and Industrial Association. (Bell, then a mining promoter, had been a railway engineer — he "had driven Prince Rupert's first train into that city."[8]) G. A. (Tommy) Thompson flew the Junkers to Hazelton, and operated it for the rest of that season on floats, the first aircraft to operate on a regular basis in central B.C. Earl MacLeod records that "The first plane to land at Queen Charlotte Islands had been George Thompson, who flew the Junkers there — just there and back."[9] According to Frank Ellis, "Spasmodic flights were made the following year [1923] by a pilot named W. H. McCardle."[10]

As it turned out, MacLeod inspected CADP at Hazelton, declared it unserviceable and, shortly afterwards was instructed to go at once to Prince Rupert to work with the Fisheries Department. In the meantime, Earl Godfrey, with mechanics Harold Davenport and Harry Bell, had flown the HS-2L, G-CYDX, to Prince Rupert, with refuelling stops at Alert Bay and Bella Bella. This was the first aircraft to fly the route up the coast from Vancouver. When he arrived, Godfrey turned the aircraft over to MacLeod and returned to Vancouver by coastal steamer.

Earl MacLeod takes up the story:

On 24 July, I selected our base at Seal Cove, a tiny sheltered lagoon at the north end of the city, where my crewmen and I were able to start operations immediately, safe from wind and storm. The base has proven, through the years, to be an excellent flying boat and seaplane base [it still is, at the time of writing].

On our patrols, we found that infractions were rampant, and that almost all fishing boats that we would land beside and inspect, would be committing one or more illegalities. At first, it was necessary for a crew member to remain on board the offending boat until a Fisheries Officer was brought to make an arrest. Later in the season, my crew and I were made "fisheries officers" with power to swear out summonses and to make arrests.[11]

So successful were the first season's fisheries patrols that the following year, 1924, two machines were based in Prince Rupert. In addition to MacLeod's machine, which this year was CYBB, Flying Officer A. H. Hull flew up in CYEB. The mechanic/air engineers were Harold Davenport and Norman Terry. By this time, the Canadian Air Force had evolved into the Royal Canadian Air Force, and the pilots all carried officer rank. Earl MacLeod was now a Flight Lieutenant. This did nothing to formalize their flying operations; their patrols still offered a variety of unforeseen developments:

I again visited the Queen Charlotte Islands. Fisheries Inspector Mackie flew with me from Prince Rupert, as he wanted to fly around the southern main island, Moresby, which flight proved to be a memorable one for me. The Fisheries Patrol Boat 'Starfish' (Captain Eburne) had preceded us to Alliford Bay carrying our gasoline supply consisting of fifty 45-gallon [205-l] steels of naphtha.... Unfortunately, she also carried one steel [drum] of distillate, a very low-grade fuel indeed, and when, on our arrival at Alliford Bay, we refuelled our 90-Gallon [410-l] fuel tank, the distillate, improperly marked, went into our tank. I had no difficulty becoming airborne while our small gravity tank fuel lasted, but the 50% naphtha/50% distillate performance for the remainder of the flight around Moresby was disturbingly poor. I was unable, despite my best piloting efforts, to attain more than a few hundred feet of altitude....[12]

Many challenges had to be met on these early bush-flying operations, and both pilots and mechanics had to be resourceful as well as bold:

Davenport and I [MacLeod] had another untoward experience at the end of our Queen Charlotte patrols, on our way back to Prince Rupert. We had a forced landing on Hecate Strait, not far from Bonilla Island, due to a broken connecting rod that tore a circular hole several inches in diameter in our crankcase. Davenport was able to disconnect the connecting rod, place the loose piston in a safe position, and using the only material available to us, plugged the hole by soaking a quantity of cleaning cloths with shellac, using a kind of tourniquet to hold the improvised material in place. When the shellac hardened, the repair proved successful and we completed our season's flying on the remaining eleven cylinders.[13]

In August, MacLeod was back in Hazelton again to inspect the Junkers seaplane. "However, I found that the pilot, Mr. McArdle, had not been able to complete the engine repairs required."[14] After this further setback, CADP remained grounded until 1929, when, presumably in pretty bad shape, it was bought by R. F. Corless, a mining promoter in Prince George. Shipped back there on a flatcar, the engine was thoroughly overhauled by air engineer Emil Kading (of whom we shall hear more later) and a local tinsmith worked on the fuselage and wings. Bill Jorss, a German ex-World-War-I pilot (of whom, too, we shall hear more), was hired to fly it.

Unfortunately, the authorities still refused to grant an airworthiness certificate and then, as Frank Ellis puts it, "she took to her wings and vanished."

Where she hopped to must remain a secret, but she did some very serviceable flying into the wilderness that summer. The headwaters of the Liard and Finlay Rivers knew the sound of her engine, but she remained a sort of ghost ship, and no one but her owners knew where she might be. She made several calls at Fort St. James on Stuart Lake, and eventually, on Sept. 20, 1929, during a landing on that lake, heavy waves jarred her so badly, the engine bearers were cracked, and she was pulled ashore for the season.[15]

This time the delinquent but durable Junkers was down for the last time. Bush flying in the late 1920s and early 1930s harboured many similarly discreet operations. Spending the money to bring an aircraft up to airworthiness standards laid down in remote offices in Ottawa was expensive; often it meant the difference between eating and not eating, and hunger is a remarkably powerful anaesthetic for a conscience. As well, Air Inspectors were thin on the ground, even thinner in the air, and people in the scattered settlements of the Canadian bush felt no particular obligation to discuss aircraft movements with licencing officials when they did happen to meet them.

The change in status which took place when the Base came under the Royal Canadian Air Force in April, 1924 — officers now had uniforms, and drill parades were the prelude to appearances in their new uniforms on ceremonial occasions — gradually brought other changes to their operations at the Jericho Beach Base. While the original CAF had been formed to provide annual refresher courses to experienced pilots, time had begun to take its toll. Many of those pilots had drifted away to other occupations; those who remained, even though they were still in their 30s, were considered too old to be fighting pilots. Before long, an important function at the Base would be to train newcomers as flying-boat pilots. And a year or so after that, private enterprise would start to take over some of their civilian flying responsibilities.

MAJOR THOMPSON.
SIMON. GUN·A·NOOT.
GEO. BEIRNES.
L. S. BELL.   HAZELTON. B.C.

E. L. MACLEOD ESTATE

The Railway Employees Investment and Industrial Association's Junkers JL-6 at Hazelton, 1923. MacLeod did not grant the certificate but there is some evidence that G. A. Thompson continued to fly it. At least one member of this crew, the celebrated outlaw, Simon Gunanoot, knew this country extremely well. For 13 years, from 1906 until 1919, he eluded the Provincial Police, who were trying to arrest him for two alleged murders. They never caught him; eventually he gave himself up in Hazelton and was acquitted at his trial in New Westminster.

VANCOUVER PUBLIC LIBRARY

When Royal Navy warships HMS *Hood* and *Repulse* visited Vancouver in April 1924, the Jericho Beach base provided an escort: a Vickers Viking and an H Boat.

HMS *Hood* and HMS *Repulse* at Victoria's Ogden Point.   RBCM

176

The transformation from mufti to uniform. Earl MacLeod on the left.

Colonel L. E. Broome, who laid out the gas caches for MacLaren's Vickers Vulture and then joined the flight at Kasumiga Ura, Japan.

HMCS *Thiepval*, the vessel that supported Stuart MacLaren's attempted round-the-world flight in 1924, docked in Vancouver before starting its voyage to lay out gas caches.

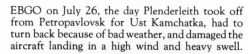
EBGO on July 26, the day Plenderleith took off from Petropavlovsk for Ust Kamchatka, had to turn back because of bad weather, and damaged the aircraft landing in a high wind and heavy swell.

MacLaren's first Vickers Vulture which crashed in Akyab, Burma. The spare machine, G-EBGO, was in a crate in Japan. Broome persuaded the United States Navy to transport it to Burma and MacLaren was able to continue with his attempt.

Japanese sailing vessels drying sails in Hakodate harbour, Japan, June 3, 1924. The well-known hunter-naturalist Hamilton Laing travelled on board the *Thiepval*, shooting and collecting specimens whenever he had the opportunity.

The Vulture, G-EBGO, just after reaching Petropavlovsk, Russia, on July 24, 1924.

What the well-dressed aviator was wearing in the 1920s. Major L. D. Taylor. Note the early model "mae west" life preserver and glove-mitten combination.

A Vickers Vedette on the Fraser River at Vancouver.

One more operation in which Earl MacLeod was involved in 1924, though only peripherally this time, is both of historical interest, as well as dramatic.

This was a period when long-distance flights were capturing headlines, and the hard-working crews in the RCAF must have felt a twinge of envy at the fame the record breakers were earning while they, in their ageing HS-2Ls, plugged away, largely unnoticed by the newspapers and the public. The first prize had been the Atlantic. This had gone to the U.S. Navy, who made the attempt with three Curtiss NC Flying boats. They took the southern route in May 1919 but only one of them reached Europe. Commander A. C. Reid flew from Newfoundland to the Azores in 15 hours, 18 minutes; then on to Lisbon, with another long flight of nine hours and 43 minutes — a triumph of endurance in an open-cockpit aircraft.

Yet it was the non-stop north-Atlantic crossing that really caught the imagination, and that had so nearly been accomplished by Hawker and Mackenzie-Grieve in May, 1919. But they were forced to ditch just short of the Irish coast because of an overheating engine; a Danish steamer rescued them, and the laurels went, only a month later, to John Alcock and Arthur Whitten Brown, who ended up with the nose of their Vickers Vimy aircraft buried in an Irish bog. After that, the next obvious challenge was to circumnavigate the globe and become the Magellan of the air age.

By 1924, several round-the-world expeditions were being mounted: the French, the Portuguese and the British were all working on it, while the United States Army Air Service was planning an all out assault with four machines: specially designed two-seater biplanes, powered by a single Liberty engine and adaptable to floats or wheels. Manufactured by Douglas, they were called World Cruisers, or more commonly, D-WCs. This expedition was to start in Seattle and head north along the British Columbia Coast, then follow the Aleutians and cross the North Pacific, before swinging back towards China, India, the Middle-East, Europe and North America.

Their progress was slow. Prince Rupert was to be their first fuelling stop but from the middle of March, the Prince Rupert newspaper reported delays: "World Aviators May Not HOP For This City Till

Next Wednesday," was a typical headline on March 29. Finally, on April 6 after eight hours in the air,

Almost on the stroke of five o'clock three of the four planes comprising the United States aerial squadron, attempting a world flight, rounded the bend at Seal Cove....

Half an hour later, the fourth which had been delayed in leaving Seattle, arrived. Everything worked without the slightest hitch, save for a mishap to the plane carrying Major Frederick L. Martin, who commands the squadron. In the snow flurry, he miscalculated distance, when approaching Buoy No. 1. He was obliged to "pancake" down. The pontoons struck with resounding impact and splash. The sudden shock snapped two of the struts.[16]

They were down for three days repairing the floats. It was the first of many delays and they wrote off two of their aircraft, but eventually two machines made it back across the United States to Seattle on September 28, 1924. It really was a triumph of courage and determination.

The British attempt, travelling in the opposite direction, was to be made by a single machine flown by Royal Air Force personnel but without official support; they were granted leave with half pay and the blessings of the service. Their aircraft was a Vickers Vulture crewed by Squadron Leader A. S. C. MacLaren, Flight Lieutenant W. N. Plenderleith and Sergeant R. Andrews. MacLaren, as leader, was to navigate, while Plenderleith flew the machine and Andrews maintained it. Only two Vultures were built. They were three-seat amphibians, powered by a single 450-horsepower Napier Lion engine.[17] The first, G-EBHO, left Southampton on March 25, heading east across Europe, the Middle-East and Asia. It was written off in a crash just after taking off from Akyab, Burma, on May 25. Fortunately, the second machine, G-EBGO, had been crated and stored in Japan as a back-up. With the help of the U.S. Navy, it was shipped to Burma and MacLaren and his crew were able to continue their flight, reaching Kasumiga Ura, Japan, on July 7.

From the beginning, the plan had been to jettison the 250-pound (115-kg) wheeled undercarriage and convert the Vulture into a conventional flying boat when it reached Japan; then it would continue the flight with a new crew member, Colonel L. E. Broome, an English mining engineer familiar with the country that lay ahead of them on the way to Canada.[18] Broome arrived in Vancouver on February 18, 1924 to make the necessary advance arrangements for the flight from Japan, particularly to lay down gasoline caches, and MacLeod was detailed to

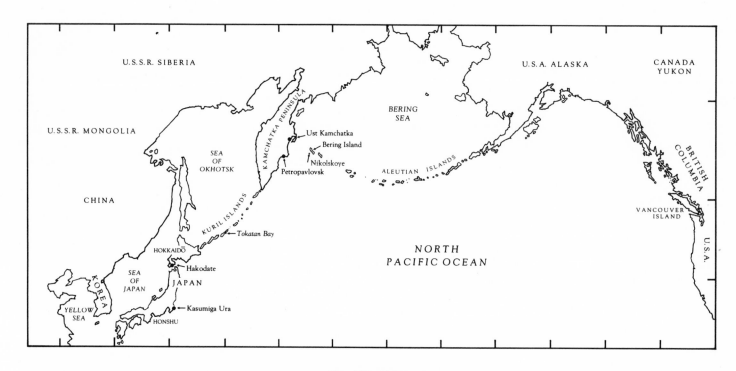

Pacific Rim

In 1924, after laying out fuel caches along what came to be known as the Pacific Rim, Colonel L. E. Broome joined Stuart MacLaren's attempt to fly round the world in Kasumiga Ura, Japan, as navigator.

From there, they flew north along the Kuril Islands to the Kamchatka Peninsula in Russia, before setting off across the Bering Sea. The attempt ended in a landing in rough water beside Bering Island, where the aircraft, a Vickers Vulture, was severely damaged by pounding waves before the crew were able to reach shore. The aircraft was salvaged and the party taken to Prince Rupert on H.M.C.S. *Thiepval.*

assist him. MacLeod travelled by train to arrange for caches at Jasper, Prince George, Burns Lake and Hazelton.

Broome was to travel in HMCS *Thiepval*, made available by the Royal Canadian Navy, to meet the Vulture, stopping at approximately 150-mile (240-km) intervals to lay out more gas caches in suitable bays and lagoons along the Alaska coast; in the Aleutians; then across the Bering Sea to Kamchatka, in Russia, and finally, along the Kuril Islands to Japan.

The voyage was no picnic because the *Thiepval* was a 125-foot (40-m), converted coal-burning trawler, normally used for tending lighthouses, and the area he was heading into does not enjoy a salubrious climate in March and April. Broome was seasick at times, and whenever the vessel took on any water at least some of it penetrated to his cabin. Nevertheless, he was successful in laying out all the gas caches along the route, met the Vulture, and left as a member of its crew from Kasumiga Ura, Japan, on July 12, 1924. By the 16th they had reached Tokatan Bay, in the Kurils, where they were held up until the 23rd, both because Plenderleith was ill — he was running a temperature as high as 104.5°F — and because the weather was atrocious. By the 24th, Plenderleith was fit again, the weather had improved and they were flying along the south-east coast of Kamchatka. Broome was able to enjoy the scenery:

. . . passing one volcano after another, each shy to part with its snow veil and each more lovely and taller than the last. A glorious flight. Given to few to see such wonders in the most wonderful way of all. The sun sets behind us as I write in the plane. Its rays slanting down golden pencils through rifts in the pink clouds. Deep bays open for a moment and disclose their wealth of valley, river and lake — each a surprise in size and shape. No trace of humans — only nature at its grandest. What a God to build such a world.[19]

Broome was entitled to enjoy the good moments that nature offered because he was in for some very bad ones in the next few days. On July 24, they reached Petropavlovsk, still on the Kamchatka Coast, where they caught up with the *Thiepval*, which was following their route to give assistance if necessary. Two days later, they took off again but had to turn back because of bad weather. The landing, in a strong wind and heavy swell, damaged the machine. "Several frames and floor braces smashed and hole forced in port side, luckily just above water line. Thankful to be alive — very near thing."[20] Repairs kept them there until August 1, when they flew to Ust Kamchatka.

The following day, August 2, turned out to be the last one for their round-the-world attempt:

Weather dull and threatening. Anything but favourable day for our long crossing to Bering I....Fog banks out to sea and on course but patchy at first. When about 2/3 across the 120 miles [190 km] that separate land from land, the fog shut down solid under us but apparently just lifted from the sea. So plane descended to 100 feet [30 m]....The further we went the lower the fog dropped till at last we were flying just above the wave tops and at a rate of 100 miles per hour [160 km/h], as we had a 20 mile [32 km] wind from the North-east and almost under our tail.

Finally fate put the lid on and we couldn't see fifty yards in any direction....Suddenly, out of the dense fog, dead ahead a small islet flashed out and Plenderleith just swerved in time. Here we were close to land so it was a case of a desperate chance of landing in the rough sea or dash against the cliffs of Bering Island. Plenderleith did his best but both wing tip floats were dashed to fragments and as the plane slewed violently round, during which process I was bounced about in the front cockpit like a pea in a pod, the port plane buried itself and splintered and the aileron was half wrenched off.

MacLaren yelled for lifebelts, which I was sitting on. These were quickly put on and we all looked anxiously inside the hull expecting to see the water rising up through a smashed bottom, but as luck would have it the hull was intact and we had a respite from a chilly death by drowning.[21]

The next two or three hours were harrowing ones. The aircraft was afloat and the engine was undamaged, so they were confident they could still taxi on the water; but they had lost their orientation in the dense fog; none of them had any idea where land was. Finally, they agreed more or less arbitrarily to head east. They started the engine again, but now they found that the wings, without their tip floats, kept digging in when they tried to taxi. Andrews was incapacitated by the same illness that had afflicted Plenderleith. He was lying, wrapped in blankets, on the floor of his cockpit; so MacLaren and Broome

...ran backwards and forwards first climbing out on one wing tip as far as we could go, till our weight brought the buried one out of the sea. Then the plane would bury her nose and threaten to dive bodily to the bottom as her tail was lifted high by the following swell and she swept down the slope of the water.

Then again the radiator would boil over and we would have to stop. And yet another failing of the poor wrecked bus was to try and broach to. What with our efforts to keep the plane from capsizing and our constant work on the starting handle we were both getting pretty well exhausted, and sometimes Plenderleith had to leave his pilot's seat to help us. During one of these interludes my old eyes caught a suspicion of a line...about where the horizon should be....I stared at it without saying a word to the others until at last a headland took dim form and I grabbed MacLaren's arm and pointed.[22]

Their troubles were nearly over. Broome, who had studied the islands carefully through his binoculars from the bridge of the *Thiepval* on his outward journey, recognized a pork-pie shaped column of basalt. It was on Torpokof Island, only a mile or two from the tiny settlement of Nikolski (Nikolskoye). "...oddly enough," Broome recorded, it was "not 20 miles [32 km] as the fulmar flies from a rotting cross which marks the grave of Vitus Bering, the Dane, who, at the command of Peter the Great, first sailed these smoky seas which bear his name and who drove ashore and died of scurvy with 18 of his men on the fifth day of November 1741."[23]

They were able to radio the faithful *Thiepval*, which had almost been able to keep up with them. Twelve hours later, the wrecked aircraft was loaded aboard and the disappointed crew of the Vulture were on their way back to Prince Rupert, and on to Vancouver — by sea.

Chapter Thirteen

The Private Sector

"I have never been killed in an airplane accident..."

MAJOR C. S. COWAN

By 1925, commercial bush flying was beginning to gain acceptance, even though salesmanship was still required to persuade industry to use aircraft. Major C. S. Cowan, a provincial Forestry Service officer who had done a good deal of flying in the Jericho Beach aircraft, addressed a lumber industry convention in Seattle and extolled the virtues of aircraft for what he called "executive work": moving supervisors around in country which had no other transportation facilities but for canoes and backpacking. He seems to have included firefighters in this category because he talks of the savings in payroll when crews of firefighters are moved by air. "I once had to go into a lake where there was a big fire and it took our men a hard day's march in order to get there at all, yet I could leave Vancouver and land on that lake in two and a half hours."[1] After stressing the savings in payroll if quick action can be taken to snuff out a small fire before it becomes a large one, and thus requires a large and expensive crew to fight it for several weeks, he faced a challenge from the floor that flying was not yet safe, and workers couldn't be persuaded to fly. "I have never been killed in an airplane accident" he responded, "and that is the best proof I can give to you that flying is pretty safe.... I think flying can be said to be just as safe as driving a Ford car on the streets of Seattle."[2]

By this time, too, purely commercial flying was beginning to make an impact on the Air Board-RCAF operations. The first really significant commercial operation had begun in eastern Canada as early as 1919.

The Laurentide Pulp and Paper Company had obtained a small grant from the Quebec provincial government and, with the loan from the Dominion government of two ex-U.S. Navy HS-2Ls — which had been stored at Halifax and Sydney since the end of World War I — began operations in the St. Maurice River area in Quebec.[3] In 1922, the lumber company decided it did not want to run its own air service, and a separate company called Laurentide Air Service Limited was formed, with marine engineer Thomas Hall as president and pilot Roy Maxwell as vice-president. The company began to expand its activities; in addition to its work in Quebec, it flew contracts for the Ontario government and contracts to produce aerial photography for the Fairchild Aerial Surveys Company of Canada; and by 1923, it was doing most of its business in Ontario. Laurentide Air Service was important because it was successful enough to prove that commercial bush flying was practicable. It was a well-run operation: crews were trained and maintenance standards were high. As a result, it attracted some of the pilots and engineers who would become the backbone of the celebrated bush-flying companies of the future. Such names as Romeo Vachon, Irenée Vachon, Roy Maxwell, C. S. Caldwell, G. A. Thompson and T. W. Siers.[4]

These men were what nowadays we would call star material. An intriguing sidelight is the way G. A. Thompson moved around the country. The last we heard of him, he was making flights of dubious legality out of Hazelton in the Junkers JL-6. More to the point, what really put Laurentide out of business was competition from the public sector. The Ontario government decided to establish their own air service. OPAS, the Ontario Provincial Air Service, was large and adequately funded from the start. It began with 13 HS-2Ls purchased from the United States Navy and, because it obviously offered more security than any other flying operation at the time, there was no shortage of applications for positions. Roy Maxwell, from Laurentide, was appointed director, and he set about hiring staff. Among the first were two other names from Laurentide, and once again they were of "star" quality: Fred Stevenson, H. A. (Doc) Oaks, Romeo Vachon, C. A. (Duke) Schiller and Tommy Siers.

Although they had now become civil servants, these people, like most bush-flying crews, worked hard and played hard. Historian Hugh Halliday gives us a hint:

...some were given over to unruly high jinks when off duty. Fred Stevenson was the prime example. Initially he was stationed in Toronto, where the HS-2Ls were to be delivered. He and two other men stayed in a rooming house. When Stevenson was later posted north, he was pursued by angry letters from his former landlady. The precise nature of her charges [and of Stevenson's activities] are not recorded in surviving records, but some hint is given in a letter written by the Minister, James Lyons, to Roy Maxwell, dated 1 August 1924:

"If some of the statements made in writing by Mrs. Johnson are at all true, especially those in reference to the condition the House was left in, the number of empty liquor bottles, and the display of discarded ladies' hose, it is my opinion that the less said about the matter publicly the better."[5]

No doubt. More pertinent, though, is that one of the most significant aspects of the OPAS operation involves a paradox. On the one hand, it deprived the private sector of a good deal of business; on the other, it provided a wonderful training ground for many of the crews who went on to found successful private-sector flying companies. At all events, it has been an enduring operation on the Canadian aviation scene; it is still in operation 75 years after it was founded.

By 1925, meanwhile, commercial operators were beginning to move into B.C. One of the first of these operations was undertaken by a United States mining syndicate, who leased an aircraft from Laurentide Air Services and had it shipped by rail to Prince Rupert, where it was assembled and test-flown. The machine was a Vickers Viking, a flying boat remarkably similar to the Vulture used by Stuart MacLaren in his round-the-world attempt the previous year. Pilot Scott Williams and Jack Caldwell (a pilot and mechanic), flew the plane from Prince Rupert to Wrangell, Alaska. From there, they moved a prospecting party in relays to Telegraph Creek, in B.C.; and then on to Dease Lake, which was to be their base for the summer.[6]

Frank Ellis records that

Flying and prospecting were carried on for six weeks and a total of 95 hours' flying was logged for the entire venture, which was the first mineral exploration mission by air in northern and western Canada.

The longest journey undertaken from the main base carried the airplane beyond the northern border of British Columbia, 150 miles [240 km] into the Yukon Territory, following the Dease and Francis rivers to the Hudson's Bay post on Francis Lake. The latitude of that outpost is between 61° and 62°N....[7]

By any measure, this was a remarkable accomplishment, particularly because they were so far removed from any maintenance or back-up facilities. The operation was clearly very well planned and very competently executed; and the mining syndicate must have assembled a hardy and seasoned group of prospectors who allowed themselves to be put out in such remote country, knowing they might well have to make their own way back without benefit of canoe or packhorse.

Nevertheless, impressive as this operation was, it represented a flash in the pan for B.C. aviation. When it was over, the Viking was dismantled and shipped back east. The first consistent commercial operation began early in February 1925, when another MacLaren who was no relative of Stuart's, Donald R. MacLaren, formed Pacific Airways Limited. Born in Calgary, he attended McGill University in 1911, joined the services in 1917 and learned to fly in the RFC, Canada, at Long Branch, Ontario. During World War I, he was one of the allies' top guns—the fourth Canadian ace in numbers of enemy aircraft shot down. His decorations included a DSO, MC and Bar and a DFC. He is described by historian S. F. Wise as "one of the last and greatest of the First World War aces...."[8] After the war, he was granted a permanent commission in the air force, but changed his mind, left the service, got married and settled down in Vancouver. The next development was interesting in the light of other claims:

By 1920, the government asked me to locate a seaplane station out here for the Ottawa Air Board, when I located the station at Jericho Beach, where they built a hangar and they started doing some work for other departments.[9]

MacLaren started his commercial flying career early in 1924, when he purchased a single-float seaplane from Earl Godfrey and "used it for taking photographs around the area."[10] Veteran pilot and instructor Hal Wilson identifies it as a Curtiss JN-4, G-CAEP;[11] and Harold Davenport dismisses it as "No good on floats," because it had an OX-5 engine, which lacked the extra power required for a successful conversion to a seaplane.[12] In any case, it was a brief venture because MacLaren tore the float off it on a sandbar, salvaged the engine and let the aircraft float out to sea and sink. Next, in 1925, MacLaren formed his company, Pacific Airways Limited, in partnership with Ernest Rogers, vice-president of the B.C. Sugar Refinery, and went down to Baltimore to buy a war-surplus HS-2L. Harold Davenport, one of the Jericho Beach mechanics, apparently tired of the air force, asked for a job. He got it and the first thing he had to do was to unpack the flying boat, which had been shipped up in one very large crate, and assemble it.

Meanwhile, MacLaren had been petitioning the federal government to turn over some of the Jericho Air Base work to private enterprise on the grounds that, while they might be training people to fly, they were doing little to encourage the growth of civil aviation. By this time, the economy was beginning to improve and the government agreed, awarding MacLaren a contract to fly the fisheries patrols in 1926 — a contract he retained for ten years — though not in the same company.

Pacific Airways set up its base with its new aircraft at Swanson Bay, near Butedale. It was an ideal place from which to launch patrols for illegal fishermen. MacLaren explains why:

Swanson Bay was the location that we used because that's where the fishery inspector lived. He had his home there. His patrol boat was moored there. There was electricity there. They kept a little generator running but the old pulp mill was falling to pieces and was abandoned. It was a handy place. Also, it was out of the eye of the fishing fleets. They didn't know where you were, you see. They couldn't see you come and go because you weren't anywhere near a cannery....[13]

The cat-and-mouse aspect of fisheries patrols, with in this case the cat clearly the winner, was obviously enjoyed by the crews. Gordon Ballentine, who joined the company in 1927 as a crewman and later became a pilot, remembers that "One of the tricks we learned was that if we flew close enough to the thickly timbered hillsides the noise of our engines would be very largely absorbed, so we could go sneaking along and drop down on some poor innocent poacher."[14]

Two years later, MacLaren very sensibly decided that it was time to move up from the by-then obsolescent HS-2L to a more efficient aircraft. Flying boats produced by the Boeing company in Seattle were beginning to make their mark, and he aspired to these, and to Junkers and Fokker seaplanes as well. Unfortunately, his partner, E. T. Rogers, was unwilling to risk the kind of money involved — these new aircraft would cost $30,000 to $40,000 apiece, according to MacLaren. To understand the next development, we have briefly to return to the east.

Gold had been discovered at Red Lake, Ontario, by Lorne and Ray Howey and something in the nature of a gold rush began. Historian Ken Molson describes the discovery as

. . . a catalyst in the development of bush flying in Canada. From there, flying operations rapidly spread throughout the provinces of Canada as a primary means of transportation for the prospector and mine developer.

The Howey brothers brought Jack E. Hammell to help develop their property and he decided that it was best to begin the exploratory work immediately. It was necessary to bring men and equipment in during the late fall of 1925 so that work could proceed during the winter months. As there was no commercial air service capable of doing the job, the Ontario Provincial Air Service was induced to take on this work. Five of its Curtiss HS-2L flying boats moved in the necessary men and material before the lake froze.[15]

Gold rushes, particularly when, as in this case, they are genuine ones, have usually influenced the course of history. Red Lake was no exception. That same winter a group of financiers decided to buy a Curtiss Lark, a two-seat, open-cockpit biplane, and incorporate Patricia Airways and Exploration Limited to service the gold field. Doc Oaks, together with mechanic S. A. Tomlinson, were persuaded to forfeit the security of OPAS to operate it.[16]

In spite of the unsuitability of the aircraft — it could carry only one passenger, or the equivalent in freight, in the front cockpit — Patricia Airways provided good service during the winter and summer of 1926. To avoid getting bogged down in the details of the flurry of new activity in aviation at the time, for our purposes it is enough to know that, towards the end of the year, Doc Oaks contacted a wealthy Winnipeg businessman, James A. Richardson, who was expressing interest in starting an air service to meet the increasing demand for mineral exploration flying. Doc Oaks was admirably qualified because he held a degree in mining engineering as well as his pilot's licence. Richardson was equally well qualified to run the proposed company. He had the financial resources, the enthusiasm for aviation and the business competence; as a result he is almost invariably referred to as the father of Canadian aviation.

This new company, to be called Western Canada Airways Limited, was incorporated late in 1926 and replaced Patricia Airways. Starting with one Fokker Universal (one of the machines MacLaren yearned for), the fleet was increased to three Fokkers in 1927, when the company was awarded a contract to fly four tons of drilling equipment from mile 350 of the Hudson Bay Railway to Churchill, Manitoba. This venture evoked high praise from Ottawa. The 1927 Report on Civil Aviation claimed that "There has been no more brilliant operation in

the history of commercial flying."[17] In fact, it turned out to be another very significant milestone in bush flying; and, because the company was well financed, and now demonstrably successful, it soon began to draw some of the best pilots and mechanics in the country. People like Fred Stevenson, Al Cheesman, Leigh Brintnell and Tommy Siers.

By 1928, a further merging of the numerous small, and marginally viable aviation companies began. The first of these was Don MacLaren's Pacific Airways. Still determined to start operating more sophisticated aircraft, MacLaren negotiated with Western Canada and eventually sold his company to them in May, together with his own and Harold Davenport's services. MacLaren became Superintendent of West Coast Operations for Western Canada Airways. In addition, three new pilots were posted to the coast: E. C. Luke, W. Neville Cumming and A. C. Upham.[18]

MacLaren wanted to buy Boeing flying boats for the west coast operation, but the Canadian government was pushing for the sale of Canadian-built Vickers aircraft, and the new company's compromise was to buy two Boeings from Seattle and lease two Vedettes from Vickers.[19]

Harold Davenport describes the immediate changes this brought about for him:

WCA acquired a wharf, a big shed at the foot of Bute Street and Beach Avenue [in Vancouver]...; there were two large sheds; then we built a slipway to launch and retrieve. Then we acquired a Boeing B1D [G-CASX] with a Wright J5 engine and a B1E [G-CATY]...[this] had a Pratt and Whitney Wasp A—best engine ever.... Also a Vedette—nice but not rugged enough for the job... it had an Armstrong Siddeley Lynx engine.[20]

Both pilots and mechanics were very taken with the Boeing but, judging by Gordon Ballentine's reaction, they were more equivocal about the Vedette.

In the Vickers Vedette and the HS2L you sat where God meant airplane drivers to sit; out in the noise and the wind. The Vickers Vedette had a horrible motion in rough air. We were, I suppose, spoiled a bit by the Boeing B1E which was quite a tough, comfortable air-plane. The RCAF used Vickers Vedettes for photography and patrols all over Canada very successfully, so there was basically nothing wrong with it, if you liked open airplanes that flapped their wings.[21]

On another occasion, Ballentine gave a more racy description of the Boeing:

First to arrive at Western Canada's English Bay base was a B1D, G-CASX. Trim and modern looking, shiny mahogany hull and cabin, a Wright Whirlwind just like Lindberg[h]'s and a wing span less than thirty three feet, the size and comparison with the old H-boat caused one old-timer to burst out, "Gawd, it's fitted up just like a whore's boudoir!" Well, I lack accurate data on the subject, but the B1D was all closed in, had windows you cranked up and down just like the latest automobiles, upholstered seats, windshield wipers and so on.[22]

In their first summer of operations under the new flag, the crews on the west coast suffered three sharp setbacks. On July 14, the B1D, G-CASX, flown by Luke, with Bill Partridge as engineer, crashed into glassy water just south of Butedale.* Luke survived, but Partridge died of his injuries. Then, only a week or so later, "The old H-boat, G-CAFH, completely re-built the previous winter and as good as new, blew parts of its Liberty engine the length of one wing and chewed up a spar so badly the aircraft was towed to Swanson Bay and Junked."[23]

Finally, on August 15, another serious accident. The Vedette, G-CASW, after an overnight stop at Prince Rupert, was headed south-west across Chatham Sound, which should have taken it between Porcher Island and Prescott Island, then across Hecate Strait for Queen Charlotte City. Neville Cumming was flying it, with engineer Alf Walker beside him and crewman Gordon Ballentine in what he called, "the round open tub in the bow . . . no charts and no windscreen, but a 100 per cent view."[24] It was a grey, overcast day, with a cloud base of about 1000 feet (300 m). Ballentine relates what happened next:

Once you could see past the islands, the grey sky and the grey sea started to blend. We were flying between two islands. All of a sudden we were in clouds, with nothing much better than a carpenter's level for instruments. . . .

Anyway, we ran into this cloud and I heard the power come off and we started down. We were between two islands and I assumed that we would simply break out over the ocean, which I'm sure is what the pilot assumed too. But the first thing I saw were the tops of trees that looked about 300 feet [90 m] high — as far as I was concerned — and about ten feet [3 m] below us. I might say that's a shocking experience. The pilot poured the coals to it then and we started to climb. What manoeuvres we went through it's impossible to say, but every few moments I'd see the trees again. Eventually, we got above the trees and smacked into the top of the mountain.

* Water is glassy when it is undisturbed by the smallest riffle of wind. A pilot looking down can not judge whether he is 10 feet [3 m] or, let's say, 200 feet [60 m] above the surface. This condition has been the cause of many bush-flying accidents. The pilot would either fly right into the water; or, if attempting a landing, flatten out far too high, stall, and then plunge into the water.

The first thing I did was get out and stumble about 50 feet [15 m], you know, thinking of fire. The airplane was a pile of junk. The air-cooled engine was flat like a pancake and still running. The gravity fuel tank, with about three or four gallons [13-18 l] of gas in it, was ruptured. The gas was steaming off this air-cooled engine, coming off in clouds of steam. Why the thing never blew up, who can tell?

I had to go around the rear of the thing; it was like crawling through a barbed-wire fence because it was just a bunch of splintered junk. I finally reached the cockpit. The pilot, Neville, was sitting with his head slumped down on his chest, some blood running all over his face. Alf Walker, who was sitting on his right, looked as though his face was made of chopped liver. He was dead as far as I was concerned. I was just reaching in to try to reach the [ignition] switch when Neville made a reflexive action, and knocked the switch off with his hand and flopped his head down again. So, I decided he must be alive if he could do that. Alf was definitely dead; I was just as sure as I am sitting here.

In my bathtub front seat was the emergency gear with axes and food and all that sort of stuff. So I crawled out through all this junk, went around to the front of the airplane again, and I couldn't get into my seat, it was such a tight fit. The top wing had come down and cut my seat in two and hadn't even touched me. Anyway, I dragged the stuff out, got the axe and started back to the cockpit. I got there and the dead man was gone! He just wasn't there. I thought, well, God, he's going to be stumbling around the mountain out of his mind. So, I went back outside again, around to the front of the airplane. As I got around to the front, I met this apparition coming around the other side, his face a mess of blood, his hands all bloody. We stood and looked at each other and we both started to laugh. You, know, a hysterical reaction. I was relatively undamaged, but Alf was a mess.

Turned out that what had happened was that he and Neville had both been hit on the back of the head by the struts from the engine when it came down. Their faces had been smashed through three-quarters of an inch [2 cm] of mahogany plywood—the instrument panel.

Anyway, Alf and I organized ourselves. Then we had to do something about the pilot who'd put us in this horrible position. Quite frankly, we didn't much care. [I became a pilot later and often wondered how close I came to making people think the same about me.] Anyway, we decided to get him out. We chopped a hole out right through the bottom of the hull and got him out that way, and stretched him out some few feet away from the airplane. Then we decided, "Well, the thing might still burn." So we dragged him another fifty feet [15 m] and stretched him out again. He was a mess and we didn't know if he was going to last or not. And we didn't know where we were; whether we were on an island, the mainland or where. So Alf and I took turns wandering around the mountain.

About five that afternoon we finally saw a glimpse down through a hole in the clouds and we saw water. We didn't know what it was, whether it was a lake, ocean or what, but it was better than where we were. So we decided that was where we had to go. We still had this guy, who had refused to die; we still had to look after him! Alf and I decided to make a stretcher, Boy Scout style. We managed to get a couple of poles. We were taking Neville's coat to use as the other half of the stretcher when he sort of came to and wanted to know what the hell was going on. We said, "We're going to carry you down the mountain." He said, "You're not. Where am I?" He said we weren't going to carry him; he was going to walk. And walk he did.

195

The Laurentide Air Services Vickers Viking, chartered by a United States mining syndicate, that flew into the far north of B.C. in 1925. The photograph was taken from the operational base at Dease Lake.

PABC

Donald R. MacLaren, who founded Pacific Airways in 1925.

Pacific Airways radio equipment at their Swanson Bay base, 1928.

E. L. MACLEOD ESTATE PHOTOS

A Junkers W34 in flight, and a Fokker Super Universal on the water at Vernon Lake on Vancouver Island — the sort of aircraft MacLaren wanted to use in Pacific Airways instead of the obsolescent H Boats.

B.C. FOREST SERVICE

The Pacific Airways HS-2L with Harold Davenport at the controls, circa 1926.

E. L. MACLEOD ESTATE

One of the new Boeing flying boats,
a B1 series, docked at Lake Union, Seattle.

GORDON PETERS COLLECTION, RBCM

Another of the new bush aircraft that was beginning to make
its name: a Fairchild FC2W in flight over Nimpkish Lake, Vancouver Island.

B.C. FOREST SERVICE

A crew at Harrison Lake in 1929, after
the merger between Pacific Airways and
Western Canada Airways. Left to right:
unidentified, Walter Gilbert, Neville
Cumming and Bill Faulkner.
Seated, Mr. Wing, B.C. Electric.

GORDON BALLENTINE, PABC

Two RCAF Vickers Vedettes being tied down for the night. E. L. MACLEOD ESTATE

Vedette G-CASW at Swanson Bay, August 14, 1928, the day before it crashed on Porcher Island.

HAROLD DAVENPORT, PABC

Gordon Ballentine, who began his career as a crewman with Pacific Airways, eventually became a pilot. By the 1940s he was Captain of a Canadian Airways de Havilland Dragon Rapide.

GORDON BALLENTINE, PABC

The wrecked Vedette on top of a mountain on Porcher Island. All three crew members, Neville Cumming, Alf Walker and Gordon Ballentine, were fortunate to escape with their lives.

A Jericho station Vedette about to be brought ashore.

The Dominion Airways de Havilland DH-60X Moth, G-CAHS. Although the Moth arrived in a crate in July 1927, and was assembled in Nelson, this photograph was taken in Vancouver shortly before the aircraft was severely damaged in a crash.

Dominion's G-CAHS at Nakusp in the late 1920s. The sternwheeler *Minto* in background.

Ted Dobbin's Moth on Kootenay Lake, 1928.

M. PARENT COLLECTION

Form P-L-8

PILOT'S LOG

NAME *Donald Page MacPhee*
ADDRESS *Permanent, Kaslo BC*
CLASSIFICATION ___
LICENSE No. *466   Canadian.*

Date	No. of Flights	Time in Air	Distance Flown	Reg. Mark or Type of Plane Used	Nature of Flights	Certified by
1929 Brought Forward		471 hr 36 min				
Sept. 2	1	30 min		CF-ABM	Landing on Phosphorus Lake	
Sept. 4	1	1 hr 40 min		CF-ABM	Welch Lake – Resolution	
Sept. 5	1	15 min		CF-ABM	Dawsons Ldg – Sulphur Point	
Sept. 6	1	2 hr 25 min		CF-ABM	Dawsons Ldg – Simpson	
Sept. 7	3	6 hr 30 min		CF-ABM	Simpson – Wrigley – Norman – Simpson	
Sept. 8	1	1 hr 10 min		CF-ABM	Resolution – Fitzgerald	
Sept. 11	1	1 hr 20 min		CF-ABM	Fitzgerald – McMurray	
Sept. 14	1	1 hr 45 min		CF-ABM	Edmonton – McMurray	
Sept. 15	2	3 hr		CF-ABM	McMurray – Fitzgerald – Resolution	
Sept. 18	1	1 hr		CF-ABM	McMurray – Waskesiu Lake	
Sept. 26	1	45 min		CF-ABM	Waskesiu – Cranberry Portage	
Oct. 5	1	1 hr		CF-ABM	South Bend – Wolleston Lake	
Oct. 10	1	2 hr		CF-ABM	Stoney Rapids – South Bend	
Oct. 10	1	1 hr 15 min		CF-AAM	South Bend – Moss Lake (Fokker)	
Oct. 11	1	30		CF-AAM	Moss Lake – Cranberry Portage	
Oct. 19	2	3 hr 30		CF-AA1	Lake – Cranberry P. Lake – Cranwr.	
Nov. 10	1	45		CF-AGD	Creston. B.C.	
Nov. 17	4	1 hr 25		CF-AGD	Creston. BC.	
Carried Forward		452 hr 21				

Entries from Page MacPhee's flying log book, 1929. By then, bush flying had come of age: crews were flying into the far north as a matter of course.   PAGE MACPHEE

Cominco's Moth at Columbia Gardens airport, near Trail, 1929. Left to right: Howard Anderson, Doug Bert, Hamilton Curry and Page MacPhee.

COMINCO COLLECTION, RBCM

So the two of us supported Neville and we stumbled downhill, something like coming down Grouse Mountain at midnight without a trail. About two in the morning, I think, we got to the beach and laid Neville out. We were pretty beat. We tried to light the standard three signal fires. We'd get one lit and the tide'd come in and put it out. We got the third one going— you know, really great Boy Scout stuff. Alf and I sat up all night by the fire signalling S-O-S off shore. When daylight came we found we were in a little bay with an island covering the whole mouth of it. So we were signalling to a vacant island all night.

We tossed a coin to see whether we'd go right or left; tossed another coin to see whether Alf would go or I would go. The toss came that Alf would go and he would go to the right. Alf came back in about two hours with his eyes all bugged out. He told me, "Some people will be coming along pretty soon to pick us up." He said he got down the beach about half a mile [800 m] and there was a launch at anchor in the bay. He'd yelled and shouted and whistled and thrown rocks at it but couldn't raise anybody, 'cause there was nobody on it. He went a little farther and came to a trail up the hill. Went up the trail about a hundred yards [90 m] and there was a telephone on a tree! So he cranked this thing, and if you can imagine Alf's feeling and the feeling of the people at the other end; you know, "Who am I?" and "Where am I?"

Well, it turned out that it was the beach site for a mining company, and that we were on Porcher Island. So they came down the hill and said they'd get a boat and come around and pick us up. They took us into Prince Rupert on this launch, and Alf and Neville into hospital. And I took the glad news back to Don MacLaren at Swanson Bay that he was short an airplane.[25]

Traumatic as this experience must have been, it did not discourage Gordon Ballentine. We will hear more of him because he went on to become one of British Columbia's notable pilots. But both he and the rest of Western Canada's staff were about to experience change. By 1930, two heavyweights in Canadian transportation began to take notice. Both the Canadian Pacific and the Canadian National Railways realized that, although there were no scheduled airlines in Canada yet, there were a number in the United States and Europe; and that, when airlines did begin operating in Canada, they would siphon off some of the railways' traffic. Historian Kaye Lamb records their response.

As early as 1919 the C.P.R. had secured authority to own and operate aircraft commercially, but no practical steps were taken until 1930, when the Canadian Pacific and the Canadian National each invested $250,000 in Canadian Airways Limited. Controlled by James Richardson of Winnipeg, a director of the C.P.R., this was a consolidation of a number of local airlines. Canadian Airways was soon operating regional services in several of the provinces, and it seemed likely that it would become a nationwide system in which the two railways would have a growing equity.[26]

The railway executives were astute men; even so, it is hard to believe that they could have foreseen, in 1930, just how much of their business would be appropriated by air transport within the next three decades.

CONQUERING THE NORTH

Flying well over a million miles the Western Canada Airways has conquered the distances of the North and made possible its early development.

WESTERN CANADA AIRWAYS
LIMITED
HEAD OFFICE **WINNIPEG**

Meanwhile, Western Canada Airways was one of the "local airlines" to be merged. Some of the others were the Aviation Corporation of Canada, Interprovincial Airways and an existing company called Canadian Airways Limited (which has since caused much confusion about the old company and the new). It became, and remained, the pre-eminent aviation company in Canada for many years to come.

While this consolidation was taking place, in British Columbia other less ambitious commercial ventures were being launched. In 1927, the four Dobbin brothers formed a company, Dominion Airways Limited. The company was incorporated in January, with Leonard A. Dobbin, his brother Edward, and Henry S. Hoffar as directors. The "plan of the operation of the company [was] to conduct a commercial aerial transportation, photography and survey service in or out of the province."[27]

They bought a float-equipped de Havilland DH-60X Moth, registered G-CAHS, a two-seat biplane. Compared to the Fairchild FC2 that was just appearing at the time, or the Fokker Universal and the Junkers W33—all of which could carry freight or up to five passengers in an enclosed cabin—it was not the most suitable aircraft for bush flying. Nevertheless, it was reliable and rugged and they operated with considerable success for two years on a provincial government forestry patrol contract out of Nelson, in the east Kootenay district of British Columbia. E. C. W. (Ted) Dobbin was the pilot and the contract was for 100 hours during the summer season at $100 an hour.[28] The Commercial Aviation section of the Department of National Defence (DND) Report for 1927 recorded that their forestry contract in Nelson had been successfully concluded; after which they flew the machine back to Vancouver, "where a small school of flying is being conducted during the winter."

The arrival of the Dobbin's Moth in Nelson that summer occasioned almost daily reports in the local newspaper, the Nelson *Daily News*. On July 20, 1927, the headline was, THRONGS WATCH ASSEMBLY OF THE SEAPLANE. "Assisted by a husky crew, Capt. Ted Dobbin and his brother Claire Dobbin broke open the crates in which the plane was shipped to Nelson from the factory in England.... Assisted by 8 or 10 husky onlookers the fuselage was lifted bodily onto arranged trestles, then pontoons were bolted on. All parts were properly aligned and securely fastened."

The following day, there was another headline: DOBBIN MAKES TEST FLIGHTS ON WEST ARM. "Several test flights, engine tuning, small adjustments were made and the aircraft flown to an anchoring site near Lakeside Park." Again on the 22nd, "Flights to altitudes above 11,000 feet [3350 m] were made during a 3 hr. 20 min. inspection of West Kootenay and Arrow Lakes areas." On July 27, "four fires were spotted from the air north of South Slocan on False Creek by air observer Percy Young flying with Ted Dobbin." And a day later, "Nakusp turned out en masse today when, for the first time in its history, a seaplane came to rest on upper Arrow Lake. The Dominion Airways seaplane piloted by Capt. Dobbin with G. P. Melrose, district forester from Nelson aroused the interest of Nakusp people. They were scouting for forest fires along the West Arm of Kootenay Lake, Trout Lake, down the Arrow Lakes, up the Kootenay River to Nelson."

Dominion Airways had made a good start. For the rest of that summer, daily flights became commonplace. First-time visits to New Denver, Kaslo, Lardeau and many other communities within the Nelson Forest District were made. For many people, this was their first opportunity to see an airplane and Dominion airways enjoyed a solid reputation with the people of the Kootenays. Unfortunately, the company did not survive for very long.

A. H. Wilson, in his "Reminiscences of a West Coast Pilot," outlines its brief career:

Dominion Airways, under "Ted" Dobbin, continued with its Forestry operations for two years at least, and in 1929 received additional financing through Norman Yarrow of Yarrow Ltd. Thereafter they expanded their fleet and commenced flying school operations and charter work. Due to a series of unfortunate accidents, however, this company finally folded up. One accident, in particular, which occurred at Vancouver 25 May 1930, was the result of Stinson CF-AMD, taxiing into two parked Moths, CF-ACC and CF-ADY. Repairs were made in due course, but they were cracked up later — the Stinson at Swanson Bay, near Butedale, on 16 July 1930, and the Moth, having been started up without chocks, took off on a pilotless flight which ended in disaster. The other Moth, CF-ADY, was crashed in 1930 by a man named Danard, who, while flying at a height of a few hundred feet, waved violently to his girl friend on the verandah of her house. By some good fortune, the pilot survived the accident which followed the inevitable stall, but this did not help the aircraft much.[29]

While Dominion Airways quickly faded away (it was officially dissolved in 1932), it left a significant legacy of pilots trained, most of whom would contribute a great deal to the growth of aviation in B.C.

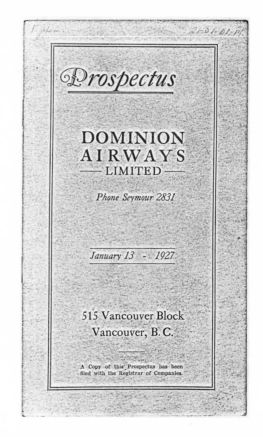

Prospectus

DOMINION AIRWAYS
——LIMITED——

Phone Seymour 2831

January 13 - 1927

515 Vancouver Block
Vancouver, B. C.

A Copy of this Prospectus has been filed with the Registrar of Companies.

Among them were many of the pilots of the Consolidated Mining and Smelting Company's air division. D. Page MacPhee, K. D. (Ken) Dewar, W. G. Jewett and W. J. Dean all earned their commercial licences at this school, as did W. M. Archibald, who learned to fly when he was 53 years old (he was granted Private Pilot Certificate No. 319, dated June 21, 1929)[30] and founded CM & S's air division. The temptation is to jump ahead and deal with this interesting story; but CM & S really began training for its bush-flying operations at Kaslo in 1930, so it is material for the future.

There is an intriguing postscript to this era. Towards the end of 1928, during the fall fair, aviation in Nelson reverted to the turn of the century. The September 21, 1928, issue of the *Daily News* carried the headline, CROWD THRILLS AS BALLOONIST DROPS TO SPACE: "Soars thousands of feet before dropping. Two swift jumps follow."

Captain Lestrange's monster hot air balloon left the earth at 4:45 yesterday afternoon on its first ascent from the ballgrounds. With a rush the big black bag rose straight up into the air. With a jump the balloonist followed it with one leg through the sling, his parachute perched above him in a neat roll. He waved farewell to the crowds around and was whisked thousands of feet above the city. Thus started the big ascent which was followed by a neat double parachute jump.

He was aided by two helpers and a swarm of youngsters who, despite the dusty blackness of the bag, clung to it for dear life to keep it on the ground until it inflated. The captain threw a can of oil into the pit under the bag, flames roared, then it bulged out, smoke and heat pouring out around it and the balloon began to rise. Then the cords holding the balloon were loosened. "Let 'er go!" Lestrange called and the excitement began.

Soaring above the highest trees and buildings the wind caught the balloon. It was carried back over the city in a southwesterly direction. Up and up it went, the captain waving as he ascended. Finally, as the balloon was getting smaller and smaller to those on the ground, the jumper was seen suddenly hurtling through space. Then a parachute opened and he came to a stop with a jerk. At this moment a second parachute opened and he began his slow descent to earth. The big bag, released of its load continued upwards for a few seconds then turned over, emptied of its smoke and heat and came crashing to earth twisting and turning in the air. The first parachute dropped like a rock past the jumper now descending. Down came Captain Lestrange. Finally he was lost to view as he neared the earth. While to the crowd in the ball grounds it seemed as though he had landed in the Kootenay Lake, he had expertly jockeyed to an open space on the CPR flats where he came to earth unharmed.

Henry Stevenson was one of the youngsters who assisted in the launching of the balloon. He recalls one of the outcomes of the experience:

Nelson boys who had witnessed the parachute jumps were captivated by the thought of floating to earth so gracefully that they decided an experiment was called for. A ten-foot square of canvas was obtained, along with a piece of clothesline rope which was tied to the four corners; now the parachute was ready for test. The five researchers drew straws and Dick McInnes was the lucky candidate who would have the honor of floating to earth. Bert Jardine, Alfred Vyse, Nelson Riddoch and Henry Stevenson were the crew that carried the parachute up into a tree where each could hang onto a corner of the canopy while the jumper swung out from the tree trunk at a height of about ten or twelve feet. When the jumper's weight pulled the chute away the canopy did not billow and McInnes dropped like a ton of bricks. When he struck the ground, the canvas covered him and he did not move. The four tree researchers scrambled quickly out of their perches, pulled the canvas off their colleague and were happy to find he was still breathing. However, for the following few days, his movements were rather slow.

Henry is ambivalent about the value of the experiment, but the history of aviation is filled with similar outcomes.

Chapter Fourteen

A Time of Optimism and Expansion

"We carried 105 passengers and took $425 in cash into the Riverside Hotel. That was okay for July 1st, 1928."

HAL WILSON

By 1928, flying training was becoming a significant factor in civil aviation. There were two avenues: one, the purely commercial training schools; the other, semi-subsidized flying clubs. In either case, the principal obstacle was lack of suitable fields from which to operate. The first licenced airfield in British Columbia, in Victoria, resulted from the formation of another new company, B.C. Airways Limited which, in 1927, purchased a field on Lansdowne Road—the same field from which W. W. Gibson had made his first flight in 1910—and opened a flying training school. The principals were Cecil and Ernest Eve, two car dealers who ran the Graham Paige agency in the city, and who received financial support from a number of other Victoria businessmen. They purchased two Eaglerocks, three-seater biplanes with Curtiss OX-5 engines, and a Driggs Dart, a very small two-seater powered by an Anzani engine.

Their operating staff was as competent as any around at the time. Hal Wilson was the instructor, and Ted Cressy, an ex-RAF fitter who had served at Jericho Beach in 1923, was the engineer. Their operations consisted of a mixture of flying training, occasional charter flights and barnstorming. According to Ted Cressy,

...every Saturday and Sunday we did barnstorming. It was $5.00 a trip, that was for a full 20 minutes from off to on; and then we did the odd charter flight now and again to Vancouver, and to Port Angeles, and to Olympia, and a couple to Everett. Every now and again to make a [buck] — in the summer particularly — if we had been a little on the slow side we'd get a scale, a weighing scale . . . and then you would fly them at a penny a pound. The passenger would come, stand on the scale, 150 pounds [68 kg]; all right, $1.50 and away you'd go for 10 minutes. And after all, it sounded cheap but we made money on it because we cut the minutes down, and took two passengers [in the Eaglerock] so it came out all right.[1]

One senses that these barnstorming sorties were a challenge to the pilot, as well as to the engineer. Hal Wilson describes a trip up Island:

Being a holiday, July 1st, I went over to Courtenay. I had Mr. Davis, who was our financial adviser of B.C. Airways, and the two Eve brothers and the engineer; that's four people rounding up passengers in the hay field there. [The field] was exactly 1,800 feet [550 m] long in all directions. So I was landing corner to corner in it, and there's no brakes on the airplane. I . . . broke the propeller on a piece of paper that was laid out to mark a circle on the field, with a rock in the middle of the paper. The prop-wash had picked up the paper and the rock hit the propeller. Where it went, I don't know, but there were no injuries other than a piece off the propeller. There was a man who had a mahogany box at home, so he took a piece of the mahogany box out and brought a couple of nails and glued them on and we carried on. We carried 105 passengers and took $425 in cash into the Riverside Hotel. That was okay for July 1st, 1928.[2]

While their flying training, barnstorming and occasional charter work — it cost $60 to fly from Victoria to Vancouver in an Eaglerock — provided a living, B.C. Airways was ambitious and decided to move into the operation of a scheduled airline.

The company bought one of the by-then celebrated Ford-Stout all-metal trimotors, capable of carrying 14 passengers — the largest land-based aircraft to operate in Canada up to that date — to inaugurate a Victoria-Seattle-Vancouver scheduled service. Its Canadian registration letters were G-CATX. Herald (known, nevertheless, as Hal) Walker, an American pilot from Seattle, was hired to fly it and he and Cressy, accompanied by Cecil Eve, went to the Ford factory at Dearborn to ferry it back to Victoria.

There was, however, a slight hiatus when they arrived at Dearborn. Maurice McGregor describes what happened:

The Eve brothers — they were great optimists — had made a $1000 down payment to buy the Ford. . . . Then they found that they had to pay the balance: $39,000. Well, my father [Fred McGregor], and Carl Pendray, the mayor, were very close friends; both were directors of the Victoria Chamber of Commerce . . . and my father was pretty active in sales, you know, money raising. So he and Carl Pendray, and the members of

featuring
THE
CANADIAN
NATIONAL
EXHIBITION
AIRCRAFT
. SHOW .
AUG 24TH to SEPT 8TH

the Chamber of Commerce, got behind the thing and they got a bank loan . . . and they shot the money down.[3]

The arrival of the Trimotor at Lansdowne was a big event. The newspapers gave it front-page headlines: THOUSANDS OF VICTORIANS WELCOME AIR LINER:

The first attempt at landing was unsuccessful, but after soaring and circling once more Pilot Walker brought the liner down and made a perfect landing, about two hundred yards [60 m] from the aerodrome [hangar].
Immediately the plane was brought to a stop thousands of people stampeded through the police, anxious to get a first glimpse of it. Police from Saanich and the city were finally successful in getting the crowd back as the plane was being brought to its parking place.[4]

Ted Cressy has a rather different recollection of that landing:

I think everybody and their brothers, cousins, uncles and sons came down to watch the Trimotor land, and we were two hours late so they were getting hot and happy, as it was a beautiful day. We had to land downwind; we couldn't land into wind at that time because of Bowker Creek [which ran across one side of the field]. So we came in a little down wind, not much down wind, . . . just over Bowker Creek and we started rolling towards where the crowd were, all around the hangar. All the dignitaries were standing there, and he yelled to me, "Pull on the brakes." So I cut the motors, and of course the motors took quite some time to unwind, and I hauled on this brake, left and right. It was like a joystick brake, and I could see that crowd coming nearer, and nearer. Faces were getting bigger and they were just standing there solid, and we stopped not more than 20-25 feet [6-8 m] from the crowd, just as if it was beautifully arranged. But little did they know how many pints of sweat were running down the back of my spine! I was seeing three propellers chewing up everybody and our hangar as well. That was an apprehensive moment — moments like that sometimes made Mrs. Cressy's little boy wish he had gone into the grocery business![5]

While B.C. Airways had given Victoria a head start with a licenced airfield, and was able to start operating a flying club in 1927, in Vancouver the genesis of the first flying club — as opposed to a commercial school — began with a loose organization called the Aero Club of British Columbia — not to be confused with the 1915-16 organization. Don MacLaren describes the development:

. . . back in 1923 or '24 . . . there was Harry Marshall, Walter Gilbert, George Dixon and one or two others and myself, and we had all been in the Flying Corps, in the Air Force, and here we were back doing jobs around [Vancouver]. . . . I was waiting for a job from General Motors . . . and Walter said, "We have a little club called the Aero Club of British Columbia." "Oh," I said. . . . It was a little room on the corner of Bute Street or Jervis, or somewhere. . . . There wasn't a thing in there except a table — a place to play poker, you see. And you bring a bottle of Scotch along with you. So I went down; they used to meet once a month. What did we meet for? Nobody had any idea except that they wanted to form a club and get some airplanes to fly.

Well, I studied this thing [the idea of a flying club] and [eventually] I talked to Colonel Godfrey [Squadron Leader Earl Godfrey]. And the next time he went to Ottawa, we put up this idea to the Air Board: "Why don't you help form these flying clubs for training?—because nobody is training anybody nowadays." So this is where the training scheme came along. The government says, "All right, you form a club; you buy a little airplane and we'll give you one." And that's the way the Aero Club of B.C. really got going.[6]

In fact, there was a little more to it than this, as the 1927 Report on Civil Aviation makes clear:

With a view to encouraging a more general knowledge and use of aviation throughout the Dominion, the Government decided to assist in the formation of light aeroplane clubs in the chief centres of population, on similar lines to those successfully operated in Great Britain and Australia....

The plan provides, in brief, for the issue to incorporated clubs or associations, which shall be responsible for their own internal management and economy, of two aircraft free of charge, provided that the club or association makes provision for their efficient maintenance, the services of a competent instructor and a suitable flying field. Should the club provide one or more aeroplanes of approved type from their own resources, the Government will each year issue one more aircraft. In addition, a grant of $100 per *ab initio** pupil trained will be made to the club.[7]

In other words, this was an early example of matching grants and it was successful. The biggest problem the clubs faced was to find "a suitable flying field." Victoria, as we have seen, beat Vancouver to the punch. The Victoria Branch of the Aero Club of B.C. was established in 1927, with one "wooden Moth, G-CAKA."[8] Sidney Pickles and A. W. Carter gave instruction at the weekend, and Hal Wilson was often called in to do so during the week when no other instructor was available. The "Light Aeroplane Clubs" section of the 1928 DND Report lists the Victoria Club as having one aircraft, training an average of 14 pupils a week and flying a total of 128 hours and 32 minutes during the year.

In Vancouver, they had to wait another year. A rather dubious field on Lulu Island, just north of the race track—known, like the one in Victoria, as Lansdowne Field—was being used by the very occasional aircraft that wanted to land near Vancouver; but it was in no condition for learners being taught to fly.

An article in *Canadian Air Review* explains how this field, which was

---

* Loosely translated, this means "from the beginning."

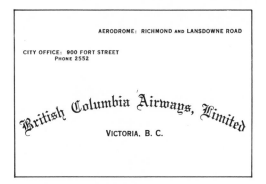

still being used to grow crops, abruptly became the municipal airport, if only temporarily.

In May [1928] the Local Branch of the Aero Club of B.C., and an official of the newly organized B.C. Airways, appeared before the City Council asking for provision of a temporary field on Lulu Island pending selection and construction of a permanent airport.

The Council agreed to lease fifty acres [20 ha] on Lulu Island and to expend $7,500.00 on a hangar and a runaway [sic]. The site was inspected by an Official of the Royal Canadian Air Force and application made to Ottawa for an airport license.

The project seemed to pause at this stage when suddenly in the middle of July the proposition, as it were, exploded in the hands of the airport committee of the Council like a giant firecracker, to which some passerby had touched a match.

The match in this case was the application of the B.C. Airways and the Commercial Air Transport Co., Everett, Wash., to use the airport for daily services between Vancouver, Victoria and Seattle, starting immediately. The Committee sprang into rapid action. Ottawa was wired for a confirmation of the license application so work could be started on the runway; the farmer from whom the site was leased was notified to cut the crop of timothy hay standing on the field. The hay was cut July 22. On July 24th the field presented a strange appearance. Parked among the haycocks [stooks] were two hundred automobiles and a large auto stage, while a thousand citizens lined the cleared strip extending the length of the field.

The Ryan 4-passenger Monoplane of the Commercial Transport, piloted by John Langdon, reached the field at 11 a.m....

On the same day a plane of the B.C. Airways, glided to a landing 40 minutes after leaving Victoria, B.C. It was flown by Harold [sic] Walker, T. H. Cressy being the mechanic....

On this inaugural trip the passengers were the popular Mayor of Vancouver, L. D. Taylor; Mayor and Mrs. Carl Pendray, of Victoria; J. E. Eve, President of B.C. Airways; G. A. Cameron, Secretary; J. H. Beatty, newly elected M.L.A. for Victoria; Major Bertram Taylor, Fred McGregor, F. J. Merrimen, of Victoria, and P. C. Rawlings, of Vancouver.[9]

It was, of course, meant to be a festive occasion; but a near tragedy occurred soon after the landing. For this reason, Ted Cressy remembers the day very clearly. He had flown over to the Vancouver Lansdowne field earlier with Hal Wilson in an Eaglerock to make sure the field was in suitable condition for a landing in the Trimotor.

When we got there, the grass was about three feet high; it was in no shape for what was supposed to be a first sked [scheduled] run. So we phoned Alderman Dean of the municipal Airport Committee, and they got cracking and had it cut.

When we went over in the Trimotor on the 24th, we found they'd cut the hay all right, but they had piled it in stooks and it was a little tricky to find a clear run for the landing. Also, I remember, we had to time our arrival so that it didn't co-incide with a race at the race track. Anyway, we taxied up to where the crowd was waiting. They were

A B.C. Airways Ltd. Alexander Eaglerock taking off from Lansdowne field, Victoria, 1928.

Ted Cressy outside the B.C. Airways' hangar at Lansdowne field, Victoria.

Ted Cressy, B.C. Airways' chief engineer, standing beside a Fairchild.

The latest in passenger comfort in 1928. Interior of the Ford trimotor. The wicker chairs had the advantage, for the operator, of being light and, for the passenger, of being comfortable.

The B.C. Airways' Driggs Dart taking part in the May 24, 1928, Victoria Day parade in Victoria.

J. ALLEN, DAVE PARKER COLLECTION

Herald Walker and Ted Cressy brought the brand-new Ford-Stout trimotor back from the Dearborn factory to another enthusiastic welcome from the public at Lansdowne field, Vancouver.

J. H. A. CHAPMAN, PABC

Victoria's elite turned out to greet the Ford
trimotor on its arrival at Lansdowne Field, July 23 1928.

T. H. CRESSY

The Vancouver branch of the Aero Club of
B.C., Lansdowne Field, Vancouver, 1930. Left
to right, standing: Frank Gilbert, Claire Dobbin,
Hal Wilson, Bill Bolton, Don Lawson, Gordon
Ballentine, George Lothian, Finny Maggar; front
row: Frank Dobbin, George Fox, ? Douglas, ?
Grabbstrom, unidentified.

GORDON PETERS COLLECTION, RBCM

B.C. Airways Aviation School's first building at Lansdowne field, Victoria, 1928.

MAURICE McGREGOR

Ernest Eve, President of B.C. Airways, left, and Herald Walker, the pilot, in the cockpit of the Ford trimotor.

PABC

The Alaska-Washington Airways of B.C.'s Fairchild 71, CF-AJP. Hal Wilson acted as pilot while the company waited for Gordon MacKenzie to earn his Canadian pilot's licence.

The Kreuzer trimotor brought up from Seattle in an attempt to revive B.C. Airways' scheduled passenger runs.

A young Maurice McGregor beside an Alexander Eaglerock, Lansdowne field, Victoria, winter 1928-29.

MAURICE McGREGOR PHOTOS

In 1927, the Department of National Defence's report on civil aviation listed 20 commercial companies operating in Canada. By 1930, the numbers had swelled to more than 100. The future looked so promising that even a firm like Sprott Shaw, hitherto renowned for its secretarial training institutions, diversified into aviation with a flying training school. Then, on October 29, the Wall Street stock market collapsed and Sprott Shaw's aviation enterprise went the way of many other contemporary aviation ventures. This photograph of a Waco 10 was taken at Lansdowne Field, Vancouver.

MAURICE McGREGOR

good this time—nobody rushed at us. When the machine came to a stop, I told everyone to sit tight, opened the door and stepped down. The door had to be swung back and locked into a latch on the fuselage and, as I turned to do this, Louis Taylor, the Mayor of Vancouver, jumped down and ran forward between the fuselage and the undercarriage towards the crowd in front of the machine. As I turned back to pull the passenger steps out from under the jump seat by the door, I saw him—but too late. Hal had already switched off the engines, but the props were still turning and, on just about the last turn, the one on the port wing whacked him right on the head.[10]

Mayor Taylor was seriously injured; his skull was fractured, but he made a complete recovery. Don MacLaren recalls that some politicians were as popular then as they are now. "Mayor Taylor ran underneath there while the prop was still going and it sliced the top of his head, you know, and [knocked] him unconscious. They said if he'd had an ounce more brains he'd have been a dead man."[11]

In any event, the club now had a suitable field from which to operate. Officially, it was known as the Vancouver Branch of the Aero Club of British Columbia, and it started off with two DH-60 Moths, G-CAKH and G-CAKW, donated by the Dominion government. P. A. (Percy) Hainstock was the first instructor and W. T. (Bill) Bolton the first engineer.[12]

The third licenced airfield in British Columbia was officially opened and dedicated by Lieutenant-Governor R. Randolph Bruce at Grand Forks on May 9, 1929. The occasion was marked by a fly-in. Nick Mamer of Spokane landed his Ford Trimotor, and he was followed by a Waco 10 and an International biplane named *City of Spokane*. In all, a total of 12 aircraft visited Grand Forks on opening day.

Apparently, the Grand Forks airfield resulted mainly from the efforts of one man, Bill Euerby, an engineer with the CPR. At the time, most pilots flying east from Vancouver landed first at Merritt, then at Penticton, both of which had serviceable though unlicenced fields. From there on, the next reasonable landing was in Cranbrook, a long way if the weather turned sour. Grand Forks was just about the right distance but, apart from cultivated fields, there were no satisfactory landings.

More or less single-handedly, Bill Euerby set out to rectify this. Over a period of years, "He cleared brush, rocks, trees and bunch grass and then levelled a runway using shovel, pick, axe and wheelbarrow." When, finally, the airfield was officially opened he set off for Missouri,

Nick Mamer with his Ford trimotor, *City of Spokane*, at the opening of Grand Forks airport, May 9, 1929.

HENRY STEVENSON

where he took flying lessons and earned his commercial licence before returning to fly out of Grand Forks.[13]

Meanwhile, back in Victoria the people were delighted with their new airline, which was gaining attention across the country. But the operating crews were less sanguine. The two Eve brothers, Ernie and Cecil, were excellent promoters, but when it came to operating an airline it was a different story. Hal Wilson describes them as "aviation enthusiasts but their practical knowledge of aviation was nil."[14] Both were over 40 years old, and Hal had what he considered the unenviable task of teaching them to fly. According to Ted Cressy, he was not entirely successful.

... because any time Ernie flew, two of Gabriel's angels were watching over him, one on each wing. He landed in more fields, false-landed in more fields than any 10 pilots in B.C. In fact, one time he came in on Lansdowne and we had a big hedge, with a fairly heavy fence at the end of it. Ernie, having no brakes, lands too long, runs right into this hedge, and the propeller just turns slowly around and over the fence, and didn't break the prop and only scratched the lower cowling. Any other man would have written the machine off.[15]

Cressy sums it up by saying that though both men were mature, they still thought they were 18; and, like some teen-aged drivers, they thought no accident could ever happen to them or their airline. They do not appear to have been unduly greedy; simply enthusiastic businessmen with rosy visions of uninterrupted scheduled flights at a time when the technology wasn't available to fulfil their dreams.

During the first few days of the tri-city service, Wilson flew with Walker as co-pilot. When he was checked out, he flew the Victoria-Vancouver run and Walker the Victoria-Seattle one. Anyone wanting to fly from Vancouver to Seattle or vice versa, had first to come to Victoria and change planes. From the beginning, there was friction between the pilots and management. Cecil Eve was the business manager and he was over-booking flights. The Trimotor had seats for 14 passengers, but he maintained they could carry more if the aircraft did not have full gas tanks. On occasions they were taking off with 17 passengers. As Wilson points out, this, while it might not mean an overload, presented other problems:

I had an unfortunate experience on one occasion when on taking off at Vancouver, I found the elevator trim exceedingly difficult to move. The aircraft had been trimmed too tail-heavy and I was unable to crank the trim due to this additional human freight strap-hanging on the trim rod, which traversed the length of the fuselage about four inches from the top of the cabin.[16]

This incident led to something of a confrontation between the two pilots and management. Cecil Eve conceded and, after that, they only carried seated passengers. But the other problem, weather limits, wasn't resolved. Characteristically, the west-coast climate provides a great deal of fog, low cloud and drizzle. By 1928, pilots without blind-flying instruments or radio aids had learned how to handle these conditions in flying boats and floatplanes over water: they flew until the weather forced them to land; then taxied until the visibility improved. On wheels, this was obviously impossible; but the Eve brothers put pressure on the pilots to keep flying in marginal weather.

The Trimotor began its scheduled flights on August 16. On August 25, Herald Walker, together with co-pilot R. L. Carson and five passengers,[17] took off from Victoria for Seattle. About an hour later, he crashed in the sea off Port Townsend, Washington. Everyone on board was killed; though, in this case, the accident doesn't seem to have resulted from any pressure by the Eve brothers. Wilson describes what happened:

...we got a telegram giving us the weather, and it was not very good. Walker had decided not to go when a passenger by the name of Scott said to him that he had been flying with Imperial Airways when you couldn't see your hand in front of your face. He said, "What's the matter with you? Can't you people fly an airplane?" And Walker said, "Get in." And they took off.

There was a big bank of fog down there at Port Townsend, and that's where they probably came to grief. As it cleared, we went to look for them and we didn't see anything, but we did find out from a fisherman that he had seen an airplane doing a violent turn and the wing tip hit the water and the airplane cartwheeled into the water. This was verified later on by a fisherman bringing up part of the undercarriage.[18]

Although Cecil Eve withdrew from any further participation in aviation, Ernest kept trying to keep the operation going; first with another Ford Trimotor from Seattle; then with a much smaller Trimotor called a Kreuzer, which had two Kinner engines outboard and a Leblond in the nose, and carried six passengers. But he lacked the finances, and now the support of the Victoria business community — who, like Cecil, had become discouraged — and these two brief attempts at a revival failed. The loss of the Ford, with its resultant fatalities, spelled the end

of the first scheduled airline on the west coast, and of British Columbia Airways. The two Eaglerocks were sold to the Vancouver Aero Club, and the Dart to the Sprott-Shaw aviation school (diversifying from their more familiar secretarial school), whose pilot Ted Luke, spun in and wrote it off on his first attempt to fly it.

During the short career of the Trimotor "1,292 paid passengers were carried between the three cities: Vancouver and Victoria supplying an estimated 75% of the traffic. Rates were $11.00 one-way or $20.00 return. In addition mail was carried, the company having its own five-cent air mail stamp, depicting a multi-engined aircraft in flight...."[19] (The federal postal service was not in the airmail business at this time, and they had no issue of air mail stamps.)

While the company lasted little more than a year, it trained a number of pilots, among whom was Maurice McGregor who was to become one of British Columbia's truly outstanding commercial pilots. He made the transition from barnstorming, through bush flying to airline flying; eventually becoming a senior executive in both Trans Canada Airlines and Canadian Pacific Airlines, and offers some very significant and interesting material for the future.

Six months after the Trimotor went down, the Victoria Aero Club Moth, flown by A. W. Carter, crash landed, putting Carter into hospital and destroying the machine. Some sporadic flying continued at the Lansdowne field by a company, Vancouver Island Airways, started by Maurice McGregor, as a flying school; but problems developed when residents in the neighbourhood of Lansdowne field began to object to the noise. "People complained their babies couldn't sleep,"[20] McGregor recalls and, in 1931, the field was closed down. A year later a new field was being used on Gordon Head, now the site of the University of Victoria.

In Vancouver, the Aero Club instructor, Percy Hainstock, was killed in an accident in 1929 and, after some hesitation, Hal Wilson accepted the vacancy. But he was still hoping to become an airline pilot, and when he was offered a temporary job, by an American company who had formed a new Canadian subsidiary, Alaska-Washington Airways of B.C., to pick up the operations of B.C. Airways on the tri-city service, he accepted. Their first aircraft was a Fairchild 71, CF-AJP. An American pilot, Gordon K. MacKenzie had been promised the job, but he lacked a Canadian licence and Wilson was taken on for the six weeks it took MacKenzie to get his licence.

This accomplished, MacKenzie took over and Wilson became the reserve pilot, flying one day a week. A few weeks later, in February 1930, MacKenzie took off on a foggy morning from English Bay in Vancouver, hit a buoy and crashed. The aircraft needed extensive repairs and Wilson was laid off. He was bitter about it because "it was the second time I had been 'crashed' out of a job."[21] Somewhat reluctantly, he returned to the Aero Club and stayed on as its chief instructor for the next ten years, earning himself a reputation as the most talented and competent instructor in western Canada — if not in the whole country. Ted Cressy also worked for Alaska Washington for a few months before joining another newly-formed aviation firm in Vancouver with the curious name of the Air Land Manufacturing Company. He was to have some remarkable experiences with this company during the next two years.

That brings us to the end of our period, a period with all the elements of human endeavour: success, failure, tragedy and comedy. It is an historian's cliché to claim that the period he or she is writing about was an era of unprecedented change. In this case, there is at least some merit to the claim because heavier-than-air flying had no precedent before 1903; and the progress from the kite-like contraption of bamboo, cloth and wire Charlie Hamilton flew in Minoru Park in 1910, to the enclosed cockpit and relatively comfortable cabin in an all-metal fuselage of the Trimotor Hal Wilson and Hal Walker flew a mere 18 years later, is certainly remarkable.

What is equally remarkable is society's perception of aviation during this period. At first, people regarded airplanes as toys; exciting and fascinating to watch because they represented the reality of a dream that was immemorial: the ability to fly. Yet no one seemed to take them seriously; they were still a stunt, or a toy. Then, in 1909, Louis Blériot flew across the English Channel and perhaps for the first time people perceived aircraft as something more than a toy. Perhaps, although it seemed far-fetched at the time, it could be used as a weapon, and the Royal Navy might no longer be quite such an invincible safeguard against aggression.

This realization was, of course, reinforced when World War I began, though even then there was considerable inertia, particularly amongst the military leaders of the time. By 1916, the air battles, or dogfights, on the Western Front had begun to have an impact on perceptions; but the actual turning point came in May 1917, when the Germans, with what seemed then to be giant Gotha bombers, attacked England. Not only the casualties and damage inflicted by these attacks, but the sense of vulnerability had a powerful effect on people. From then on, aircraft were seen primarily as weapons.

When World War I ended, there was a period of ambivalence. Because of a revulsion to anything military, there was something of a retreat to the toy perception: the Aerial League exhibition meets in Vancouver and Victoria in 1919 were, once again, stunts. Then came barnstorming, in which the purpose was to carry passengers; but even here, it was not for utilitarian purposes; it was for the thrill of the experience. Some time was to pass before any perception of the aircraft as a practical vehicle to move people and materials more rapidly than they had ever been moved before began to emerge.

The most recognizable turning point can be identified as the day in May 1927 when a slim and handsome young American, Charles Lindbergh, took off solo in a single-engined monoplane from New York and landed 33 hours later in Paris. The symbolic effect on people can hardly be exaggerated. Almost overnight, aircraft were now perceived as a practical means of transport over land or ocean, and over very long distances. An airplane was no longer only a toy or a weapon — it was also a vehicle with all the potential, and much more, of an automobile, a train or a ship.

Lindbergh's accomplishment was a milestone and, in Canada, it coincided with a rising economy and was followed by some of the accomplishments that began to make Canadian bush-flying crews famous throughout the world. One flight, in particular, made the headlines. On August 28, C. H (Punch) Dickins, in a Western Canada Airways Fokker Super Universal, left Winnipeg with Colonel C. D. H. MacAlpine, president of the mining company, Dominion Explorers; Richard Pearce, editor of the *Northern Miner*; and air engineer, W. B. Nadin — and headed north. The route he took is outlined in the DND report for 1928:

The aircraft left Winnipeg on August 28 and flew to Norway House; from Norway

House along the Nelson River to Jackfish Islands, thence to Churchill on Hudson bay; from Churchill along the shores of Hudson bay to Mistake Bay and Corbet Inlet to Chesterfield Inlet, and west to Baker Lake, north of latitude 64. From Baker Lake west and south, over the Barren Lands following the course of the Dubawnt River as far as Wholediah; west over the height of land to Stony Rapids on Lake Athabaska, and onwards west and north to Fort Smith on the Slave River; returning by Fort Chipewyn, Stony Rapids, Reindeer Lake, Cold Lake, The Pas and south to Winnipeg.[22]

Dickins flew 3,960 miles (6370 km) in 12 days, a good deal of it over unexplored and unmapped territory. More importantly, for the first time he had traversed the forbidding Barrens. The impact of this flight on Canadians was almost as powerful as Lindbergh's conquest of the Atlantic, and aviation began to expand rapidly. DND Reports listed "Firms chiefly operating aircraft." In 1927 there were 20; in 1928, 53; and by 1929, 81.[23] It looked as though aviation was going to make giant strides within two or three years—until the Wall Street stockmarket collapsed in October 1929.

A year earlier, journalist F. Smith had made a surprisingly accurate forecast just after the B.C. Airways scheduled service had been inaugurated:

Thus Vancouver aviation history opens with four round trip daily services. How much additional history will be written in the next two or three years is difficult to predict. It seems logical that there should be an extension of sea plane services to points on the Island and north along the coast, and ultimately a connection with the East, perhaps via Edmonton and Jasper. However, judging from the trend of present events, it seems probable that Vancouver will be linked to a well developed air system extending from Southern California to Alaska before the extension of air services westward from Montreal will have time to reach the coast.[24]

He was right about the east-west route. Eleven years were to pass before, on April 2, 1939, the first commercial, passenger-carrying aircraft, a Trans Canada Airlines Lockheed 14H which had taken off from Montreal the day before, landed in Vancouver—the beginning of a consistent trans-continental air service. Canada finally had an airline of its own.

But that's a story for another day.

Notes

CHAPTER 1, pp. 15-22

1 G. A. Fuller, J. A. Griffin and K. M. Molson, *125 Years of Canadian Aeronautics: A Chronology, 1840-1965*, 1983, p. 13.

2 Frank W. Goodale, "Reminiscences of an Early Bird," *The Rotarian*, April, 1933. Reprinted as "Reminiscences of an Early Dirigible Pilot," *Canadian Aviation Historical Society Journal*, Vol. 23, No. 1, Spring 1985, pp. 25-28,.

3 Harold E. Morehouse, "The Flying Pioneers: Charles K. Hamilton," *Journal of the American Aviation Historical Society*, Vol. 14, No. 3, Fall 1969, p. 159.

4 The Vancouver *Daily News-Advertiser*, March 26, 1910, p. 11.

5 Vancouver *Daily Province*, March 26, 1910, p. 21.

6 Frank H. Ellis, "Pioneer Flying in British Columbia: 1910-1924," *British Columbia Historical Quarterly*, October 1939, p. 230.

7 The Vancouver *Daily World*, March 24, 1910, pp. 3-4.

8 The Vancouver *Daily News-Advertiser*, March 26, 1910, p. 12.

CHAPTER 2, pp. 23-32

1 Frank H. Ellis, *Canada's Flying Heritage*, 1954, p. 23.

2 *Ibid.*, p. 24.

3 *Ibid.*

4 *Ibid.*, p. 25.

5 The Victoria *Daily Times*, September 9, 1910, pp. 1 & 16.

6 The Victoria *Daily Colonist*, September 25, 1910, p. 3.

7 F. H. Ellis, *Canada's Flying Heritage*, p. 28.

8 The Victoria *Daily Colonist*, June 2, 1911, p. 9.

9 The Kamloops *Inland Sentinel*, June 30, 1911, p. 1.

10 F. H. Ellis, *Canada's Flying Heritage*, p. 31.

11 The Calgary *Daily Herald*, August 8, 1911, p. 1.

12 *Ibid.*, August 12, 1911, p. 1.

13 The Victoria *Daily Colonist*, September 24, 1910, p. 2.

14 The Vancouver *Daily News-Advertiser*, May 7, 1911, p. 21.

15 F. H. Ellis, *Canada's Flying Heritage*, pp. 32-33.

CHAPTER 3, pp. 33-44

1 The Vancouver *Daily News-Advertiser*, April 15, 1911, p. 1.

2 *Ibid.*

3 The Victoria *Daily Colonist*, April 16, 1911, p. 1.

4 The Vancouver *Daily Province*, April 17, 1911, p. 2.

5 *Ibid.*, April 18, 1911, p. 12.

6 The Vancouver *Daily News-Advertiser*, April 14, 1911, p. 13.

7 The Vancouver *Daily World*, April 15, 1911, p. 4.

8 The Vancouver *Daily Province*, April 15, 1911, p. 34.

9 The Victoria *Daily Colonist*, May 31, 1911, p. 9.

10 The Victoria *Daily Times*, June 1, 1911, p. 7.

11 *Ibid.*

12 The Vancouver *Daily World*, April 15, 1912, p. 14.

13 C. R. Roseberry, *Glenn Curtiss: Pioneer of Flight*, 1972, p. 228.

14 The Vancouver *Daily Province*, April 15, 1912, p. 30.

15 *Ibid.*, April 25, 1912, p. 10.

16 *Ibid.*, May 6, 1912, p. 11.

17 *Ibid.*

18 The Vancouver *Daily World*, May 8, 1912, p. 4.

19 Newspapers described it as a Wright biplane, but photographs show it to have a front-mounted engine with a single propeller; Fuller, *et al.*, describe it as a "Gage tractor biplane." See: the Vancouver *Daily Province*, May 7, 1912, p. 11; the Vancouver *Daily News-Advertiser*, May 26, 1912, p. 2; and Fuller, *et al.*, *Canadian Aeronautics: A Chronology, 1840-1965*, p. 51.

20 Henry R. Palmer, Jr., "Lighter-Than-Air Flight in America: 1784-1910," *Journal of the American Aviation Historical Society*, Vol. 24, No. 3, Fall 1979, pp. 162-186. To paraphrase, in the early nineteenth century, ballooning was known as "aerostation," and was generally recognized as a science. Consequently, practitioners of balloon ascents and parachute drops adopted the title "Professor."

21 The Vancouver *Daily World*, May 25, 1912, p. 10.

22 The Vancouver *Daily Province*, May 31, 1912, p. 22.

23 *Ibid.*, June 3, 1912, p. 2.

CHAPTER 4, pp. 45-60

[1] The Armstrong *Advertiser*, July 4, 1912. p. 1.

[2] *Ibid.*

[3] *Ibid.*

[4] The Nelson *Daily News*, September 20, 1912, p. 8.
Ibid., September 21, p. 1.
Ibid., September 23, pp. 1, 3-4.
Ibid., September 24, p. 1.
Ibid., September 25, p. 1.
Ibid., September 26, p. 1.
Ibid., September 27, p. 1.
Ibid., September 28, pp. 1 & 4.

[5] Personal interviews, January, 1989.

[6] The Vancouver *Daily Province*, August 1, 1913, p. 12.

[7] The Victoria *Daily Colonist*, August 6, 1913, p. 10.

[8] The Victoria *Daily Times*, August 6, 1913, p. 16.

[9] The Victoria *Daily Colonist*, August 7, 1913, pp. 2 & 10.

[10] The Chilliwack *Progress*, July 9, 1914, pp. 1 & 9.

[11] In the trade jargon called Chinook, Chahko-Mika meant "All of you come."

[12] Nelson *Daily News*, July 14, 1914, p. 1.

[13] *Ibid.*, July 15, p. 1.

[14] *Ibid.*, July 18, p. 1.

[15] Ellis, p. 104.

CHAPTER 5, pp. 61-70

[1] Robert B. Johnston, "The Wrights: The First Aeronautical Engineers," *Journal of the American Aviation Historical Society*, Vol. 23, No. 4, Winter 1978, p. 303.

[2] Sherwood Harris, *The First to Fly: Aviation's Pioneer Days*, 1970, pp. 159-61.

[3] Thomas W. Ray, "First Year of Naval Aviation," *Journal of the American Aviation Historical Society*, Vol. 12, No. 3, Fall 1967, p. 205.

[4] J. H. Parkin, *Bell and Baldwin: Their Development of Aerodromes and Hydrodromes at Baddeck, Nova Scotia*, Toronto, 1964, p. 35.

[5] J. H. Parkin, *Bell and Baldwin*, and C. R. Roseberry, *Glenn Curtiss*, both deal with the activities of the A.E.A. in depth.

[6] These descriptions of the respective control systems of the Wright and Curtiss machines are generalizations. Over the years in question, a good deal of experimentation was still in progress. For example, an article in the *Scientific American* (Vol. CIII, No. 17, October 22, 1910, pp. 315-17) reports that "The tail surface is fixed," on the Curtiss, as does C. H. Gibbs-Smith (*Aviation*, 1970, p. 144); whereas Beckwith Havens (see note 10), describes the advantage gained when the front elevator — of inter-connected front-and-rear horizontal elevators — was disconnected.

Similarly with the Wright machine: before 1909 it had elevators only on the front boom. In 1909, French-built Wrights had first a fixed tailplane behind the rudder, then experimental inter-connected front-and-rear elevators; finally, the Wrights themselves discarded the front elevators and settled for a single tail-mounted elevator in 1910.
More confusing still was, or were, the Wright's wing-warping and rudder controls. While the *Scientific American* article has the wing-warping controlled by the articulating joint on top of the right-hand lever — and the rudder by a fore-and-aft movement — Thomas Ray in his article, (see note 3) has the wing-warping controlled by a fore-and-aft motion of the right-hand lever, and "If additional rudder control was needed . . . the operator simply moved a handle hinged at the top of the wing-warping and rudder control stick in the direction of the turn" (p. 205). In fact, the Wrights had two different systems; so both the above descriptions are correct. Either way, I would contend that the Curtiss machine was easier to control than the Wright.
For anyone interested in pursuing the mechanics of these control systems, by far the best place to start is C. H. Gibbs-Smith, *The Wright Brothers: A Brief Account of their Work, 1899-1911*, 1987.

[7] Thomas Ray, "First Year of Naval Aviation," p. 206.

[8] C. H. Gibbs-Smith, *A History of Flying*, 1953, pp. 237-38 and C. R. Roseberry, *Glenn Curtiss*, p. 97.

[9] Sherwood Harris, *The First to Fly*, p. 226.

[10] *Ibid.*

[11] "The Deperdussin Monoplane," *Flight*, No. 33, Vol. III, August 19, 1911, p. 713.

CHAPTER 6, pp. 71-80

[1] S. F. Wise, *Canadian Airmen and the First World War: The Official History of the Royal Canadian Air Force*, Vol. 1, 1980, p. 10.

[2] *Ibid.*

[3] *Ibid.*, p. 13.

[4] *Ibid.*, pp. 26-27.

[5] *Ibid.*, p. 27.

[6] *Ibid.*

[7] Bartlett Gould, "The Burgess Story," *Journal of the American Aviation Historical Society*, Vol. 11, No. 4, Winter 1966, p. 274.

[8] F. H. Ellis, "Canada's First Military Aeroplane," *The Beaver*, Autumn 1974, p. 49.

[9] S. F. Wise, *Canadian Airmen . . .*, p. 28.

[10] F. H. Ellis, "Canada's First . . .," p. 50.

[11] H. A. Farr, "Canada's Air Force and the World War," *Canadian Air Review*, Vol. 1, No. 5, July 1928, p. 13.

[12] S. F. Wise, *Canadian Airmen . . .*, p. 28.

[13] *Ibid.*, p. 29.

14 Geoffrey Norris, *The Royal Flying Corps: A History*, 1965, p. 16.

15 S. F. Wise, *Canadian Airmen . . .*, p. 15.

16 J. A. Chamier, *The Birth of the Royal Air Force: The Early History and Experiences of the Flying Services*, 1943, p. 5.

17 G. Norris, *The Royal Flying Corps . . .*, p. 25.

18 *Ibid.*

19 *Ibid.*, pp. 28-29.

20 J. M. Bruce, *The Aeroplanes of the Royal Flying Corps*, 1982, p. 199.

21 G. Norris, *The Royal Flying Corps . . .*, p. 29.

22 Robert Casari, "The First 59," *Journal of the American Aviation Historical Society*, Vol. 16, No. 1, 1st Quarter, 1971, p. 11.

23 *Ibid.*

24 G. Norris, *The Royal Flying Corps . . .*, p. 31.

CHAPTER 7, pp. 81-104

1 F. H. Ellis, *Canada's Flying Heritage*, p. 110.

2 W. P. Anderson, "Early Aviation in B. C.: 1910-1931," *Canadian Aviation Historical Society Journal*, Vol. 21, No. 2, Summer, 1983. p. 38.

3 F. H. Ellis, *Canada's Flying Heritage*, p. 114.

4 K. M. Molson and H. A. Taylor, *Canadian Aircraft Since 1909*, 1982, p. 372.

5 F. H. Ellis, *Canada's Flying Heritage*, p. 115.

6 The Vancouver *Daily Province*, January 14, 1916, p. 4.

7 *Aerial Age Weekly*, July 12, 1915, in Molson and Taylor, *Canadian Aircraft*, p. 373.

8 British Columbia Register of Companies, File 2962.

9 British Columbia Aviation Limited Prospectus, December 15, 1915 (Royal British Columbia Museum, Historical Collections).

10 Molson and Taylor, *Canadian Aircraft . . .*, p. 374.

11 F. H. Ellis, *Canada's Flying Heritage*, p. 115. However, Clarence Hilborn came from Quesnel, B. C., and there is evidence to suggest that he was never in the United States before the end of World War I.

12 *Ibid.*

13 Molson and Taylor, *Canadian Aircraft . . .*, p. 374.

14 "The Avro Biplane," *Flight*, No. 44, Vol. III, November 4, 1911, p. 951. "The New Avro Biplane," *Flight*, No. 13, Vol. IV, March 30, 1912, pp. 281-83. "Hydro-Aeroplane Experiments at Barrow," *Flight*, No. 16, Vol. IV, April 20, 1912, p. 359. "Designer's Autographs in Wing Sections," *Flight*, No. 42, Vol. IV, October 19, 1912, p. 944. I am indebted to Geoffrey Rowe for this information.

15 Molson and Taylor, *Canadian Aircraft . . .*, pp. 382-83.

16 *Ibid.*, p. 383.

17 C. R. Roseberry, *Glenn Curtiss: Pioneer of Flight*, 1972, p. 227.

18 Molson and Taylor's account, although the source is not cited, of this first flight of the H-1 appears to come from a three-page, typewritten, undated and unsigned "manuscript" by Henry Hoffar, a copy of which is in the collections of the British Columbia Aviation Museum, Sidney, B.C. This paper, which gives the date of construction as 1915, was presented at a meeting of the Coal Harbour Old Timers, *circa* 1976, by Henry's son, Norman Hoffar, and published as an article, "Vancouver's First Aeroplane," *Raincoast Chronicles*, No. 9, [1981], more than 50 years after the events described, and I suspect memory, after this time span, may have simplified matters.

19 This confusion seems to have originated with James Hoffar. In a letter (dated August 8, 1953) to Major J. S. Matthews, Vancouver City Archivist, Frank Ellis has this to say: "Now for the Hoffar date. Yes, July 17, 1917 is correct [*sic*]. When I mentioned to you that I THOUGHT it was in March 1914 I was only repeating what Hoffar had wished me to think, as at the time I was under the belief that he might be eligible as a member in the Early Birds organization, by virtue of any flights he had made prior to August 4, 1914. However when I began to dig into things, I quickly learned he was way off the beam in his dates, kidding me I suppose" (City of Vancouver Archives).

20 The Vancouver *Sun*, January 16, 1916, p. 10.

21 E. L. MacLeod, "Early Flying in British Columbia," *Canadian Aviation Historical Society Journal*, Vol. 12, No. 4, Winter 1974, p. 100. However, there appears to be no supporting evidence for this report.

22 The Vancouver *Sun*, Magazine Section, July 25, 1953, p. 17.

23 The Vancouver *Daily Province*, July 10, 1917, p. 18.

24 Henry Hoffar "Manuscript," p. 2.

25 Alan Sullivan, *Aviation in Canada: 1917-1918*, 1919, p. 15.

26 *Ibid.*, p. 21.

27 *Ibid.*, pp. 44 & 48.

28 *Ibid.*, p. 49.

29 J. R. Lincke, *Jenny Was No Lady*, 1970, p. 167.

30 F. Kostenuk and J. Griffin, *RCAF: Squadron Histories and Aircraft: 1924-1968*, 1977, p. 1.

31 *Ibid.*, p. 2.

32 *Ibid.*

33 *Ibid.*

34 Alan Sullivan, *Aviation in Canada*, p. 125.

CHAPTER 8, pp. 105-112

1 "Report of the Forest Branch, Department of Lands," *British Columbia Legislative Assembly Sessional Papers*, 1919, Vol. II, pp. 5-7.

2 John Parminter, "Guardians in the Sky: Aircraft and their Use in Forestry in B. C., 1918-1926," *Whistle Punk*, Spring 1986, p. 3.

3 *Ibid.*, p. 3.

4 K. M. Molson and H. A. Taylor, *Canadian Aircraft*... , p. 382, rated the Roberts engine at 75 horsepower.

5 J. Parminter, "Guardians in the Sky," p. 4.

6 K. M. Molson and H. A. Taylor, *Canadian Aircraft*... , p. 384.

7 The confusion is understandable. On August 27, 1918, p. 2, the Vancouver *Daily World* carried a photograph of the H-2 and the caption reported that it "Made a successful flight last Sunday [August 25] and will be flown by Captain McKenzie from this city to Victoria," and that the aircraft "... was taken over by P. Caverhill of the Forestry Branch on behalf of the government." In the August 29 issue of the same newspaper, there were two reports: one on page 1; the other on page 14. The first listed only McKenzie as the pilot on the Sunday flights; the second, that "... last Sunday J. B. Hoffar made the first flight... [and] Capt. McKenzie then took the machine up."

8 V. A. Bishop personal diaries and *RNAS-RAF Pilot's Flying Log Book*, 1917-1919 (V. A. Bishop Estate).

9 J. Parminter, "Guardians in the Sky," p. 4.

10 The Vancouver *Daily Province*, September 4, 1918, p. 1.

11 J. Parminter, "Guardians in the Sky," p. 4.

12 Henry Hoffar "Manuscript," p. 3.

13 An advertisement by United Aircraft of British Columbia Limited offered a landplane for $2,500 f.o.b. Vancouver. Victoria *Daily Colonist*, May 18, 1919, p. 27. This price soon dropped as more war-surplus JN-4s came on the market.

CHAPTER 9, pp. 113-132

1 G. A. Fuller, J. A. Griffin and K. M. Molson, *125 Years of Canadian Aeronautics: A Chronology*, 1983, p. 95.

2 The Vancouver *Daily Province*, May 19, 1919, p. 7.

3 *Ibid.*, May 13, 1919, p. 5.

4 The Vancouver *Daily World*, May 19, 1919, p. 3.

5 The Victoria *Daily Colonist*, May 20, 1919, p. 7.

6 *Ibid.*

7 The Vancouver *Daily World*, February 28, 1919, p. 1.

8 *Ibid.*, March 3, 1919, p. 1.

9 F. H. Ellis, *Canada's Flying Heritage*, 1954, p. 157.

10 The Vancouver *Daily Province*, May 17, 1919, p. 10.

11 The Vancouver *Daily World*, May 21, 1919, p. 1.

12 The Vancouver *Daily Province*, May 28, 1919, p. 6.

13 The Vancouver *Daily World*, June 2, 1919, p. 10.

14 F. H. Ellis, *Canada's Flying Heritage*, p. 179.

15 The Vancouver *Daily World*, August 4, 1919, pp. 1 & 16.

16 *Ibid.*, p. 16.

17 *Ibid.*, August 5, 1919, p. 1.

18 *Ibid.*, August 7, 1919, p. 1.

19 *Ibid.*

20 The Vernon *News*, August 14, 1919, p. 7.

21 F. H. Ellis, *Canada's Flying Heritage*, p. 179.

22 The Vancouver *Daily World*, August 8, 1919, p. 1.

23 The Golden *Star*, August 14, 1919, p. 1.

24 *Ibid.*

25 *Ibid.*

26 The Prince George *Citizen*, August 13, 1919, p. 1.

CHAPTER 10, pp. 133-154

1 F. H. Hitchins, *Air Board, Canadian Air Force and Royal Canadian Air Force*, 1972, p. 2.

2 D. Lovegrove, "The RCAF: 1918-1939—A Political History," *Canadian Aviation Historical Society Journal*, Vol. 25, No. 1, Spring 1987, pp. 4-5.

3 J. R. K. Main, *Voyageurs of the Air*, 1967, p. 28.

4 D. Lovegrove, "The RCAF: 1918-1929...," p. 5.

5 *Ibid.*

6 *Hansard*, Debates, House of Commons, Dominion of Canada, Session 1919, Vol. II, pp. 1864-5.

7 *Ibid.*, Vol. III, p. 2051.

8 *Ibid.*, p. 2052.

9 *Ibid.*, p. 2053.

10 *Ibid.*, p. 2058.

11 *Ibid.*, p. 2061.

12 F. H. Hitchins, *Air Board*... , p. 4.

13 *Ibid.*, p. 5.

14 S. Kostenuk and J. Griffin, *RCAF: Squadron Histories and Aircraft, 1924-1968*, 1977, p. 9.

15 *Hansard*, 1920 Session, Vol. V, p. 4553.

16 *Report of the Air Board*, 1921, p. 9-10.

17 *Hansard*, 1920 Session, Vol. V, p. 4554.

18 *Ibid.*

19 *Ibid.*, p. 4555.

20 F. H. Hitchins, *Air Board*... , p. 5-6.

21 *Ibid.*, p. 5.

22 S. Kostenuk and J. Griffin, *Squadron Histories*... , p. 9.

23 *The Magnificent Distances: Early Aviation in British Columbia, 1910-1940*, 1980, p. 15.

24 E. L. MacLeod, "Early Flying in British Columbia," *Canadian Aviation Historical Society Journal*, Vol. 12, No. 4, Winter 1974, p. 101.

25 Provincial Archives of British Columbia Transcript (E. L. MacLeod, interviewed by Paul Stoddart): Accession No. 3215, Tape No. 2, p. ah2-17. However, in his article, "Early Flying in British Columbia,"

MacLeod states that he assisted Hobbs in choosing the site for the base, but that it was MacLaurin "...who had played a key role at Ottawa in the planning stage of the Canadian Air Board, and had been allowed the privilege of choosing the base of his choice" (p. 101).

26 F. H. Hitchins, *Air Board...*, p. 34.

27 E. L. MacLeod, "Early Flying...," p. 101.

28 F. H. Hitchins, *Air Board...*, pp. 34-35.

29 *Ibid.*, p. 35.

30 F. H. Ellis, *Canada's Flying Heritage*, p. 187.

31 *Ibid.*, p. 190.

32 *Ibid.*

33 *Ibid.*, p. 191.

34 *Ibid.*

35 C. F. O'Brien, "Northwest Staging Route," *Alberta Historical Review*, Vol. 17, No. 4, Autumn 1969, p. 15.

36 F. H. Hitchins, *Air Board...*, p. 42.

37 *Ibid.*, p. 43.

38 *Ibid.*, p. 48.

39 *Ibid.*, p. 35.

40 The Victoria *Daily Times*, October 21, 1920, p. 7.

CHAPTER 11, pp. 155-170

1 John Stroud, "The Beginning of the Air Lines," *History of Aviation: Air Transport Before the Second World War*, p. 12.

2 *Ibid.*

3 *Ibid.*, p. 14.

4 John Stroud, "Opening up the Airways," *History of Aviation...*, p. 23.

5 The Victoria *Daily Times*, May 13, 1920, p. 5.

6 *Ibid.*, September 22, 1920, p. 12.

7 *Ibid.*, September 27, 1920, pp. 2 & 4.

8 *Ibid.*

9 J. R. Ellis, *The Canadian Civil Aircraft Register*, Fall 1972.

10 E. L. MacLeod, "Early Flying in British Columbia," p. 101.

11 *Ibid.*, p. 102.

12 *Ibid.*

13 *Ibid.*

14 *Ibid.*, p. 103.

15 Provincial Archives of British Columbia Transcript (E. L. MacLeod, interviewed by Paul Stoddart), Accession No. 3215, Tape No. 1, Track No. 1, p. 9.

16 *Sessional Papers*, "Report of the Forest Branch," Department of Lands, British Columbia, 1921, p. I 37.

17 PABC Transcript 3215, 2, 1, pp. ah2 & 7-8.

18 E. L. MacLeod, "Early Flying in British Columbia," p. 103.

19 P. Corley-Smith and D. Parker, *Helicopters: The British Columbia Story*, 1985, pp. 23-26.

20 PABC Transcript, No. 3215, 1, 2, p. 11.

21 E. L. MacLeod, "Early Flying...," p. 104.

22 A good overview of this subject is given in D. W. Thomson, *Skyview Canada: A Story of Aerial Photography in Canada*, 1975. Another good source is E. W. Stedman, *From Boxkite to Jet*, a Canadian War Museum Mercury Series publication, 1972.

23 PABC Transcript, No. 3215, 1, 2, p. 15.

24 E. L. MacLeod, "Early Flying...," p. 104.

25 *Ibid.*, p. 106.

26 The Forest Branch Report for 1922 talks of "The appalling loss by fire this year..." (*Sessional Papers*, p. L 47.)

27 *Sessional Papers*, 1922, Forest Branch Report, pp. L 51-52.

28 PABC Transcript 3215, 1, 2, p. 17.

29 E. L. MacLeod, "Early Flying...," p. 106.

CHAPTER 12, pp. 171-186

1 The Vancouver *Province*, September 12, 1922, p. 1.

2 *Ibid.*, September 13, 1922, p. 7.

3 *Ibid.*, p. 1.

4 F. H. Hitchins, *Air Board, Canadian Air Force and Royal Canadian Air Force*, p. 71.

5 J. M. Larson of New York had obtained the North American rights for Junkers. To minimize the German connection (post-war animosity still existed), he called the aircraft Junkers-Larson 6. However, except for the propeller, an American Hartzell, the aircraft was identical to the successful post-war German model, Junkers F-13 (see K. M. Molson, note 6).

6 C. E. Taylor, Imperial's western development manager, initiated this aviation "Division." The "Vick" was named after Taylor's daughter, Victoria, and the "René" after his secretary. In K. M. Molson, "Early Flying Along the Mackenzie: the 'René' and the 'Vic'," *Canadian Aviation Historical Society Journal*, Vol. 20. No. 2, Summer 1982, p. 44.

7 The story of this arduous operation—which culminated in the hand crafting of two propellers at Fort Simpson, using oak sleigh boards bonded with moosehide glue, by the air engineer Bill Hill and the Hudson's Bay post carpenter and cabinet maker Walter Johnson—is recounted in most Canadian aviation histories. Frank Ellis, in *Canada's Flying Heritage*, and in his articles, "Illustrious Twins..." (see note 9), and "The Birth of British Columbia Bush Flying," (*Northwest Digest*, February 1958), gives it full coverage, as does K. M. Molson in "Early Flying Along the Mackenzie" (see note 6).

8 E. L. MacLeod, "Early Flying in British Columbia," p. 107.

9 PABC Transcript No. 3215 (E. L. MacLeod, interviewed by Paul Stoddart), Tape 1, Track 2, p. 16.

10 F. H. Ellis, "Illustrious Twins Were RENE and VIC," *Canadian Aviation*, May 1945, p. 97. MacLeod recalls the pilot's name as McArdle. Both were almost certainly referring to W. H. McCardell, licence #118 (see, Molson, *The First 500 Canadian Civil Pilots*, CAHS, 1983, p. 22).

11 E. L. MacLeod, "Early Flying in British Columbia," pp. 106-7.

12 *Ibid.*, p. 107.

13 *Ibid.*, p. 108.

14 *Ibid.*, p. 107.

15 F. H. Ellis, "Illustrious Twins...", p. 97.

16 The Prince Rupert *Evening Empire*, April 27, 1924, p. 1.

17 A. J. Jackson, *British Civil Aircraft: 1919-59*, 1960, Vol. 2, p. 454. McKay erroneously describes it as the Vickers Vulcan, a very different aircraft (see note 18).

18 E. A. McKay, *A World to Conquer*, New York, 1981, p. 49.

19 L. E. Broome Diary, Part 2, p. 7 (E. L. MacLeod Estate).

20 *Ibid.*, p. 8.

21 *Ibid.*, p. 11.

22 *Ibid.*, p. 12.

23 *Ibid.*, p. 14.

15 K. M. Molson, *Pioneering in Air Transport*, 1974, p. 5.

16 *Ibid.*

17 "Report on Civil Aviation," *Report of the Department of National Defence*, 1927, p. 28.

18 K. M. Molson, *Pioneering in Canadian Air Transport*, p. 39.

19 *Ibid.*

20 PABC Transcript 3182, 2, 2, pp. 16-17.

21 Duffy, *et al.*, *Magnificent Distances*, p. 24.

22 Gordon Ballentine, "Those Early Boeing Boats," *Canadian Aviation Historical Society Journal*, Vol. 26, No. 2, Summer 1988, p. 50.

23 Gordon Ballentine, "Crash!" *Canadian Aviation Historical Society Journal*, Vol. 23, No. 3, Fall 1985. p. 87.

24 *Ibid.*

25 Duffy, *et al.*, *The Magnificent Distances*, pp. 26-29.

26 W. Kaye Lamb, *History of the Canadian Pacific Railway*, 1977, p. 356. See also: G. R. Stevens, *History of the Canadian National Railways*, 1973, p. 371.

27 *British Columbia Register of Companies*, File No. 9167.

28 A. H. Wilson, "Reminiscences of a West Coast Pilot," p. 67.

29 *Ibid.*

30 A. G. Sutherland, *Canada's Aviation Pioneers: 50 Years of McKee Trophy Winners*, 1978, p. 86.

CHAPTER 13, pp. 187-206

1 *The Timberman*, November 1925, p. 57.

2 *Ibid.*

3 H. A. Halliday, "Laurentide Air Service Limited: Commercial Pioneer," *Canadian Geographical Journal*, Vol. 80, No. 4, April, 1970, p. 110.

4 *Ibid.*, p. 115.

5 H. A. Halliday, "The First Twenty Years... The O. P. A. S.," *Canadian Aviation Historical Society Journal*, Vol. 12, No. 3, Fall 1974, pp. 70-71.

6 F. H. Ellis, *Canada's Flying Heritage*, p. 212.

7 *Ibid.*

8 S. F. Wise, *Canadian Airmen and the First World War*, 1980, p. 444.

9 PABC Transcript No. 3217 (D. R. MacLaren, interviewed by Paul Stoddart), Tape 1, Track 1, p. 2.

10 *Ibid.*

11 A. H. Wilson, "Reminiscences of a West Coast Pilot," *Canadian Aviation Historical Society Journal*, Vol. 3, No. 3, Fall 1965, p. 67.

12 PABC Transcript 3182 (H. E. Davenport, interviewed by Paul Stoddart), Tape 2, Track 2, p. 8.

13 Don MacLaren, Transcript 3217, 1, 1, p. 8.

14 Duffy, *et al.*, *The Magnificent Distances*, 1980, p. 25.

CHAPTER 14, pp. 207-224

1 PABC Transcript No. 3366 (T. H. Cressy, interviewed by D. N. Parker), Tape 1, Track 1, p. 13.

2 PABC Transcript No. 3218 (A. H. Wilson, interviewed by Paul Stoddart), Tape 1, Track 1, p. 19.

3 Personal interview, August 1989.

4 The Victoria *Daily Colonist*, July 24, 1928, p. 1.

5 PABC Transcript 3366, 1, 1, p. 15.

6 PABC Transcript 3217 (D. R. MacLaren, interviewed by Paul Stoddart), Tape 1, Track 1, p. 17.

7 "Light Aeroplane Clubs," *Report of the Department of National Defence*, 1927, p. 61.

8 A. H. Wilson, "Reminiscences of a West Coast Pilot," *Canadian Aviation Historical Society Journal*, Vol.3, No. 3, p. 68.

9 F. Smith, "The Air Traffic Situation On the Western Coast," *Canadian Air Review*, Vol. 1, No. 6, August 1928, pp. 16-17.

10 Personal interview, June 28, 1989.

11 PABC Transcript 3217, 2, 2, p. 4.

12 A. H. Wilson, "Reminiscences of a West Coast Pilot," p. 68.

13 Communicated by Henry Stevenson, who knows the Euerby family.

14 A. H. Wilson, "Reminiscences...", p. 67.

15 PABC Transcript 3366, Tape 1, Track 1, p. 5. (Nevertheless, by World War II, Ernest Eve was proficient enough to become an instructor in a Service Flying Training School, teaching all aspects of flying, including aerobatics.)

16 A. H. Wilson, "Reminiscences...", p. 68.

17 Hal Wilson, quoted in *Magnificent Distances*, cites five passengers; however, the Victoria *Daily Colonist* (August 26, 1928, p. 1) lists four, as does the Vancouver *Daily Province* (August 27, 1928, p. 1). They were: Mr. and Mrs. A. M. Scott, London, England; Dr. D. B. Holden, Victoria; and Thomas E. Lake, San Francisco.

18 Duffy, *et al.*, *The Magnificent Distances*, p. 38.

19 A. H. Wilson, "Reminiscences...", p. 68.

20 Personal interview, 1989.

21 A. H. Wilson, "Reminiscences...", p. 69.

22 "Commercial Aviation," *Report of the Department of National Defence*, 1928, p. 26.

23 *Ibid.*

24 F. Smith, "The Air Traffic Situation On the Western Coast," p. 17.

GERALD LUXTON

Bibliography

BOOKS

Bowers, P. *Boeing Aircraft Since 1916*. Putnam, Toronto, Ont., 1966.

Bruce, J. M. *The Aeroplanes of the Royal Flying Corps (Military Wing)*. Putnam, London, U.K., 1982.

Chamier, J. A. *The Birth of the Royal Air Force: The Early History and Experiences of the Flying Services*. Sir Isaac Pitman & Sons, Ltd., London, U.K., 1943.

Corley-Smith, P., and D. Parker. *Helicopters: The British Columbia Story*. CANAV Books, Toronto, Ont., 1985.

Davies, R. E. G. *A History of the World's Airlines*. Oxford University Press, London, U.K., 1964.

Downs, A., ed. *Pioneer Days in British Columbia*. Vol. 4, Heritage House, Vancouver, B.C., 1979.

Duffy, Dennis and Carol Crane, eds., commentary by David Parker. *The Magnificent Distances: Early Aviation in British Columbia, 1910-1940*. Sound Heritage Series No. 28, Provincial Archives of British Columbia, Victoria, B.C., 1980.

Ellis, F. H. *Canada's Flying Heritage*. University of Toronto Press, Toronto, Ont., 1954.

Ellis, J. R. *The Canadian Civil Air Register*. Canadian Aviation Historical Society, Willowdale, Ont., 1972-1975.

Fuller, G. A., J. A. Griffin and K. M. Molson. *125 Years of Canadian Aeronautics: A Chronology, 1840-1965*. Canadian Aviation Historical Society, Willowdale, Ont., 1983.

Gibbs-Smith, C. H. *A History of Flying*. B. T. Batsford Ltd., London, U.K., 1953.

———. *Aviation: An Historical Survey from its Origins to the End of World War II*. H.M.S.O., London, U.K., 1970.

———. *The Wright Brothers: A Brief Account of their Work, 1899-1911*. H.M.S.O., London, U.K., 1987.

Harris, Sherwood. *The First to Fly: Aviation's Pioneer Days*. Simon and Schuster, New York, NY, 1970.

Hitchins, F. H. *Air Board, Canadian Air Force and Royal Canadian Air Force*. Mercury Series: Canadian War Museum Paper No. 2, National Museums of Canada, Ottawa, Ont., 1972.

Jackson, A. J. *British Civil Aircraft: 1919-59*. Vol. 2, Putnam, London, U.K., 1960.

Kostenuk, F., and J. Griffin. *RCAF: Squadron Histories and Aircraft: 1924-1968*. Historical Publication 14, Canadian War Museum, published by Samuel Stevens Hakkert & Company, Toronto, Ont., 1977.

Lamb, W. Kaye. *History of the Canadian Pacific Railway*. Macmillan, New York, NY, 1977.

Lincke, J. R. *Jenny Was No Lady*. N. W. Norton Co., New York, NY, 1970.

Main, J. R. K. *Voyageurs of the Air*. Queen's Printer, Ottawa, Ont., 1967.

McFarland, M. W., ed. *The Papers of Orville and Wilbur Wright*. Vols. 1 and 2, Arno Press, New York, NY, 1972.

McKay, E. A. *A World to Conquer*. Arco Publishing, Inc., New York, NY, 1981.

Molson, K. M. *Pioneering in Air Transport*. J. M. Richardson & Sons, Winnipeg, Man., 1974.

———, and H. A. Taylor. *Canadian Aircraft Since 1909*. Canada's Wings Inc., Stittsville, Ont., 1982.

Norris, Geoffrey. *The Royal Flying Corps: A History*. Frederick Muller Ltd., London, U.K., 1965.

Parkin, J. H. *Bell and Baldwin: Their Development of Aerodromes and Hydrodromes at Baddeck, Nova Scotia*. University of Toronto Press, Toronto, Ont., 1964.

Roseberry, C. R. *Glenn Curtiss: Pioneer of Flight*. Doubleday & Co., New York, NY, 1972.

Stedman, E. W. *From Boxkite to Jet*. Mercury Series, Canadian War Museum, Ottawa, Ont., 1972.

Stevens, G. R. *History of the Canadian National Railways*. Macmillan, New York, NY, 1973.

Sullivan, Alan. *Aviation in Canada: 1917-1918: Being a Brief Account of the Work of the Royal Air Force Canada, the Aviation Department of the Imperial Munitions Board and the Canadian Aeroplanes Limited*. Rous & Mann Ltd., Toronto, Ont., 1919.

Sutherland, A. G. *Canada's Aviation Pioneers: 50 Years of McKee Trophy Winners*. McGraw-Hill Ryerson, Toronto, Ont., 1978.

Taylor, J. W. R., K. Munson and John Stroud, eds. *History of Aviation: Air Transport Before the Second World War*. New English Library, London, U.K., 1975.

Thomson, D. W. *Skyview Canada: A Story of Aerial Photography in Canada*. Federal Department of Energy Mines and Resources, Ottawa, Ont., 1975.

Wise, S. F. *Canadian Airmen and the First World War: The Official History of the Royal Canadian Air Force*. Vol. 1, University of Toronto Press, Department of National Defence and Canadian Government Publishing Centre, Ottawa, Ont., 1980.

JOURNALS AND DIARIES

Anderson, W. P. "Early Aviation in B.C.: 1910-1931," *Canadian Aviation Historical Society Journal*, Vol. 21, No. 2, Summer, 1983.

Ballentine, G. "Crash!" *Canadian Aviation Historical Society Journal*, Vol. 23, No. 3, Fall 1985.

———. "Those Early Boeing Boats," *Canadian Aviation Historical Society Journal*, Vol. 26, No. 2, Summer 1988.

Bishop, V. A. Personal Diary and RNAS-RAF Pilot's Flying Log Book (V. A. Bishop Estate).

Broome, L. E. Personal Diary (E. L. MacLeod Estate).

Casari, R. "The First 59," *Journal of the American Aviation Historical Society*, Vol. 16, No. 1, 1st Quarter, 1971.

Ellis, F. H. "The Birth of British Columbia Bush Flying," *Northwest Digest*, February 1958.

———. "Canada's First Military Aeroplane," *The Beaver*, Autumn 1974.

———. "Illustrious Twins Were RENE and VIC," *Canadian Aviation*, May 1945.

———. "Pioneer Flying in British Columbia: 1910-1924," *British Columbia Historical Quarterly*, October 1939.

Farr, H. A. "Canada's Air Force and the World War," *Canadian Air Review*, Vol. 1, No. 5, July 1928.

Fribourg, A. W. "Fighting Forest Fires from the Air," *Western Lumberman*, April 1930.

Goodale, F. W. "Reminiscences of an Early Bird," *The Rotarian*, April, 1933. Reprinted as "Reminiscences of an Early Dirigible Pilot," *Canadian Aviation Historical Society Journal*, Vol. 23, No. 1, Spring 1985.

Gould, B. "The Burgess Story," *Journal of the American Aviation Historical Society*, Vol. 11, No. 4, Winter 1966.

Halliday, H. A. "The First Twenty Years . . . The O.P.A.S.," *Canadian Aviation Historical Society Journal*, Vol. 12, No. 3, Fall 1974.

——. "Laurentide Air Service Limited: Commercial Pioneer," *Canadian Geographical Journal*, Vol. 80, No. 4, April, 1970.

Hoff, N. J. "Who Invented the Airplane?" *Journal of the American Aviation Historical Society*, Vol. 23, No. 1, Spring 1978.

Hopping, G. R. "Dusting by Airplane in British Columbia," *The Timberman*, January 1931.

Johnston, R. B. "The Wrights: The First Aeronautical Engineers," *Journal of the American Aviation Historical Society*, Vol. 23, No. 4, Winter 1978.

Logg, H. "Wings and the Lumber Industry," *Western Lumberman*, February, 1930.

Lovegrove, D. "The RCAF: 1918-1939—A Political History," *Canadian Aviation Historical Society Journal*, Vol. 25, No. 1, Spring 1987.

MacLeod, E. L. "Early Flying in British Columbia," *Canadian Aviation Historical Society Journal*, Vol. 12, No. 4, Winter 1974.

McDarment, C. P. "Around the World by Air: The Details of the American Army Aviators' Experience, and the Lessons Learned, *Scientific American*, October 1924.

McLaren, D. "Dependable Power," *Canadian Aviation Historical Society Journal*, Vol. 26, No. 3, Fall 1988.

Molson, K. M. "Early Flying Along the Mackenzie: The 'Rene' and the 'Vic'," *Canadian Aviation Historical Society Journal*, Vol. 20, No. 2, Summer 1982.

Morehouse, H. E. "The Flying Pioneers: Charles K. Hamilton," *Journal of the American Aviation Historical Society*, Vol. 14, No. 3, Fall 1969.

O'Brien, C. F. "Northwest Staging Route," *Alberta Historical Review*, Vol. 17, No. 4, Autumn 1969.

Parminter, J. "Guardians in the Sky: Aircraft and their Uses in B.C.: 1918-1926," *Whistle Punk*, Spring, 1986.

Palmer, H. R., Jr. "Lighter-Than-Air Flight in America: 1784-1910," *Journal of the American Aviation Historical Society*, Vol. 24, No. 3, Fall 1979.

Ray, T. W. "First Year of Naval Aviation," *Journal of the American Aviation Historical Society*, Vol. 12, No. 3, Fall 1967.

Smith, F. "The Air Traffic Situation On the Western Coast," *Canadian Air Review*, Vol. 1, No. 6, August 1928.

Wilson, A. H. "Reminiscences of a West Coast Pilot," *Canadian Aviation Historical Society Journal*, Vol. 3, No. 3, Fall 1965.

"Leading French and American Aeroplanes: Their Construction and Methods of Control," *Scientific American*, Vol. CIII, No. 17, October 22, 1910.

"The Deperdussin Monoplane," *Flight*, No. 33, Vol. III, August 19, 1911.

"The Avro Biplane," *Flight*, No. 44, Vol. III, November 1911.

"The New Avro Biplane," *Flight*, No. 13, Vol. IV, March 30, 1912.

"Hydro-Aeroplane Experiments at Barrow," *Flight*, No. 16, Vol. IV, April 20, 1912.

"Designers' Autographs in Wing Sections," *Flight*, No. 42, Vol. IV, October 19, 1912.

The Timberman, November 1925.

"Getting the Bird's-Eye View," *Pacific Pulp & Paper Industry*, June 1929.

"Vancouver's First Aeroplane," *Raincoast Chronicles*, No. 9, [1981].

NEWSPAPERS

The Armstrong *Advertiser*.

The Calgary *Daily Herald*.

The Chilliwack *Progress*.

The Cowichan *Leader*.

The Golden *Star*.

The Kamloops *Inland Sentinel*.

The Lethbridge *Herald*.

The Nelson *Daily News*.

The Prince George *Citizen*.

The Prince Rupert *Evening Empire*.

The Revelstoke *Review*.

The Vancouver *Daily News-Advertiser*.

The Vancouver *Daily Province*.

The Vancouver *Sun*.

The Vancouver *Daily World*.

The Vernon *News*.

The Victoria *Daily Colonist*.

The Victoria *Daily Times*.

OFFICIAL PUBLICATIONS

British Columbia Aviation Limited Prospectus, 1915.

British Columbia Legislative Assembly Sessional Papers: 1919-1927.

British Columbia Register of Company Files: 1910-1920.

Hansard, Debates: House of Commons, Dominion of Canada: 1919-1920.

Reports of the Air Board, 1920-1921.

Reports of the Department of National Defence, 1927-1930.

INTERVIEWS

Provincial Archives of British Columbia Transcripts:
    3182, H. E. Davenport, interviewed by Paul Stoddart.
    3215, E. L MacLeod, interviewed by Paul Stoddart.
    3217, D. R. McLaren, interviewed by Paul Stoddart.
    3218, A. H. Wilson, interviewed by Paul Stoddart.
    3219, Gordon Ballentine, interviewed by Paul Stoddart.
    3220, Margaret Rutledge, interviewed by Paul Stoddart.
    3222, Maurice McGregor, interviewed by Paul Stoddart.
    3366, T. H. Cressy, interviewed by David Parker.
All of the above interviews were conducted during 1977-78.

Personal Interviews by the Author:
    Doris Coombes (daughter of V. A. Bishop), 1989.
    T. H. Cressy, 1985 and 1989.
    Laura Donaldson, 1989.
    Russ Fletcher, 1989.
    Norman Hoffar (son of Henry), 1989.
    Diana Kennedy (daughter of V. A. Bishop), 1989.
    John M. MacLeod (son of E. L. MacLeod), 1989.
    Maurice McGregor (with David Parker), 1985 and 1989.
    Page and Ethel MacPhee, 1989.
    Lillian Reid-Hoffar (daughter of Henry Hoffar), 1989.
    Margaret Rutledge (with David Parker), 1989.
    Margaret Sawyer (daughter of Clarence Hilborn), 1989.

Streett, St. Clair **143**, 147-48
Stringer, A. **162**, 166
Stuart Lake, B.C. 175
Sturdee, Alta. 152
Sullivan, Alan 100, 102
Sumas Lake Reclamation Dyking Scheme 167
Sumas Lake, B.C. 167
Sumas Mountain, B.C. 166
Sunshine Coast, B.C. 166
Swanson Bay, B.C. 191, 194, **196**, **199**, 202, 204
Sweden **86**, **154**, 158
Sweeney, Miss Marie 126
Switzerland 156
Sydney, N.S. 138, 188

Tacoma, Washington 127
Tall, W. 159
Taylor, B. 211
Taylor, H. A. 83, 87, 98, 106
Taylor, L. D. **179**, 211, 218
Telegraph Creek, B.C. 149, 189
Templeton brothers 158
Templeton, William 31, 158-59, **161**
Templeton, Winston 31, 158
Terra Nova, B.C. 82, 87
Terry, N. 159, 174
Texada Island, B.C. 164
Texas 102
The Pas, Man. 224
Theatre Alley, Victoria, B.C. 57
Thiepval, H.M.C.S. **177-78**, 183-85
Titanic, S.S. 36
Thompsett, Mr. 126
Thompson, G. A. **145**, 151-52, 173, **176**, 188
Thompson, S. **118**
Three Rivers, P.Q. 74
Tokatan Bay, Japan 183
Tomlinson, S.A. 192
Topographic Survey, British Columbia 166
Toronto, Ont. 81-82, 100-01, 114, 116, 155, 189
Torpokof Island, Russia 185
Trail, B.C. **201**
Trans Canada Airlines 221, 224
Trans-Canada Flight 147, 150, 152
Trim, G. K. 116-17, **119**, **123**, 128
Trout Lake, B.C. 204
Trucilla, S.S. 164

Turpin, Clifford **42**, 43
Tylee, A. K. **145**, 150-52
TWA Airlines 156

United Aircraft of British Columbia, Limited 110
United Airlines 156
United States 75, 79, 102, 137, 147, 155-56, 181, 202
United States Army 66
United States Army Air Service **143**, 147, 180
United States Naval Flying Corps 138
United States Navy 101, **178**, 180-81, 188
United States post Office 156
United States Signal Corps 79
University of Victoria 221
Upavon, U.K. 74
Upham, A.C. 193
Upper Arrow Lake, B.C. 204
Upper Heyford, U.K. 133
Ust Kamchatka, Russia 178, 183

Vachon, I. 188
Vachon, R. 188
Valcartier, P.Q., 72
Vancouver Aerial Transportation Company 115, 117, 128, 157
Vancouver Airport, B.C. 82, 158, **161**
Vancouver District, Forest Branch 168
Vancouver General Hospital 107
Vancouver Harbour 166
Vancouver Harbour Board **163**, 166-67
Vancouver Island Aerial Service Limited 157
Vancouver Island Aerial Transport Company 158
Vancouver Island Airways 221
Vancouver Island, B.C. 114, 165-66, 168-69
Vancouver Post Office 115
Vancouver, B.C. 30-32, 36-37, 42, 46, **52**, 56, 82-83, **89**, 100, 106-07, 114-15, **119-20**, **123**, **125**, 126-28, 136-37, 139, **142**, 147, 150-53, 159, 164, 168-69, 172-73, **176-77**, **179**, 181, 185, 187, 190, **200**, 203-04, 208-11, 218-19, 221-24
Vendome, France 106
Verdun, France 100
Vernon Lake, B.C. **197**

Vernon, B.C. 128-30
Victoria Beach, Man. 137, 159
Victoria Chamber of Commerce 208
Victoria, B.C. 23-24, **28**, 30, 32, 35-36, 42, 56, 110, 114, **118-19**, 126, 146, 152-53, 156-58, **176**, 207-11, 219-21, 223

Walker, A. 159, 194-95, **199**, 202
Walker, H. 208-09, 211, **213**, **215**, 218-20, 222
Wall Street Stock Exchange **217**, 224
Walleach Lake, B.C. 166
Walsh, C. F. **28**, 35-36
War Measures Act 134
Washington, D.C. 156
Watson Lake, Y.T. 150
Watson, J. 42
Webb, V. 128
Webster, Clifford 73, 74
Weimer, Germany 156
Wellburn, Gerry 57
West Kootenay Lake, B.C. 204
West Point Lighthouse 164
West Vancouver, B.C. 74
Western Canada Airways Limited 192-93, **198**, 203, 223
Western Front **90**, **95-96**, 100, **107**, 223
Western Motor & Supply Company, Victoria, B.C. 31-32
White pine blister rust 169
Whitehorse, Y.T. 144, 149-50
Wholediah, N.W.T. 224
Williams, S. 189
Willows Park, Victoria, B.C. 35, 42, 56, 114, 117, **122**, 126, 158
Wilson, A. H. 190, 204, 207-08, 210-22, **214**, **216**, 219-22
Wing, Mr. **198**
Winnipeg River, Man. 151
Winnipeg, Man. 16, 150-51, 192, 202, 223-24
Wisconsin 105
Wise, S. F. 72, 74, 190
Wiseman, F. J. 35
World War I 45, **53**, 61, 69, **70**, 71, **76**, 79-81, **97**, 100, 105-06, 110, 112, 134, 139, 155, 190, 222-23
Wrangell, Alaska 148-49, 189
Wright brothers 15-16, 22-23, 42, 59, 61-62, **62-63**, 66-67
Wright, Orville **62**

ENDSHEETS

The enactment of the Canadian Air Board Act on June 6, 1919, was a pivotal event in the development of aviation in British Columbia, as well as the rest of Canada. By establishing Air Stations across the country—this is Jericho Beach, in Vancouver's English Bay—it launched the beginnings of bush flying, for which Canadian aircrews became celebrated throughout the world.

E. L. MACLEOD ESTATE